Lecture Notes in Computer Science   14155

Founding Editors

Gerhard Goos
Juris Hartmanis

The series Lecture Notes in Computer Science (LNCS), including its subseries Lecture Notes in Artificial Intelligence (LNAI) and Lecture Notes in Bioinformatics (LNBI), has established itself as a medium for the publication of new developments in computer science and information technology research, teaching, and education.

LNCS enjoys close cooperation with the computer science R & D community, the series counts many renowned academics among its volume editors and paper authors, and collaborates with prestigious societies. Its mission is to serve this international community by providing an invaluable service, mainly focused on the publication of conference and workshop proceedings and postproceedings. LNCS commenced publication in 1973.

Hossein Hojjat · Erika Ábrahám

Editors

Fundamentals of Software Engineering

10th International Conference, FSEN 2023
Tehran, Iran, May 4–5, 2023
Revised Selected Papers

Editors
Hossein Hojjat 🔟
Tehran Institute for Advanced Studies
Tehran, Iran

Erika Ábrahám 🔟
RWTH Aachen University
Aachen, Germany

ISSN 0302-9743   ISSN 1611-3349 (electronic)
Lecture Notes in Computer Science
ISBN 978-3-031-42440-3   ISBN 978-3-031-42441-0 (eBook)
https://doi.org/10.1007/978-3-031-42441-0

© IFIP International Federation for Information Processing 2023

This Springer imprint is published by the registered company Springer Nature Switzerland AG
The registered company address is: Gewerbestrasse 11, 6330 Cham, Switzerland

Preface

The growing complexity of modern software and hardware systems and their ever more central role in society poses many challenges concerning their reliability, safety, correctness, and robustness. Based on a variety of fundamental concepts from theoretical computer science, formal methods techniques aim at making a significant contribution to better-quality systems. The development and use of formal methods promotes mathematically sound methods and tools for system analysis and verification.

The present volume contains the post-proceedings of the 10th IPM International Conference on Fundamentals of Software Engineering (FSEN 2023). This event was held as a mixed virtual/physical event in Tehran, Iran, during May 4–5, 2023. This two-yearly event is organized by the School of Computer Science at the Institute for Research in Fundamental Sciences (IPM) in Iran, in cooperation with ACM SIGSOFT and IFIP WG2.2. The topics of interest in FSEN span over all aspects of formal methods, especially those related to advancing the application of formal methods in the software industry and promoting their integration with practical engineering techniques.

The Program Committee of FSEN 2023 consisted of 42 top researchers from 20 countries. This edition of FSEN received 19 submissions. Each submission was single-blind reviewed by at least three independent referees, for its quality, originality, contribution, clarity of presentation, and relevance to the conference topics. In accordance with ACM SIGSOFT rules, PC chairs and the general chair were not permitted to submit papers. Two papers included PC members as coauthors; in these cases the PC members in question were excluded from discussion of the paper to avoid a conflict of interests. After thorough discussions on each individual paper, the Programme Committee selected 9 regular full papers and 2 short papers for presentation at the conference. Four distinguished keynote speakers were invited at FSEN 2023: Wolfgang Ahrendt, Dines Bjørner, Mohammad Reza Mousavi, and Heike Wehrheim.

Many people contributed to making FSEN 2023 a success. First of all, we would like to thank the many authors that submitted high-quality papers. Special thanks also go to the Institute for Research in Fundamental Sciences (IPM) in Tehran, Iran, for their financial support and local organization of FSEN 2023. We also thank the members of the Program Committee for their time, effort, and excellent and timely contributions to making FSEN a high-quality international conference and the Steering Committee of FSEN for their valuable support and feedback during all phases of the organisation. We are also grateful to IFIP, the IFIP Working Group 2.2 and ACM for their continuing support of the FSEN conference series. Furthermore, we thank the providers of the EasyChair conference management system, whose facilities greatly helped us run the review process and facilitate the preparation of these post-proceedings.

Finally, we are indebted to all conference attendees for their active and lively participation in the FSEN research community, ultimately contributing to the success of this special conference series.

June 2023   Hossein Hojjat
                                                                   Erika Abraham

Organization

Program Chairs

Hossein Hojjat   Tehran Institute for Advanced Studies, Iran
Erika Abraham   RWTH Aachen University, The Netherlands

Program Committee

Erika Abraham	RWTH Aachen University, The Netherlands
Ebru Aydin Gol	Middle East Technical University, Turkey
Ezio Bartocci	TU Wien, Austria
Simon Bliudze	INRIA, France
Maria Paola Bonacina	Università degli Studi di Verona, Italy
Borzoo Bonakdarpour	Michigan State University, USA
Marcello Bonsangue	Leiden University, The Netherlands
Mario Bravetti	University of Bologna, Italy
Georgiana Caltais	University of Twente, The Netherlands
Erik de Vink	Eindhoven University of Technology, The Netherlands
Fathiyeh Faghih	University of Tehran, Iran
Wan Fokkink	Vrije Universiteit Amsterdam, The Netherlands
Adrian Francalanza	University of Malta, Malta
Fatemeh Ghassemi	University of Tehran, Iran
Jan Friso Groote	Eindhoven University of Technology, The Netherlands
Kim Guldstrand Larsen	Aalborg University, Denmark
Hassan Haghighi	Shahid Beheshti University, Iran
Osman Hasan	National University of Sciences and Technology, Pakistan
Hossein Hojjat	Tehran Institute for Advanced Studies, Iran
Mohammad Izadi	Sharif University of Technology, Iran
Einar Broch Johnsen	University of Oslo, Norway
Amir Kafshdar Goharshady	Hong Kong University of Science and Technology, China
Narges Khakpour	Newcastle University, UK
Ehsan Khamespanah	University of Tehran, Iran
Ramtin Khosravi	University of Tehran, Iran

Eva Kühn	Vienna University of Technology, Austria
Mieke Massink	CNR-ISTI, Pisa, Italy
Jedidiah McClurg	Colorado State University, USA
Rosemary Monahan	Maynooth University, Ireland
Mohammad Mousavi	King's College London, UK
Ali Movaghar	Sharif University of Technology, Iran
Luigia Petre	Åbo Akademi University, Finland
José Proença	CISTER-ISEP and HASLab-INESC TEC, Portugal
Anne Remke	WWU Münster, Germany
Philipp Ruemmer	University of Regensburg, Germany
Asieh Salehi Fathabadi	University of Southampton, UK
Cristina Seceleanu	Mälardalen University, Sweden
Marjan Sirjani	Mälardalen University, Sweden
Meng Sun	Peking University, China
Carolyn Talcott	SRI International, USA
Tayssir Touili	LIPN, CNRS & Sorbonne Paris North University, France
Martin Wirsing	Ludwig Maximilian University of Munich, Germany
Lijun Zhang	Institute of Software, Chinese Academy of Sciences, China
Peter Ölveczky	University of Oslo, Norway

Additional Reviewers

Barrett, Clark
Blanchette, Jasmin
Leofante, Francesco
Luan, Xiaokun
Turrini, Andrea

Contents

Structured Specification of Paraconsistent Transition Systems

Juliana Cunha[1], Alexandre Madeira[1(✉)], and Luís Soares Barbosa[2]

[1] CIDMA, Department of Mathematics, Aveiro University, Aveiro, Portugal
{juliana.cunha,madeira}@ua.pt
[2] INESC TEC and Department of Informatics, Minho University, Braga, Portugal
lsb@di.uminho.pt

Abstract. This paper sets the basis for a compositional and structured approach to the specification of paraconsistent transitions systems, framed as an institution. The latter and theirs logics were previously introduced in [CMB22] to deal with scenarios of inconsistency in which several requirements are on stake, either reinforcing or contradicting each other.

1 Introduction

In Software Engineering it is often a challenge to cope with modelling contexts in which the classical bivalent logic distinction is not enough. Several modal logics have been proposed [BEGR09] to address such a challenge, namely to capture vagueness or uncertainty. Typically, their semantics is based on residuated lattices, i.e. complete lattices equipped with a commutative monoidal structure such that the monoid composition has a right adjoint, the residue. The lattice carrier stands for the set of truth values, a typical example being the real $[0, 1]$ interval.

Often, however, there is also a need to go further and equip the underlying Kripke structure with both *positive* and *negative* accessibility relations, one weighting the possibility of a transition to be present, the other weighting the possibility of being absent. Moreover, in a number of real situations, such weights are not complementary, and thus both relations should be formally taken into consideration. For this purpose, in a previous work [CMB22] we introduced *paraconsistent transition systems*, abbreviated to PLTS, and the corresponding modal logic, which generalises Belnap-Dunn four-valued logic [RJJ15] in a very generic way. Actually, all the relevant constructions are parametric in a class of residuated lattices, thus admitting different instances according to the structure of the truth values domain that better suits each modelling problem at hands.

The present study was developed in the scope of the Project "Agenda ILLIANCE" [C644919832-00000035 | Project no. 46], financed by PRR – Plano de Recuperação e Resiliência under the Next Generation EU from the European Union. FCT, the Portuguese funding agency for Science and Technology suports with the projects UIDB/04106/2020 and PTDC/CCI-COM/4280/2021.

H. Hojjat and E. Ábrahám (Eds.): FSEN 2023, LNCS 14155, pp. 1–17, 2023.
https://doi.org/10.1007/978-3-031-42441-0_1

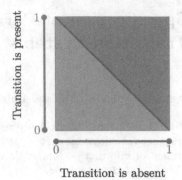

Fig. 1. The vagueness-inconsistency square [CMB22].

To exemplify suppose, for example, that weights for both transitions come from a residuated lattice over the real $[0, 1]$ interval.
Then, the two accessibility relations jointly express a scenario of

- *inconsistency*, when the positive and negative weights are contradictory, i.e. they sum to some value greater than 1 (cf, the upper triangle in Fig. 1 filled in grey). Exploring this area of the square
- *vagueness*, when the sum is less than 1 (cf, the lower, periwinkle triangle in Fig. 1);
- *strict consistency*, when the sum is exactly 1, which means that the measures of the factors enforcing or preventing a transition are complementary, corresponding to the red line in the figure.

Exploring the upper triangle calls for paraconsistent logics [Jas69, CCM07], in which inconsistent information is considered as potentially informative. Introduced more than half a century ago, through the pioneering work of F. Asenjo and Newton da Costa, such logics are becoming increasingly popular (see, for example, reference [Aka16], a recent book on engineering applications). This paper goes a step ahead. First the modal logic associated to PLTS is extended to the multi-modal case. Then it is prepared to act as a *structured specification logic* [ST12] equipped with specific versions of the standard structured specification operators *à la CASL* [MHST03]. This offers to the working software engineer the (formal) tools to specify, in a compositional way, paraconsistent transition systems. The approach builds on previous work documented in reference [JGMB21] where a similar agenda is proposed for the specification of fuzzy transition systems. Technically, the price to be paid to support this move consists of framing the logic as an institution [GB92].

The rest of the paper is divided in two sections. Section 2 characterizes an institution for paraconsistent transition systems $L(\mathcal{A})$. The formalism is parametric to the truth space $\mathcal{A}$, formalised as a metric twisted structure. Then, in Sect. 3, the usual structured specification operators [ST12] are re-built on top of this institution. These are the basic (technical) results for supporting a specification framework for this sort of systems, within the well-established tradition of algebraic specification. Going a step further into the specification methodology and engineering practices will be discussed in a twin publication.

2 An Institution for Paraconsistent Transitions Systems

We start by recalling the notion of an institution, followed, in Sect. 2.2, by a characterization of metric twisted algebras which continue the semantic domain upon which the logic is parametrised, as mentioned in the introduction. Such structures amount to a particular class of residuated lattices in which the lattice meet and the monoidal composition coincide, equipped with a metric which entails a concrete meaning to the vagueness-inconsistency square informally described in the introduction. Finally, in sub-sect. 2.3, the relevant institution(s) for L($\mathcal{A}$) is built in a step by step way and suitably illustrated.

2.1 Institutions

An institution abstractly defines a logic system by describing the kind of signatures in the system, the kind of models and a satisfaction relation between models and sentences.

Definition 1 ([GB92]). *An institution I is a tuple*

$$I = (\mathsf{Sign}_I, \mathsf{Sen}_I, \mathsf{Mod}_I, \models_I)$$

consisting of

- *a category Sign_I of signatures*
- *a functor $\mathsf{Sen}_I : \mathsf{Sign}_I \to \mathsf{Set}$ giving a set of Σ − sentences for each signature $\Sigma \in |\mathsf{Sign}_I|$. For each signature morphism $\sigma : \Sigma \to \Sigma'$ the function*

$$\mathsf{Sen}_I(\sigma) : \mathsf{Sen}_I(\Sigma) \to \mathsf{Sen}_I(\Sigma')$$

translates Σ − sentences to Σ' − sentences
- *a functor $\mathsf{Mod}_I : \mathsf{Sign}_I^{op} \to \mathsf{Cat}$ assigns to each signature Σ the category of Σ − models. For each signature morphism $\sigma : \Sigma \to \Sigma'$ the functor*

$$\mathsf{Mod}_I(\sigma) : \mathsf{Mod}_I(\Sigma') \to \mathsf{Mod}_I(\Sigma)$$

translates Σ' − models to Σ − models
- *a satisfaction relation $\models_I^\Sigma \subseteq |\mathsf{Mod}_I(\Sigma)| \times \mathsf{Sen}_I(\Sigma)$ determines the satisfaction of Σ − sentences by Σ − models for each signature $\Sigma \in |\mathsf{Sign}_I|$.*

Satisfaction must be preserved under change of signature that is for any signature morphism $\sigma : \Sigma \to \Sigma'$, for any $\varphi \in \mathsf{Sen}_I(\Sigma)$ and $M' \in |\mathsf{Mod}_I(\Sigma')|$

$$\left(M' \models_I^{\Sigma'} \mathsf{Sen}_I(\sigma)(\varphi) \right) \Leftrightarrow \left(\mathsf{Mod}_I(\sigma)(M') \models_I^\Sigma \varphi \right) \tag{1}$$

Actually, when formalising multi-valued logics as institutions, the equivalence on the satisfaction condition (1) can be replaced by an equality (c.f. [ACEGG91]):

$$\left(M' \models_I^{\Sigma'} \mathsf{Sen}_I(\sigma)(\varphi) \right) = \left(\mathsf{Mod}_I(\sigma)(M') \models_I^\Sigma \varphi \right) \tag{2}$$

The institution formalisation several logics, including Propositional, Equational, First-order, High-Order, etc., can be found in reference [ST12].

2.2   (Metric) Twisted Algebras

A residuated lattice $\langle A, \sqcap, \sqcup, 1, 0, \odot, \rightarrow, e \rangle$ over a set A is a complete lattice $\langle A, \sqcap, \sqcup, 1, 0 \rangle$, equipped with a monoid $\langle A, \odot, e \rangle$ such that $\odot$ has a right adjoint, $\rightarrow$, called the residuum. We will, however, focus on a particular class of residuated lattices in which the lattice meet ($\sqcap$) and monoidal composition ($\odot$) coincide. Thus the adjunction is stated as $a \sqcap b \leqslant c$ iff $b \leqslant a \rightarrow c$. Additionally, we will enforce a pre-linearity condition

$$(a \rightarrow b) \sqcup (b \rightarrow a) = 1 \tag{3}$$

A residuated lattice obeying prelinearity is known as a MTL-algebra [EG01]. With a slight abuse of nomenclature, the designation iMTL-algebra, from *integral MTL-algebra*, will be used in the sequel for the class of semantic structures considered, i.e. prelinear, residuated lattices such that $\sqcap$ and $\odot$ coincide. Examples of iMTL-algebras are:

- the Boolean algebra $\mathbf{2} = \langle \{0,1\}, \wedge, \vee, 1, 0, \rightarrow \rangle$

- $\mathbf{3} = \langle \{\top, u, \bot\}, \wedge_3, \vee_3, \top, \bot, \rightarrow_3 \rangle$, where

$\wedge_3$	$\bot$	u	$\top$
$\bot$	$\bot$	$\bot$	$\bot$
u	$\bot$	u	u
$\top$	$\bot$	u	$\top$

$\vee_3$	$\bot$	u	$\top$
$\bot$	$\bot$	u	$\top$
u	u	u	$\top$
$\top$	$\top$	$\top$	$\top$

$\rightarrow_3$	$\bot$	u	$\top$
$\bot$	$\top$	$\top$	$\top$
u	$\bot$	$\top$	$\top$
$\top$	$\bot$	u	$\top$

- $\ddot{\mathbf{G}} = \langle [0,1], \min, \max, 0, 1, \rightarrow \rangle$, with implication defined as

$$a \rightarrow b = \begin{cases} 1 & if\, a \leqslant b \\ b & otherwise \end{cases}$$

We focus on *iMTL-algebras* $\mathbf{A}$ whose carrier A supports a metric space (A, d), with suitable choice of d. Where $d \colon A \times A \to \mathbb{R}^+$ such that $d(x, y) = 0$ iff $x = y$ and $d(x, y) \leqslant d(x, z) + d(z, y)$.

In order to operate with pairs of truth weights, it was introduced in [CMB22] the notion of $\mathbf{A}$-*twisted algebra*. This algebraic structure will play a crucial role in the semantics of our institution, consists of an enrichment of a twist-structure [Kra98] with a metric. The latter is relevant to interpret the consistency operator of the logic:

Definition 2 ([CMB22]). *Given a iMTL-algebra $\mathbf{A}$ enriched with a metric d, a $\mathbf{A}$-twisted algebra $\mathcal{A} = \langle A \times A, \sqcap\!\!\sqcap, \sqcup\!\!\sqcup, \Longrightarrow, /\!/, D \rangle$ is defined as:*

- $(a, b) \,\sqcap\!\!\sqcap\, (c, d) = (a \sqcap c, b \sqcup d)$
- $(a, b) \,\sqcup\!\!\sqcup\, (c, d) = (a \sqcup c, b \sqcap d)$
- $(a, b) \Longrightarrow (c, d) = (a \rightarrow c, a \sqcap d)$
- $/\!/(a, b) = (b, a)$
- $D((a, b), (c, d)) = \sqrt{d(a, c)^2 + d(b, d)^2}$

The order in $\mathbf{A}$ is lifted to $\mathcal{A}$ as $(a, b) \preceq (c, d)$ iff $a \leqslant c$ and $b \geqslant d$.

2.3   Institutional Framing of L($\mathcal{A}$)

Let us fix a given twisted algebra $\mathcal{A}$. In the following subsections we will introduce the ingredients for an institution $\mathrm{L}(\mathcal{A}) = (\mathsf{Sign}, \mathsf{Sen}, \mathsf{Mod}, \models)$.

Signatures

Definition 3. *A signature Σ is a pair* (Prop, Act) *where* Prop *is a set of propositions and* Act *is a set of action symbols. A signature morphism* $\sigma : \Sigma \to \Sigma'$ *is a pair of functions* $\sigma_{\text{Prop}} : \text{Prop} \to \text{Prop}'$ *and* $\sigma_{\text{Act}} : \text{Act} \to \text{Act}'$.

The category of signatures and their morphisms will be called signature category and will be denoted by Sign.

The Models

Definition 4. *Let* (Prop, Act) *be a signature. A* (Prop, Act)-L($\mathcal{A}$) *paraconsistent labelled transition system, is a tuple* $M = (W, R, V)$ *such that,*

- *W is a non-empty set of states,*
- *$R = (R_a : W \times W \to A \times A)_{a \in \text{Act}}$ is an Act-indexed family of partial functions, given any pair of states $(w_1, w_2) \in W \times W$ and an action $a \in$ Act, relation R assigns a pair $(tt, ff) \in A \times A$ such that tt represents the evidence degree of the transition from w_1 to w_2 occurring through action a and ff represents the evidence degree of the transition being prevented from occurring.*
- *$V : W \times$ Prop $\to A \times A$ is a valuation function, that assigns to a proposition $p \in$ Prop at a given state w a pair $(tt, ff) \in A \times A$ such that tt is the evidence degree of p holding in w and ff the evidence degree of not holding*

The images of a state through an action a is the set of states for which the transition is defined, i.e. the set $R_a[w] = \{w' \in W \mid R_a(w, w') = (tt, ff)$ for some $tt, ff \in A\}$. For any pair $(tt, ff) \in A \times A$, $(tt, ff)^+$ denotes tt and $(tt, ff)^-$ denotes ff.

Definition 5. *Let $M = (W, R, V)$ and $M' = (W', R', V')$ be two* (Prop, Act)-*PLTS. A morphism between M and M' is a function $h : W \to W'$ compatible with the source valuation and transition functions, i.e.*

- *for each $a \in$ Act, $R_a(w_1, w_2) \preccurlyeq R'_a(h(w_1), h(w_2))$, and*
- *for any $p \in$ Prop, $w \in W$, $V(w, p) \preccurlyeq V'(h(w), p)$.*

We say that M and M' are isomorphic, in symbols $M \cong M'$, whenever there are morphisms $h : M \to M'$ and $h^{-1} : M' \to M$ such that $h' \circ h = id_{W'}$ $h \circ h' = id_W$.

(Prop, Act)-PLTSs and the corresponding morphisms form a category denoted by Mod, which acts as the model category for our L($\mathcal{A}$) logic.

Definition 6. *Let $\sigma : $ (Prop, Act) $\to$ (Prop', Act') be a signature morphism and $M' = (W', R', V')$ a* (Prop', Act')-*PLTS. The σ-reduct of M' is the* (Prop, Act)-*PLTS $M|_\sigma = (W, R, V)$ where*

- *$W = W'$,*
- *for $p \in$ Prop, $w \in W$, $V(w, p) = V'(w, \sigma(p))$, and*
- *for $w, v \in W$ and $a \in$ Act, $R_a(w, v) = R'_{\sigma(a)}(w, v)$.*

Reducts preserve morphism. Hence, each signature morphism $\sigma : (\text{Prop}, \text{Act}) \to$ $(\text{Prop}', \text{Act}')$ defines a functor $\text{Mod}(\sigma) : \text{Mod}(\text{Prop}', \text{Act}') \to \text{Mod}(\text{Prop}, \text{Act})$ that maps systems and morphisms to the corresponding reducts. This lifts to a functor, $\text{Mod} : (\text{Sign})^{op} \to \text{CAT}$, mapping each signature to the category of its models, and each signature morphism to its reduct functor.

The Sentences. Once characterised models for $L(\mathcal{A})$. Let us define its syntax and the satisfaction relation.

Definition 7. *Given a signature* $(\text{Prop}, \text{Act})$ *the set* $\text{Sen}(\text{Prop}, \text{Act})$ *of sentences is given by the following grammar*

$$\varphi ::= p \mid \bot \mid \neg\varphi \mid \varphi \to \varphi \mid \varphi \vee \varphi \mid \varphi \wedge \varphi \mid [a]\varphi \mid \langle a \rangle\varphi \mid [\![a]\!]\varphi \mid \langle\!\langle a \rangle\!\rangle\varphi \mid \circ\varphi$$

with $p \in \text{Prop}$ *and* $a \in \text{Act}$. *Note that* $\top = \neg\bot$ *and* $\varphi_1 \leftrightarrow \varphi_2 = (\varphi_1 \to \varphi_2) \wedge (\varphi_2 \to \varphi_1)$.

Each signature morphism $\sigma : (\text{Prop}, \text{Act}) \to (\text{Prop}', \text{Act}')$ induces a sentence translation scheme $\text{Sen}(\sigma) : \text{Sen}(\text{Prop}, \text{Act}) \to \text{Sen}(\text{Prop}', \text{Act}')$ recursively defined as follows:

- $\text{Sen}(\sigma)(p) = \sigma_{\text{Prop}}(p)$
- $\text{Sen}(\sigma)(\bot) = \bot$
- $\text{Sen}(\sigma)(\neg\varphi) = \neg\text{Sen}(\sigma)(\varphi)$
- $\text{Sen}(\sigma)(\varphi \odot \varphi') = \text{Sen}(\sigma)(\varphi) \odot \text{Sen}(\sigma)(\varphi'), \odot \in \{\vee, \wedge, \to\}$
- $\text{Sen}(\sigma)([a]\,\varphi) = [\sigma_{Act}(a)]\,\text{Sen}(\sigma)(\varphi)$
- $\text{Sen}(\sigma)(\langle a \rangle\varphi) = \langle\sigma_{Act}(a)\rangle\,\text{Sen}(\sigma)(\varphi)$
- $\text{Sen}(\sigma)([\![a]\!]\,\varphi) = [\![\sigma_{Act}(a)]\!]\,\text{Sen}(\sigma)(\varphi)$
- $\text{Sen}(\sigma)(\langle\!\langle a \rangle\!\rangle\varphi) = \langle\!\langle\sigma_{Act}(a)\rangle\!\rangle\,\text{Sen}(\sigma)(\varphi)$
- $\text{Sen}(\sigma)(\circ\varphi) = \circ\,\text{Sen}(\sigma)(\varphi)$

which entails a functor $\text{Sen} : \text{Sign} \to \text{Set}$ mapping each signature to the set of its sentences, and each signature morphism to the corresponding translation of sentences.

The Satisfaction Relation

Definition 8. *Given a signature* $(\text{Prop}, \text{Act})$, *and a* $(\text{Prop}, \text{Act})$-*PLTS* $M = (W, R, V)$, *the satisfaction relation*

$$\models\; : \text{Mod}(\text{Prop}, \text{Act}) \times \text{Sen}(\text{Prop}, \text{Act}) \to A \times A$$

is defined by

$$(M \models \varphi) = \bigsqcap_{w \in W} (M, w \models \varphi)$$

where the relation $\models$ is recursively defined as follows:

- $(M, w \models p) = V(w, p)$
- $(M, w \models \bot) = (0, 1)$
- $(M, w \models \neg\varphi) = /\!\!/ (M, w \models \varphi)$
- $(M, w \models \varphi \rightarrow \varphi') = (M, w \models \varphi) \Longrightarrow (M, w \models \varphi')$
- $(M, w \models \varphi \vee \varphi') = (M, w \models \varphi) \sqcup (M, w \models \varphi')$
- $(M, w \models \varphi \wedge \varphi') = (M, w \models \varphi) \sqcap (M, w \models \varphi')$
- $(M, w \models [a]\varphi) = (\,[a^+](M, w, \varphi^+), \langle a^+\rangle(M, w, \varphi^-)\,)$
- $(M, w \models \langle a\rangle\varphi) = (\langle a^+\rangle(M, w, \varphi^+), [a^+](M, w, \varphi^-)\,)$
- $(M, w \models [\![a]\!]\varphi) = (\langle a^-\rangle(M, w, \varphi^-), [a^-](M, w, \varphi^+)\,)$
- $(M, w \models \langle\!\langle a\rangle\!\rangle\varphi) = (\,[a^-](M, w, \varphi^-), \langle a^-\rangle(M, w, \varphi^+)\,)$
- $(M, w \models \circ\varphi) = \begin{cases} (1, 0) & \text{if } (M, w \models \varphi) \in \Delta_C \\ (0, 1) & \text{otherwise} \end{cases}$

where

- $[a^+](M, w, \varphi^*) = \displaystyle\bigsqcap_{w' \in R_a[w]} (R_a^+(w, w') \rightharpoonup (M, w' \models \varphi)^*)$
- $[a^-](M, w, \varphi^*) = \displaystyle\bigsqcap_{w' \in R_a[w]} (R_a^-(w, w') \rightharpoonup (M, w' \models \varphi)^*)$
- $\langle a^+\rangle(M, w, \varphi^*) = \displaystyle\bigsqcup_{w' \in R_a[w]} (R_a^+(w, w') \sqcap (M, w' \models \varphi)^*)$
- $\langle a^-\rangle(M, w, \varphi^*) = \displaystyle\bigsqcup_{w' \in R_a[w]} (R_a^-(w, w') \sqcap (M, w' \models \varphi)^*)$
- $\Delta_C = \{(a, b) \mid D((a, b), (0, 0)) \leqslant D((a, b), (1, 1))\}$

with $* \in \{^+, ^-\}$. *Hence* φ *is valid in* M *if for any* $w \in W$, $(M, w \models \varphi) = (1, 0)$.

The following examples serve to illustrate the satisfaction relation in our logic.

Example 1. Consider **2** the underlying *iMTL-algebra*, a signature $(\{p, q\}, \{a\})$ and a PLTS $M = (\{s_0, s_1\}, R, V)$ depicted in the figure below:

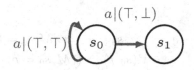

where $V(s_0,p) = (\top,\bot)$, $V(s_0,q) = (\bot,\top)$, $V(s_1,p) = (\top,\top)$ and $V(s_1,q) = (\bot,\bot)$.

$$M, s_0 \models \langle a \rangle p \vee q$$
$$=(M, s_0 \models \langle a \rangle p) \sqcup\!\sqcup (M, s_0 \models q)$$
$$=([a^-](M, s_0, p^-), \langle a^- \rangle(M, s_0, p^+)) \sqcup\!\sqcup V(s_0, q)$$
$$=\Big((R_a^-(s_0, s_0) \rightarrow (M, s_0 \models p)^-) \sqcap (R_a^-(s_0, s_1) \rightarrow (M, s_1 \models p)^-),$$
$$(R_a^-(s_0, s_0) \sqcap (M, s_0 \models p)^+) \sqcup (R_a^-(s_0, s_1) \sqcap (M, s_1 \models p)^+) \Big) \sqcup\!\sqcup (\bot, \top)$$
$$=\Big((\top \rightarrow \bot) \sqcap (\bot \rightarrow \top), (\top \sqcap \top) \sqcup (\bot \sqcap \top) \Big) \sqcup\!\sqcup (\bot, \top)$$
$$=(\bot \sqcap \top, \top \sqcup \bot) \sqcup\!\sqcup (\bot, \top) = (\bot, \top) \sqcup\!\sqcup (\bot, \top) = (\bot \sqcup \bot, \top \sqcap \top) = (\bot, \top)$$

At state s_0 the sentence $\langle a \rangle p \vee q$ holds with evidence degree $\bot$ and doesn't hold with evidence degree $\top$ so we are in a case where the pair of weights are consistent!

Example 2. Let **3** be the underlying iMTL-algebra and $M = (\{s_0, s_1\}, R, V)$ be a $(\{p, q, r\}, \{a, b\})$-PLTS depicted in the figure below. Where $V(s_0, p) = (\top, \top)$, $V(s_0, q) = V(s_1, p) = (\bot, u)$, $V(s_0, r) = V(s_1, r) = (u, u)$, $V(s_1, q) = (\bot, \bot)$

$$a|(\top, \bot)$$

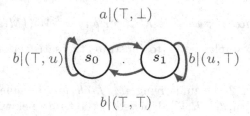

$$b|(\top, \top)$$

$$(M, s_0 \models r \rightarrow (p \vee q)) = (M, s_0 \models r) \Rightarrow (M, s_0 \models (p \vee q))$$
$$= V(s_0, r) \Rightarrow ((M, s_0 \models p) \sqcup\!\sqcup (M, s_0 \models q))$$
$$= V(s_0, r) \Rightarrow (V(s_0, p) \sqcup\!\sqcup V(s_0, q))$$
$$= (u, u) \Rightarrow ((\top, \top) \sqcup\!\sqcup (\bot, u))$$
$$= (u, u) \Rightarrow (\top \sqcup \bot, \top \sqcap u)$$
$$= (u, u) \Rightarrow (\top, u)$$
$$= (u \rightarrow \top, u \sqcap u) = (\top, u)$$

At state s_0 the sentence $r \rightarrow (p \vee q)$ has an evidence degree $\top$ of holding and it's unknown, u, the evidence degree in which it doesn't hold.

Notice that,

$$\langle b^+\rangle(M, s_1, p^+) = \bigsqcup_{s \in R_b[s_1]} (R_b^+(s_1, s) \sqcap (M, s \models p)^-)$$

$$= (R_b^+(s_1, s_1) \sqcap (M, s_1 \models p)^-) \sqcup (R_b^+(s_1, s_0) \sqcap (M, s_0 \models p)^-)$$

$$= \left((u, \top)^+ \sqcap (\top, u)^-\right) \sqcup \left((\top, \top)^+ \sqcap (\top, \top)^-\right)$$

$$= (u \sqcap u) \sqcup (\top \sqcap \top) = \top$$

Analogously, we can see that $([b^+](M, s_1, p^-)) = \top$. Therefore, $(M, s_1 \models \langle b\rangle p) = (\langle b^+\rangle(M, s_1, p^+), [b^+](M, s_1, p^-)) = (\top, \top)$. That is, in state s_1 the sentence $\langle b\rangle p$ has evidence degree $\top$ of holding and evidence degree $\top$ of not holding.

Proposition 1. *Let $\sigma : (\mathrm{Prop}, \mathrm{Act}) \to (\mathrm{Prop}', \mathrm{Act}')$ be a signature morphism, M' a $(\mathrm{Prop}', \mathrm{Act}')$-PLTS, and $\varphi \in \mathrm{Sen}(\mathrm{Prop}, \mathrm{Act})$ a formula. Then, for any $w \in W$,*

$$(M'|_\sigma, w \models \varphi) = (M', w \models \mathrm{Sen}(\sigma)(\varphi)) \tag{4}$$

Proof. The proof, given by induction on the structure of sentences, is in the appendix.

Theorem 1. *For a given metric twisted structure $\mathcal{A}$, $\mathrm{L}(\mathcal{A})$ is an institution.*

Such abstraction is necessary to get away from the particular syntax of the logic and to focus on building larger specifications in a structured manner.

3 Structured Specification with $\mathrm{L}(\mathcal{A})$

Usually one starts with flat specifications, that consist of a signature and a set of sentences in a logic, new specifications are then built through a composition of operators. These specification building operators are defined in an arbitrary but fixed institution which allows this theory to be applicable to a wide range of logics that can be framed as institutions.

Definition 9. *A specification is a pair*

$$SP = (Sig(SP), Mod(SP))$$

where $Sig(SP)$ is a signature in Sign and the models of SP is a function

$$Mod(SP) : \mathsf{Mod}(Sig(SP)) \to A \times A.$$

For some model $M \in \mathsf{Mod}(Sig(SP))$ we have that $Mod(SP)(M) = (\mathit{tt}, \mathit{ff})$, with tt representing the evidence degree of M being a model of SP and the value ff representing the evidence degree of M not being a model of SP.

Specifications are built in a structured way as follows:

Flat Specifications If $\Sigma \in |\text{Sign}|$ is a signature and $\Phi \subseteq \text{Sen}(\Sigma)$ is a set of Σ-sentences, often called axioms, then $SP = (\Sigma, \Phi)$ is a flat specification consequently
- $Sig(SP) = \Sigma$
- $Mod(SP)(M) = \left(\underset{\varphi \in \Phi}{\sqcap}(M \models \varphi) \right) = \left(\underset{\varphi \in \Phi}{\sqcap} \underset{w \in W}{\sqcap} (M, w \models \varphi) \right)$

Flat specifications are a basic tool to build small specifications.

Union Let SP and SP' be two specifications over the same signature, Σ. Then $SP \cup SP'$ is
- $Sig(SP \cup SP') = \Sigma$
- $Mod(SP \cup SP')(M) = Mod(SP)(M) \sqcap Mod(SP')(M)$

If $SP_1 = \langle \Sigma, \Phi_1 \rangle$ and $SP_2 = \langle \Sigma, \Phi_2 \rangle$ are flat specifications then:

$$Mod(\langle \Sigma, \Phi_1 \rangle \cup \langle \Sigma, \Phi_2 \rangle)(M) = Mod(\langle \Sigma, \Phi_1 \cup \Phi_2 \rangle)(M)$$

Translation If SP is a Σ-specification and $\sigma : \Sigma \to (\text{Prop}', \text{Act}')$ a signature morphism. Then,
- $Sig(SP \text{ with } \sigma) = (\text{Prop}', \text{Act}')$
- $Mod(SP \text{ with } \sigma)(M') = Mod(SP)(M'|_\sigma)$

Note that M' is a $(\text{Prop}', \text{Act}') - model$.

Hiding If SP' is a Σ'-specification and $\sigma : (\text{Prop}, \text{Act}) \to \Sigma'$ is a signature morphism then,
- $Sig(SP' \text{ hide via } \sigma) = (\text{Prop}, \text{Act})$
- $Mod(SP' \text{ hide via } \sigma)(M) = \left(\underset{N \in M^\sigma}{\sqcup} Mod(SP')(N) \right)$

where M^σ is the class of all σ-expansions of M, i.e. $M^\sigma = \{N \in Mod(SP') \mid N|_\sigma = M\}$.

The following examples illustrate some of the structured specifications operators defined above.

Example 3. Consider **2** the underlying iMTL-algebra. Given the signature $\Sigma = (\{p, q\}, \{b, c\})$, the specification $SP = \langle \Sigma, \Phi \rangle$ where $\Phi = \{[c]\langle b \rangle \top, \neg(p \vee q), q \to \langle c \rangle q\}$ and the inclusion morphism $\sigma : (\{p, q\}, \{b, c\}) \to (\{p, q\}, \{a, b, c\})$. Let $M' = (\{s_0, s_1, s_2\}, R', V')$ be a $(\{p, q\}, \{a, b, c\})$-transition model depicted below.

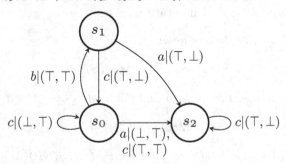

where $V'(s_0, p) = V'(s_0, q) = V'(s_1, q) = (\top, \top)$, $V'(s_1, p) = (\bot, \bot)$, $V'(s_2, p) = (\top, \bot)$ and $V'(s_2, q) = (\bot, \top)$.

The following Σ-model $M'|_\sigma = (W, R, V)$ is the σ-reduct of M':

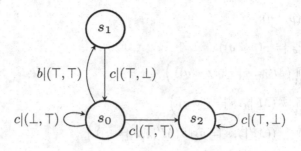

By the definition of σ-reduct: $W = W'$ and $V(s,r) = V'(s,r)$ for any $s \in W$ and $r \in \{p,q\}$.
Then,

- $Sig(SP \text{ with } \sigma) = (\{p,q\}, \{a,b,c\})$

- $Mod(SP \text{ with } \sigma)(M') = Mod(SP)(M'|_\sigma) = \left(\underset{\substack{\varphi \in \Phi \\ s \in W}}{\sqcap} (M'|_\sigma, s \models \varphi) \right)$

Notice that,

$$M'|_\sigma, s_0 \models \langle\!\langle b \rangle\!\rangle \top$$
$$= ([b^-](M'|_\sigma, s_0, \top^-), \langle b^- \rangle(M'|_\sigma, s_0, \top^+))$$
$$= (R_b^-(s_0, s_1) \to (M'|_\sigma, s_1 \models \top)^-, R_b^-(s_0, s_1) \wedge (M'|_\sigma, \models \top)^+)$$
$$= (\top \to \bot, \top \wedge \top) = (\bot, \top)$$

Similarly, we find that $(M'|_\sigma, s_1 \models \langle\!\langle b \rangle\!\rangle \top) = (\top, \bot) = (M'|_\sigma, s_2 \models \langle\!\langle b \rangle\!\rangle \top)$.
Hence,

$$M'|_\sigma, s_0 \models [c] \langle\!\langle b \rangle\!\rangle \top$$
$$= ([c^+](M'|_\sigma, s_0, (\langle\!\langle b \rangle\!\rangle \top)^+), \langle c^+ \rangle(M'|_\sigma, s_0, (\langle\!\langle b \rangle\!\rangle \top)^-))$$
$$= (R_c^+(s_0, s_2) \to (M'|_\sigma, s_2 \models \langle\!\langle b \rangle\!\rangle \top)^+, R_c^+(s_0, s_2) \wedge (M'|_\sigma, s_2 \models \langle\!\langle b \rangle\!\rangle \top)^-)$$
$$= (\top \to \top, \top \wedge \bot) = (\top, \bot)$$

Similarly, we can check that $(M'|_\sigma, s_1 \models [c] \langle\!\langle b \rangle\!\rangle \top) = (\bot, \top)$ and that $(M'|_\sigma, s_2 \models [c] \langle\!\langle b \rangle\!\rangle \top) = (\top, \bot)$. Therefore, there is $\bot$ evidence of sentence $[c] \langle\!\langle b \rangle\!\rangle \top$ being true in model $M'|_\sigma$ and evidence $\top$ of being false:

$$(M'|_\sigma \models [c] \langle\!\langle b \rangle\!\rangle \top) = \underset{s \in W}{\sqcap} (M'|_\sigma, s \models [c] \langle\!\langle b \rangle\!\rangle \top) = (\top \wedge \bot \wedge \top, \bot \vee \top \vee \bot) = (\bot, \top)$$

For sentence $\neg(p \vee q)$:

$$(M'|_\sigma \models \neg(p \vee q))$$

$$= \left(\underset{s \in W}{\text{⊓}} (M'|_\sigma, s \models \neg(p \vee q)) \right)$$

$$= \left(\underset{s \in W}{\text{⊓}} \mathbin{/\!\!/} (M'|_\sigma, s \models p \vee q) \right)$$

$$= \left(\underset{s \in W}{\text{⊓}} \mathbin{/\!\!/} ((M'|_\sigma, s \models p) \sqcup (M'|_\sigma, s \models q)) \right)$$

$$= (\mathbin{/\!\!/}(\top \wedge \top, \top \vee \top)) \text{⊓} (\mathbin{/\!\!/}(\bot \wedge \top, \bot \vee \top)) \text{⊓} (\mathbin{/\!\!/}(\top \wedge \bot, \bot \vee \top))$$

$$= (\mathbin{/\!\!/}(\top, \top)) \text{⊓} (\mathbin{/\!\!/}(\bot, \top)) \text{⊓} (\mathbin{/\!\!/}(\bot, \top))$$

$$= (\top, \top) \text{⊓} (\top, \bot) \text{⊓} (\top, \bot) = (\top \wedge \top \wedge \top, \top \vee \bot \vee \bot) = (\top, \top)$$

For sentence $q \to \langle c \rangle q$:

$$M'|_\sigma, s_0 \models q \to \langle c \rangle q$$

$$= (M'|_\sigma, s_0 \models q) \implies (M'|_\sigma, s_0 \models \langle c \rangle q)$$

$$= (\top, \top) \implies (\langle c^+ \rangle(M, s_0, q^+), [c^+](M, s_0, q^-))$$

$$= (\top, \top) \implies$$

$$\left(\underset{s \in W}{\bigvee} (R_c^+(s_0, s) \wedge (M'|_\sigma, s \models q)^+), \underset{s \in W}{\bigwedge} (R_c^+(s_0, s) \to (M'|_\sigma, s \models q)^-) \right)$$

$$= (\top, \top) \implies ((\bot \wedge \top) \vee (\bot \wedge \top) \vee (\top \wedge \bot), (\bot \to \top) \wedge (\bot \to \top) \wedge (\top \to \top))$$

$$= (\top, \top) \implies (\bot, \top) = (\top \to \bot, \top \wedge \top) = (\bot, \top)$$

Similarly, we have that $(M'|_\sigma, s_1 \models q \to \langle c \rangle q) = (\top, \top)$ and $(M'|_\sigma, s_2 \models q \to \langle c \rangle q) = (\top, \bot)$. Therefore, $(M'|_\sigma \models q \to \langle c \rangle q) = (\bot, \top) \text{⊓} (\top, \top) \text{⊓} (\top, \bot) = (\bot, \top)$. In conclusion,

$$Mod(SP)(M'|_\sigma)$$

$$= (M'|_\sigma \models [c]\langle b \rangle \top) \text{⊓} (M'|_\sigma \models \neg(p \vee q)) \text{⊓} (M'|_\sigma \models q \to \langle c \rangle q)$$

$$= (\top \wedge \bot \wedge \bot, \top \vee \top \vee \top) = (\bot, \top)$$

$$= Mod(SP \text{ with } \sigma)(M')$$

The degree of which there is evidence that model M' is a model of SP **with** σ, i.e. specification SP translated via the morphism σ, is $\bot$ and the degree to which there is evidence of M' not being a model of the specification is $\top$.

Notice that in this case we have *consistency*, we are completely certain that M' is not a model of SP **with** σ, that is, model M' doesn't satisfy the requirements/axioms demanded by SP **with** σ.

The following example is adapted from [MBHM18] to suit paraconsistent systems and specifications.

Example 4. Let **3** be the underlying iMTL-algebra and $\langle \text{Act}, \varnothing \rangle$ a signature where the set of propositions is empty and the set of actions is $\text{Act} = \{in, out\}$ with $\{in\}$ standing for the input of a text file and $\{out\}$ standing for the output of a zip-file.

This example considers a file compressing service working only with text files. Starting with a loose specification SP_0 whose requirements are that at any state:

0.1 $[in]\langle out \rangle \top$, whenever a text file is received for compression there has to exist an action where there is an output of a zip-file

0.2 $\langle a \rangle \top$, for some $a \in \{in, out\}$, that is, the system should never terminate

Let M_0 be the following model such that the information regarding the input action is inconsistent and the information regarding the output action is vague.

$$in|(\top, \top) \ \ \boxed{w} \ \ out|(u, u)$$

It's possible to check that $(M_0, w \models \langle in \rangle \top) = (\top, \bot)$ and $(M_0, w \models [in]\langle out \rangle \top) = (u, \bot)$. Hence,

$$Mod(SP_0)(M_0) = (u, \bot) \sqcap (\top, \bot) = (u \wedge \top, \bot \vee \bot) = (u, \bot)$$

As stated, SP_0 is a very loose specification that doesn't demand, for example, that immediately after an output action must come an input action. Because of that we will now consider a new specification. Let SP_1 be a specification over Σ whose requirement is that at any state:

1.1 $[out](\langle in \rangle \top \wedge [out] \bot)$, whenever there is an output action the system must go on with an input

Let $SP = SP_0 \cup SP_1$ be the union of both specifications. Then,

$$Mod(SP)(M_0) = Mod(SP_0 \cup SP_1)(M_0)$$
$$= Mod(SP_0)(M_0) \sqcap Mod(SP_1)(M_0)$$
$$= (u, \bot) \sqcap (\bot, u) = (\bot, u)$$

If we now consider the following PLTS, M_1:

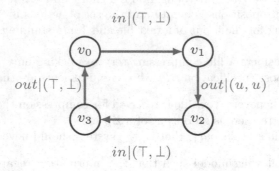

For model M_1 we have that:

$$Mod(SP_0 \cup SP_1)(M_1) = Mod(SP_0)(M_1) \sqcap Mod(SP_1)(M_1)$$
$$= (u, \bot) \sqcap (\top, \bot) = (u, \bot)$$

Since SP results from the union of SP_0 and SP_1, both flat specifications. SP_0 axioms consists of the union of the axioms of SP_0 and SP_1, (0.1)+(0.2)+(1.1). Note that $Mod(SP)(M_0) \preccurlyeq Mod(SP)(M_1)$, thus there is a higher evidence degree that M_1 is a model of SP and a lower evidence degree that M_1 isn't a model of SP, compared to M_0.

4   Conclusions

Paraconsistent transition systems [CMB22] were revisited in an institutional framework in order to develop a compositional, structured specification approach for engineering their composition.

Current work includes the study of horizontal and vertical refinement in this institution, as well as normalization structured specifications. Another important extension goes into the domain of observational abstraction: behavioural specifications resort to a notion of observational satisfaction for the axioms of a specification, whereas abstractor specifications define an abstraction from the standard semantics of a specification w.r.t. an observational equivalence relation between algebras.

Adding abstractor and behavioural operators [HMW18] and investigating a proper notion of observational equivalence for these systems is in order.

Appendix

Proposition 1 Let $\sigma : (\mathrm{Prop}, \mathrm{Act}) \to (\mathrm{Prop}', \mathrm{Act}')$ be a signature morphism, M' a $(\mathrm{Prop}', \mathrm{Act}')$-PLTS, and $\varphi \in \mathrm{Sen}(\mathrm{Prop}, \mathrm{Act})$ a formula. Then, for any $w \in W$,

$$(M'|_\sigma, w \models \varphi) = (M', w \models \mathrm{Sen}(\sigma)(\varphi)) \tag{5}$$

Proof. The proof is by induction over the structure of sentences. To simplify notation we will write $\sigma(p)$ instead of $\sigma_{\text{Prop}}(p)$ for any $p \in \text{Prop}$ and $\sigma(a)$ instead of $\sigma_{\text{Act}}(a)$ for any $a \in \text{Act}$. The case of $\perp$ is trivial, by the definition of $\models$ and Sen we have that $(M'|_\sigma, w \models \perp) = (0, 1) = (M', w \models \text{Sen}(\sigma)(\perp))$. For sentences $p \in \text{Prop}$, one observes that by defn of Sen, of $\models$ and of reducts, $(M', w \models \text{Sen}(\sigma)(p)) = (M', w \models \sigma(p)) = V'(w, \sigma(p)) = V(w, p) = (M'|_\sigma, w \models p)$. For sentences $\neg\varphi$ we observe that, by definition of Sen and of $\models$, we have that $(M', w \models \text{Sen}(\sigma)(\neg\varphi)) = M', w \models \neg\text{Sen}(\sigma)(\varphi) = (/\!\!/(M', w \models \text{Sen}(\sigma)(\varphi)))$. By induction hypothesis $(/\!\!/(M', w \models \text{Sen}(\sigma)(\varphi))) = /\!\!/(M'|_\sigma, w \models \varphi)$ and, again, by definition of Sen and of $\models$, we have $/\!\!/(M'|_\sigma, w \models \varphi) = (M'|_\sigma, w \models \neg\varphi)$.

Let us consider now formulas composed by Boolean operators. Firstly, we can observe that, by definition of Sen and of $\models$, $(M', w \models \text{Sen}(\sigma)(\varphi \wedge \varphi')) = (M', w \models \text{Sen}(\sigma)(\varphi) \wedge \text{Sen}(\sigma)(\varphi')) = (M', w \models \text{Sen}(\sigma)(\varphi)) \sqcap (M', w \models \text{Sen}(\sigma)(\varphi'))$. By I.H. we have that $(M', w \models \text{Sen}(\sigma)(\varphi')) = (M'|_\sigma, w \models \varphi) \sqcap (M'|_\sigma, w \models \varphi')$ and by definition of $\models$, it is equal to $M'|_\sigma, w \models (\varphi \wedge \varphi')$. The proof for sentences $\varphi \vee \varphi'$ and $\varphi \rightarrow \varphi'$ is analogous.

$M', w \models \text{Sen}(\sigma)([a]\,\varphi)$

$= \{\text{defn of Sen}\}$

$M', w \models [\sigma(a)]\,\text{Sen}(\sigma)(\varphi)$

$= \{\text{defn of } \models\}$

$([\sigma(a)^+](M', w, \text{Sen}(\sigma)(\varphi)^+), \langle\sigma(a)^+\rangle(M', w, \text{Sen}(\sigma)(\varphi)^-))$

$= \{\text{def. of } [a^+] \text{ and } \langle a^+\rangle\}$

$$\left(\bigsqcap_{w' \in R'_{\sigma(a)}[w]} (R'^+_{\sigma(a)}(w, w') \rightarrow (M', w' \models \text{Sen}(\sigma)(\varphi))^+), \right.$$

$$\left. \bigsqcup_{w' \in R'_{\sigma(a)}[w]} (R'^+_{\sigma(a)}(w, w') \sqcap (M', w' \models \text{Sen}(\sigma)(\varphi))^-) \right)$$

$= \{(\text{step } \star)\}$

$$\left(\bigsqcap_{w' \in R_a[w]} (R^+_a(w, w') \rightarrow (M'|_\sigma, w \models \varphi)^+), \bigsqcup_{w' \in R_a[w]} (R^+_a(w, w') \sqcap (M'|_\sigma, w \models \varphi)^-) \right)$$

$= \{\text{def. } [a^+] \text{ and } \langle a^+\rangle\}$

$([a^+](M'|_\sigma, w, \varphi^+), \langle a^+\rangle(M'|_\sigma, w, \varphi^-))$

$= \{\text{defn of } \models\}$

$M'|_\sigma, w \models [a]\,\varphi$

(step $\star$) We have by reduct that $R'_{\sigma(a)}[w] = R_a[w]$. Moreover, by I.H., it is true that $(M', w \models \text{Sen}(\sigma)(\varphi)) = (M'|_\sigma, w \models \varphi)$, and hence

$$\left((M', w \models \text{Sen}(\sigma)(\varphi))^+, (M', w \models \text{Sen}(\sigma)(\varphi))^- \right) =$$

$$\left((M'|_\sigma, w \models \varphi)^+, (M'|_\sigma, w \models \varphi)^- \right) \tag{6}$$

Therefore, $M', w \models \mathsf{Sen}(\sigma)(\varphi))^+ = (M'|_\sigma, w \models \varphi)^+$ and
$(M', w \models \mathsf{Sen}(\sigma)(\varphi))^- = (M'|_\sigma, w \models \varphi)^-$.

$$M', w \models \mathsf{Sen}(\sigma)([a]\,\varphi)$$
$$= \{\text{defn of Sen}\}$$
$$M', w \models [\sigma(a)]\,\mathsf{Sen}(\sigma)(\varphi)$$
$$= \{\text{defn of } \models\}$$
$$(\langle \sigma(a)^- \rangle (M', w, \mathsf{Sen}(\sigma)(\varphi)^-), [\sigma(a)^-](M', w, \mathsf{Sen}(\sigma)(\varphi)^+))$$
$$= \{\text{def. of } [a^-] \text{ and } \langle a^- \rangle\}$$
$$\left(\bigsqcup_{w' \in R'_{\sigma(a)}[w]} (R'^-_{\sigma(a)}(w,w') \sqcap (M', w' \models \mathsf{Sen}(\sigma)(\varphi))^-),\right.$$
$$\left. \prod_{w' \in R'_{\sigma(a)}[w]} (R'^-_{\sigma(a)}(w,w') \to (M', w' \models \mathsf{Sen}(\sigma)(\varphi))^+) \right)$$
$$= \{\text{analogous to (step } \star)\}$$
$$(\langle a^- \rangle (M'|_\sigma, w, \varphi^-),\, [a^-](M'|_\sigma, w, \varphi^+))$$
$$= \{\text{defn of } \models\}$$
$$M'|_\sigma, w \models [a]\,\varphi$$

The proofs for sentences $\langle a \rangle \varphi$ and $\langle\!\langle a \rangle\!\rangle \varphi$ are analogous.

Finally, let us consider the proof for sentences $\circ\,\varphi$. By definition of Sen, $M', w \models \mathsf{Sen}(\sigma)(\circ\,\varphi) = (M', w \models \circ\,\mathsf{Sen}(\sigma)(\varphi))$. By definition of $\models$, this evaluates to $(1,0)$, if $(M', w \models \mathsf{Sen}(\sigma)(\varphi)) \in \Delta_C$ and to $(0,1)$ otherwise. Hence, by I.H. it evaluates to $(1,0)$ when $(M'|_\sigma, w \models \varphi) \in \Delta_C$ and to $(0,1)$, i.e., we have $(M'|_\sigma, w \models \circ\,\varphi)$.

References

[ACEGG91] Agustí-Cullell, J., Esteva, F., Garcia, P., Godo, L.: Formalizing multiple-valued logics as institutions. In: Bouchon-Meunier, B., Yager, R.R., Zadeh, L.A. (eds.) IPMU 1990. LNCS, vol. 521, pp. 269–278. Springer, Heidelberg (1991). https://doi.org/10.1007/BFb0028112

[Aka16] Akama, S. (ed.): Towards Paraconsistent Engineering. ISRL, vol. 110. Springer, Cham (2016). https://doi.org/10.1007/978-3-319-40418-9

[BEGR09] Bou, F., Esteva, F., Godo, L., Rodríguez, R.O.: On the minimum many-valued modal logic over a finite residuated lattice. J. Logic Comput. **21**(5), 739–790 (2009)

[CCM07] Carnielli, W., Coniglio, M.E., Marcos, J.: Logics of formal inconsistency. In: Handbook of Philosophical Logic, pp. 1–93 (2007)

[CMB22] Cruz, A., Madeira, A., Barbosa, L.S.: A logic for paraconsistent transition systems. In: Indrzejczak, A., Zawidzki, M. (eds.) 10th International Conference on Non-Classical Logics. Theory and Applications, vol. 358 of EPTCS, pp. 270–284 (2022)

[EG01] Esteva, F., Godo, L.: Monoidal t-norm based logic: towards a logic for left-continuous t-norms. Fuzzy Sets Syst. **124**, 271–288 (2001)

[GB92] Goguen, J.A., Burstall, R.M.: Institutions: abstract model theory for specification and programming. J. ACM **39**(1), 95–146 (1992)

[HMW18] Hennicker, R., Madeira, A., Wirsing, M.: Behavioural and abstractor specifications revisited. Theor. Comp. Sc. **741**, 32–43 (2018)

[Jas69] Jaskowski, S.: Propositional calculus for contradictory deductive systems (communicated at the meeting of march 19, 1948). Studia Logica: Int. J. Symb. Logic **24**, 143–160 (1969)

[JGMB21] Jain, M., Gomes, L., Madeira, A., Barbosa, L.S.: Towards a specification theory for fuzzy modal logic. In: International Symposium on Theoretical Aspects of Software Engineering, TASE 2021, pp. 175–182. IEEE (2021)

[Kra98] Kracht, M.: On extensions of intermediate logics by strong negation. J. Phil. Logic **27**(1), 49–73 (1998)

[MBHM18] Madeira, A., Barbosa, L.S., Hennicker, R., Martins, M.A.: A logic for the stepwise development of reactive systems. Theor. Comput. Sci. **744**, 78–96 (2018)

[MHST03] Mossakowski, T., Haxthausen, A., Sannella, D., Tarlecki, A.: CASL, the common algebraic specification language: semantics and proof theory. Comput. Inf. **22**, 285–321 (2003)

[RJJ15] Rivieccio, U., Jung, A., Jansana, R.: Four-valued modal logic: Kripke semantics and duality. J. Logic Comput. **27**(1), 155–199 (2015)

[ST12] Sannella, D., Tarlecki, A.: Foundations of Algebraic Specification and Formal Software Development. Monographs on TCS, an EATCS Series. Springer, Heidelberg (2012). https://doi.org/10.1007/978-3-642-17336-

Towards a Basic Theory for Partial Differentiation in the Prototype Verification System

Andrea Domenici[✉][iD]

Department of Information Engineering, University of Pisa, Pisa, Italy
andrea.domenici@unipi.it

Abstract. This paper presents preliminary work on theories supporting partial differentiation of scalar fields, which will be based upon, and add to, the large library of mathematical theories supported by the Prototype Verification System theorem-proving environment. These theories include mathematical analysis of functions of one real-valued variable, but not, currently, theories on partial differentiation. In this paper, the issue of defining *partial derivatives* in the strongly typed, higher-order language of PVS is discussed, and a straightforward, pragmatic approach is proposed, introducing the formalizations of some basic concepts.

1 Introduction

Current (and future) applications of formal verification involve highly complex systems, where software is embedded in *continuous* physical systems, whose control software must integrate systems of differential equations.

Logic languages are a class of formalisms used to model both the physical and software aspects of complex systems, at the different levels of abstraction required at different phases of development. The work presented in this paper relies on the *Prototype Verification System* (PVS), an interactive theorem-proving environment for a higher-order logic language that has been applied to a range of different engineering problems [2,3]. A large number of PVS libraries contain proved results in mathematics and application fields that can be used to prove further results of theoretical or application-specific interest. However, the existing libraries currently offer no direct support for partial differentiation (PD).

Developing a full-fledged theory of PD from fundamental definitions, general enough to verify partial derivatives (PDv) of real-valued functions over domains of arbitrary dimensionality, is a large and complex task. This preliminary work has the less ambitious goal of producing a set of basic definitions for differentiation of scalar fields $\mathbb{R}^n \to \mathbb{R}$, built upon the existing PVS theories. The theory presented in this paper (`pderiv_basic`) has been developed as a basis for future extended theories that designers would use in most practical applications. For this reason, some definitions follow the approach used in introductory textbooks on calculus rather than more fundamental formalizations. The theory defines,

© IFIP International Federation for Information Processing 2023
Published by Springer Nature Switzerland AG 2023
H. Hojjat and E. Ábrahám (Eds.): FSEN 2023, LNCS 14155, pp. 18–24, 2023.
https://doi.org/10.1007/978-3-031-42441-0_2

in the specification language of PVS, (i) a minimal set of concepts about scalar fields and derivatives, and (ii) a few predicates and functions to support the verification of PD results.

In the following, Sect. 2 presents related work, Sect. 3 introduces the PVS environment, Sect. 4 gives an overview of the theory developed in this work, and Sect. 5 discusses the limits of this work to propose further research.

2 Related Work

Computer algebra systems, such as MATLAB, Maple, Mathematica, and Maxima can compute PDvs symbolically, but they do not address the issue of *verification*, which is the motivation for the present work. Even when a problem is solved automatically with computer algebra, checking the solutions also on a verification system increases our confidence in their correctness.

The full description of the PVS environment is given by the manuals available from the PVS site (pvs.csl.sri.com). Among the works on mathematical analysis with PVS, we mention Dutertre [5] and Gottliebsen [8]. Examples of applications to control systems can be found in [1,2]. In paper [4] the PDvs defining the system's Jacobian had been written in PVS but their correctness had not been verified.

Extensive theories on real analysis, including ordinary differentiation, are available for the Coq proof assistant [9] and the HOL [7] theorem provers.

The KeYmaera X theorem prover [6] supports *differential dynamic logic* (d$\mathcal{L}$) [10], a modal specification language featuring ordinary differentiation.

3 The PVS Theorem Proving Environment

The Prototype Verification System is an interactive theorem proving environment, providing a higher-order logic specification language and an extensive set of inference rules based on sequent calculus. A user proves a theorem by choosing a PVS rule at each proof step, and each step transforms the current goal according to the chosen rule. A PVS theory is a named collection of *definitions* and *formulas*. Definitions declare symbols for types, variables, and constants. Variable and constant symbols may range over functions and relations. Formulas are logical expressions identified by a name and labeled by keywords such as AXIOM, THEOREM, or LEMMA. The theorem prover takes AXIOMs as proved formulas, while the other formulas are to be proved interactively. Formulas are built with the usual arithmetic and logical operators and quantifiers, together with operators for sets, tuples, records, and lists, and conditional operators. The *overriding* operator (WITH) enables pointwise redefinition of a function. For example, from

```
f(x: real): real = 0
```

we can define a function g that takes the same values as f for all real values except zero, where it takes the value 1:

```
g: [real -> real] = f WITH [ (0) := 1]
```

A given theory may refer to other theories with IMPORTING directives, inheriting their definitions and formulas with the stored proofs for the verified formulas. Theories can be parametric in types and constants (including functions) and the parameters can be instantiated for the whole theory (in the IMPORTING directives) or for single occurrences of the imported symbols. Theories can be grouped in *libraries*. Name conflicts among theories are resolved by prefixing the name of the defining theory (and library, if needed) to identifiers. For example, structures@listn[real].list(n) is the fully qualified name for finite lists with n elements, defined in theory listn[real] of library structures.

The type system includes the fundamental arithmetic types, such as *naturals*, *integers*, and *reals*, and also user-definable types, such as *records* and *lists*. The different arithmetic types represent mathematical concepts defined axiomatically. *Uninterpreted* types are identified by a name but give no information about their possible values. Likewise, *uninterpreted constants* are names of single, but unspecified members of a given type. *Subtypes* are defined by set comprehension.

Constants are declared by specifying their type and optionally their value and variables may be declared *globally* as in n: VAR natural, or *locally*, within a quantifier, a λ-expression, or a function argument declaration. Function types are specified as, e.g.,

```
int2real: TYPE = [int -> real]
intrat2real: TYPE = [[int, rational] -> real]
int2_int2int: TYPE = [int -> [int -> int]]
```

where int2real and intrat2real are the functions of signature $\mathbb{Z} \to \mathbb{R}$ and $\mathbb{Z} \times \mathbb{Q} \to \mathbb{R}$, respectively, and int2_int2int are the functions that map integers to functions of signature $\mathbb{Z} \to \mathbb{Z}$.

Named function constants are defined, e.g., with this syntax:

```
incr(n: int): int = n + 1
```

Anonymous function constants are denoted as λ-expressions, e.g.,

```
LAMBDA (n: int): n + 1
```

Proofs based on the sequent calculus are constructed as trees, rooted at the formula to be proved, of *sequents*, expressions of the form $\Gamma \vdash \Delta$, where Γ and Δ are sequences of *antecedent* and *consequent* formulas, respectively.

The PVS type checker ensures that the conditions for applicability of the inference rules are satisfied, producing *type check conditions* (TCC), i.e., assumptions on certain expressions that must be discharged to complete a proof.

The NASALIB libraries [5] are an important collection of PVS definitions and theorems from various branches of mathematics, including, e.g., linear algebra, vectors, and metric spaces. In particular, the analysis library defines the basic concepts for differentiation and integration of real functions of one variable, and the differentiation rules for standard mathematical functions. It should be noted that proofs involving these differentiation rules require proving TCCs.

4   The pderiv_basic Theory

The pderiv_basic theory is divided in two parts. The first part is an embryonic set of concepts about scalar fields and their derivatives, while the second part introduces a few predicates and functions to support the practical process of verifying PD results. The theory is parametric in the dimensionality n of a scalar field $\mathbb{R}^n \to \mathbb{R}$, where $\mathbb{R}^n$ is represented by the PVS type Vector[n], from the NASALIB theory vectors. A function $f(x_1, \ldots, x_n)$ must be rewritten as a function $f(p)$, where each occurrence of x_i $(1 \le i \le n)$ must be replaced by $p(i-1)$. This produces a parametric theory, applicable to domains of any dimensionality. Scalar fields are represented as:

```
vect: TYPE = Vector[n];       Rn2R: TYPE = [vect -> real]
```

We define a vector as an anonymous function that maps an Index argument to an element of a NASALIB list of type listn(n). Vectors are created with this constructor, where nth accesses the i-th element of list l:

```
list2vect(l: listn[real].listn(n)): Vector = LAMBDA(i: Index): nth(l, i)
```

Unit vectors are defined as follows:

```
u(i: Index[n]): vect = LAMBDA(j: Index[n]): IF j= i THEN 1 ELSE 0 ENDIF
```

Various concepts can be defined after the patterns of similar concepts from one-variable calculus. For example, the set of adherence points of a set S of vectors is defined as:

```
vadh(S: setof[vect]): setof[vect] = {z: vect | FORALL (e: posreal):
    EXISTS (v: vect): member(v, S) AND norm(v - z) < e}
```

where norm is the norm of a vector, defined in theory vectors. The following lemma, similar to the NASALIB lemma adherence_prop1, can then be proved:

```
vadherence_prop1: LEMMA FORALL (e:posreal, E:setof[vect], (a:(vadh(E)))):
    EXISTS (x: vect): member(x, E) AND norm[n](x - a) < e
```

Assuming c to be an interior point of the domain S of a scalar field f, and v a vector such that $c + v$ lies within a ball centered at c and contained in S, f is *differentiable* at c if there exist a linear map (the *total derivative*) $T_c : \mathbb{R}^n \to \mathbb{R}$ and a scalar function $E : \mathbb{R}^n \times \mathbb{R}^n \to \mathbb{R}$ such that $f(c + v) = f(c) + T_c(v) + ||v||E(c, v)$, where $E(c, v) \to 0$ as $||v|| \to 0$.

Linear maps $\mathbb{R}^n \to \mathbb{R}^m$ are represented by Map, a NASALIB record with fields n, m, and mp, which contains a function from n-vectors to m-vectors. Functions v2r and sf2vf are introduced to convert from one-vectors to reals and from functions [vect->real] to functions [vect->Vector[1]]. Differentiability at a point c is then defined as:

```
differentiable_at?(f: Rn2R, c: vect): bool =
  EXISTS (Tc: [vect -> Map(n, 1)], Ec: Rn2R): FORALL (v: vect):
    f(c + v) = f(c) + v2r(Tc(c)'mp(v)) + norm(v)*Ec(v)
    AND lim(sf2vf(Ec), c) = zero
```

The difference quotient of f at c in the direction of u is defined as:

```
diffquot(f, c, u)(h): real = abs(f(c + h*u) - f(c))/(abs(h)*norm(u))
```

The directional derivative at a point c in the direction of vector u is then:

```
dderiv_at(f, c, (u: {u0: vect | norm(u0) = 1})): real =
    lim(diffquot(f, c, u), 0)
```

PDvs can then be defined as directional derivatives:

```
pderiv_at(i, f, c): real = dderiv_at(f, c, u(i))
```

The above definitions sketch a basic theory of PD, but a full-fledged theory at that level of abstraction would be of little use in the daily work of people designing, say, a state-space model for a plant controller, as they need the familiar textbook-style differentiation rules.

Elementary textbooks define the PDv $D_i f$ of a function $f : \mathbb{R}^n \rightarrow \mathbb{R}$ with respect to x_i at a point $P_0 = (x_{01}, \ldots, x_{0n})$ as the ordinary derivative of the *restriction* $\phi_i : \mathbb{R} \rightarrow \mathbb{R}$ of f to the set $\{x_{01}, \ldots, x_i, \ldots, x_{0n}\}$, expressed as "*differentiate f with respect to x_i, keeping the other variables constant*". Yet, the PVS type checker does not allow a function of n variables to be treated as a function of one variable, "keeping the other variables constant". In this work, we formalize the concept of *restriction* with the PVS overriding operator and define a few predicates using the NASALIB function `deriv`:

```
restrcn?(i, phi, f, P): bool = FORALL(r:real): phi(r) = f(P WITH[(i):=r])
pder_at?(i: Index[n], pd_at: Rn2R, f: Rn2R, p: vect): bool =
    EXISTS (phi, dphi: R2R): restrcn?(i, phi, f, p) AND
        dphi = deriv(phi) AND restrcn?(i, dphi, pd_at, p)
pder?(i, pd, f): bool = EXISTS (p: vect): pder_at?(i, pd, f, p)
```

The correctness of a PD $D_i f$ can be proved as follows:

1. write the definitions of f (e.g., `f`) and $D_i f$ (`df_x`),
2. choose an uninterpreted constant point P;
3. write ϕ_i (`phi_x`) and ϕ_i' (`dphi_x`), the restrictions at P of f and $D_i f$ wrt x_i;
4. verify that ϕ_i' is the ordinary derivative of ϕ_i:

   ```
   lem1: LEMMA dphi_x_f = deriv(phi_x_f)
   ```

5. verify that ϕ_i and ϕ_i' are the restrictions of f and $D_i f$:

   ```
   restr_phi_x_f: LEMMA restrcn?(0, phi_x_f, f, P)
   restr_dphi_x_f: LEMMA restrcn?(0, dphi_x_f, df_x, P)
   ```

6. verify that $D_i f$ is the PDv of f:

```
pder_df_x_f: LEMMA pder?(0, df_x, f)
```

It should be stressed that, to verify that ϕ_i is a restriction of f at P with respect to x_i, a user must instantiate P as an uninterpreted constant. *This is crucial for the soundness of this procedure.* The PVS environment currently does not provide means to verify if a constant symbol is uninterpreted or it represents a concrete numerical value, so it is the user's responsibility to apply the procedure correctly. *It is acknowledged that this is a major loophole in the procedure.*

5 Discussion and Further Work

This paper has introduced a proof-of-concept PVS theory aimed at supporting PD of scalar fields. Its main objective is to provide practical means to verify results of PD in the context of complex systems, in the PVS environment. The verification procedure has been devised to circumvent the constraints imposed by the PVS typechecker, by providing a quasi-formalization of the familiar definition of PD in terms of ordinary differentiation. Unfortunately, this approach requires the user to define a vector of uninterpreted constants to replace the variables "kept constant". An inadvertent user might choose a vector of *interpreted* constants, like, say, $(0, 0, 0)$, which clearly would make the procedure unsound. At the moment, two approaches are possible: (i) a formalization of PD from first principles, or (ii) a modification of the PVS prover. The first approach would require a great effort, and it could not reuse the simple differentiation rules already available in PVS. The second one is probably easier, requiring the developers of the PVS prover to make the property of uninterpretedness accessible in some way. Or, a prover rule to produce "safe" restrictions of a multi-variable function could be implemented.

References

1. Bernardeschi, C., Dini, P., Domenici, A., Saponara, S.: Co-simulation and verification of a non-linear control system for cogging torque reduction in brushless motors. In: Camara, J., Steffen, M. (eds.) SEFM 2019. LNCS, vol. 12226, pp. 3–19. Springer, Cham (2020). https://doi.org/10.1007/978-3-030-57506-9_1
2. Bernardeschi, C., Dini, P., Domenici, A., Palmieri, M., Saponara, S.: Formal verification and co-simulation in the design of a synchronous motor control algorithm. Energies **13**(16), 4057 (2020). https://doi.org/10.3390/en13164057
3. Bernardeschi, C., Domenici, A., Saponara, S.: Formal verification in the loop to enhance verification of safety-critical cyber-physical systems. Electron. Commun. EASST **77**, 10 (2019). https://doi.org/10.14279/tuj.eceasst.77.1106
4. Domenici, A., Bernardeschi, C.: A logic theory pattern for linearized control systems. Electron. Proceed. Theoret. Comput. Sci. **338**, 46–52 (2021). https://doi.org/10.4204/eptcs.338.7

5. Dutertre, B.: Elements of mathematical analysis in PVS. In: Goos, G., Hartmanis, J., van Leeuwen, J., von Wright, J., Grundy, J., Harrison, J. (eds.) TPHOLs 1996. LNCS, vol. 1125, pp. 141–156. Springer, Heidelberg (1996). https://doi.org/10.1007/BFb0105402
6. Fulton, N., Mitsch, S., Quesel, J.-D., Völp, M., Platzer, A.: KeYmaera X: an axiomatic tactical theorem prover for hybrid systems. In: Felty, A.P., Middeldorp, A. (eds.) CADE 2015. LNCS (LNAI), vol. 9195, pp. 527–538. Springer, Cham (2015). https://doi.org/10.1007/978-3-319-21401-6_36
7. Gordon, M.J., Melham, T.F.: Introduction to HOL: a theorem proving environment for higher order logic. Cambridge University Press (1993)
8. Gottliebsen, H.: Automated theorem proving for mathematics: real analysis in PVS, Ph. D. thesis, University of St Andrews (2002)
9. The Coq development team: The Coq proof assistant reference manual (2004)
10. Platzer, A.: Differential dynamic logic for hybrid systems. J. Autom. Reason. **41**, 143–189 (2008). https://doi.org/10.1007/s10817-008-9103-8

Case Studies of Development of Verified Programs with Dafny for Accessibility Assessment

João Pascoal Faria[1,2]([⊠]) [iD] and Rui Abreu[1,3] [iD]

[1] Faculty of Engineering of the University of Porto, Porto, Portugal
{jpf,rma}@fe.up.pt
[2] INESC TEC - Institute for Systems and Computer Engineering,
Technology and Science, Porto, Portugal
[3] INESC ID, Lisbon, Portugal

Abstract. Formal verification techniques aim at formally proving the correctness of a computer program with respect to a formal specification, but the expertise and effort required for applying formal specification and verification techniques and scalability issues have limited their practical application. In recent years, the tremendous progress with SAT and SMT solvers enabled the construction of a new generation of tools that promise to make formal verification more accessible for software engineers, by automating most if not all of the verification process. The Dafny system is a prominent example of that trend. However, little evidence exists yet about its accessibility. To help fill this gap, we conducted a set of 10 case studies of developing verified implementations in Dafny of some real-world algorithms and data structures, to determine its accessibility for software engineers. We found that, on average, the amount of code written for specification and verification purposes is of the same order of magnitude as the traditional code written for implementation and testing purposes (ratio of 1.14) – an "overhead" that certainly pays off for high-integrity software. The performance of the Dafny verifier was impressive, with 2.4 proof obligations generated per line of code written, and 24 ms spent per proof obligation generated and verified, on average. However, we also found that the manual work needed in writing auxiliary verification code may be significant and difficult to predict and master. Hence, further automation and systematization of verification tasks are possible directions for future advances in the field.

Keywords: Formal verification · Dafny · Accessibility · Case studies

1 Introduction

1.1 Motivation

Given the increasing dependence of our society on software-based systems, it is ever more important to assure their correct, secure and safe functioning, particularly for high-integrity systems [1]. Since software development is a knowledge-intensive activity and software-based systems are increasingly complex, errors

© IFIP International Federation for Information Processing 2023
Published by Springer Nature Switzerland AG 2023
H. Hojjat and E. Ábrahám (Eds.): FSEN 2023, LNCS 14155, pp. 25–39, 2023.
https://doi.org/10.1007/978-3-031-42441-0_3

are inevitable, so several techniques need to be applied along the process to catch and fix defects as early as possible.

Testing and reviews are the most widely applied techniques in the software industry for defect detection. However, since "program testing can be used to show the presence of bugs, but never to show their absence" [2], testing alone cannot be considered sufficient for high-integrity systems. If properly applied [3], reviews are a cost-effective technique for defect detection and knowledge sharing, but, like with testing, they cannot be used to show the absence of bugs.

By contrast, formal verification techniques aim at formally proving the correctness of a computer program, i.e., show the absence of defects. To that end, we need a formal specification of the program intent and a logic reasoning framework, usually based on Hoare logic [4]. But the expertise and effort required for applying formal specification and verification techniques and scalability issues have limited their practical application. In recent years, the tremendous progress with SAT and SMT solvers [5], such as Z3 [6], enabled the construction of a new generation of tools that promise to make formal verification accessible for software engineers, like Dafny [7], Frama-C [8] and Why3 [9], by automating most if not all of the verification process. However, little evidence exists yet about their accessibility, regarding the expertise and effort required to apply them.

The authors have used formal specification languages and automated reasoning tools for several years in software engineering research, education, and practice [10–14]. E.g., in [11], Alloy [15] was used to automatically generate unit tests and mock objects in JUnit[1] from algebraic specifications of generic types. Although model-based testing approaches such as this one do not guarantee the absence of bugs, they provide a higher assurance than manual test generation and seem to be currently more accessible than formal verification.

From an educational perspective, the authors are also interested in assessing the feasibility of embedding computer-supported formal specification and verification techniques in undergraduate programs, namely in courses dedicated to studying algorithms and data structures.

1.2 Objectives and Methodology

To help fill the gap in the current state of the art regarding accessibility studies, we conducted a set of case studies of developing verified implementations in Dafny of some well-known algorithms and data structures of varying complexity, with the goal of determining its accessibility for software engineering practitioners, students and researchers, with limited training in formal methods.

Table 1 shows the list of case studies. The source code is available in GitHub[2] and [16]. The case studies explore formal specification and verification features of increasing complexity. In the paper, we provide some highlights for selected features. For each case study, we collected a few metrics and lessons learned, to help answer our main question, regarding Dafny accessibility. Those metrics and lessons learned are aggregated and discussed at the end of the paper.

---

[1] https://junit.org/.

[2] https://github.com/joaopascoalfariafeup/DafnyProjects.

Table 1. List of case studies.

Category	Case study
Numerical algorithms	o Integer division (Euclidean division)
	o Natural power of a number (divide and conquer algorithm)
Searching & sorting algorithms	o Binary search
	o Insertion sort
Collections	o Priority queue implemented with a binary heap
	o Unordered set implemented with a hash table (Hash Set)
	o Ordered set implemented with a binary search tree (Tree Set)
Matching problems	o Stable marriage problem solved by the Gale-Shapley algorithm
	o Teachers placement problem reduced to stable marriage
Graph algorithms	o Topological sorting (Khan's algorithm [17])
	o Eulerian circuit (Hierholzer's algorithm)

1.3 Structure of the Paper

Section 2 presents some highlights about specification and verification features of increasing complexity in the case studies. Section 3 consolidates the metrics collected and lessons learned, and draws conclusions regarding our research goal. Related work is discussed in Sec. 4. Conclusions and future work are presented in Sec. 5.

2 Case Studies Highlights

2.1 An Introductory Example (Integer Division)

The self-explanatory program in Fig. 1 explores some basic features of Dafny and serves as our first case study.

Dafny[3] [7] is a multi-paradigm programming language and system for the development of verified programs. The functional style is typically used for writing specifications, using value types and side-effect-free expressions, functions, and predicates. The procedural and object-oriented styles are typically used for writing implementations, using reference types (arrays, classes, etc.), and methods and statements with side effects. The Dafny programming system comprises a verifier (based on Z3), compilers that produce code in several target languages (C#, Java, JavaScript, Go, and C++), and an extension for Visual Studio Code.

The semantics of a method (`div` in this case) is formally specified by means of pre and postconditions, indicated with the `requires` and `ensures` clauses, respectively. The Dafny verifier is in charge of checking (with the help of the Z3 theorem prover) if such pre and postconditions are satisfied. When the implementation involves a loop, the user has to provide a loop invariant (with the `invariant` clause) and, in some cases, a loop variant (with the `decreases` clause), to help the verifier accomplish its job.

---

[3] https://github.com/dafny-lang/dafny.

```
// Computes the quotient q and remainder r of the integer division
// of a (non-negative) dividend n by a (positive) divisor d.
method div(n: nat, d: nat) returns (q: nat, r: nat)
  requires d > 0
  ensures q * d + r == n && r < d
{
  q := 0;
  r := n;
  while r >= d
    decreases r
    invariant q * d + r == n
  {
    q := q + 1;
    r := r - d;
  }
}
// Main program, with a simple test case (checked statically!).
method Main() {
    var q, r := div(15, 6);
    assert q == 2 && r == 3;
    print "q=", q, " r=", r, "\n";
}
```

Fig. 1. A simple program in Dafny for performing integer division.

The `Main` method is the entry point of a program in Dafny. In this example, it exercises the `div` method for some inputs, and checks (with `assert`) and prints the corresponding outputs. Like with pre and postconditions, `assert` statements are checked statically by the Dafny verifier. In this example, the verifier will try to prove the assertion based only on the postcondition of the `div` method (i.e., the method body is opaque for this purpose); this makes the verification modular and scalable. Since assertions are checked statically, test cases such as the one shown do actually test the specification in pre-compile time, and not the implementation at run-time; such *static test cases* are useful to detect problems in the specification, e.g., incomplete postconditions.

All the specification constructs and assertions mentioned above (indicated with the `requires`, `ensures`, `invariant`, `decreases`, and `assert` clauses) are used as annotations for verification purposes only (during static analysis), but are not compiled into the executable program, so do not cause runtime overhead.

2.2 Lemmas and Automatic Induction (Power of a Number)

In this case study, the goal is to prove the correctness of a well-known $O(log\ n)$ divide-and-conquer algorithm to compute the natural power of a real number (x^n). Self-explanatory excerpts are shown in Fig. 2 and the full code is available in GitHub. It illustrates the usage of lemmas, to specify properties that Dafny alone cannot deduce, and automatic induction, i.e., the ability of Dafny to automatically prove some properties by induction (directive `:induction a`).

```
// Recursive definition of x^n in functional style.
function power(x: real, n: nat) : real {
    if n == 0 then 1.0 else x * power(x, n-1)
}
// Computation of x^n in time and space O(log n).
method powerDC(x: real, n: nat) returns (p : real)
    ensures p == power(x, n)
{ ...
    if n % 2 == 0 {
        productOfPowers(x,  n/2, n/2); // recall lemma
        var temp := powerDC(x, n/2);
        return temp * temp;
    } ...
}
// States the property x^a * x^b = x^(a+b), used by 'powerDC'.
// The property is proved by automatic induction on 'a'.
lemma {:induction a} productOfPowers(x: real, a: nat, b: nat)
    ensures power(x, a) * power(x, b)  == power(x, a + b)
{/*Proof should go here, but is discovered by Dafny!*/}
```

Fig. 2. Excerpts of a program in Dafny for computing the natural power of a number.

2.3   Modules, Mutable Objects and Generics (Insertion Sort)

In this case study, we explore Dafny features for working with mutable objects (in this case, arrays) and generics, and separating specification, implementation, and test code with modules. Self-explanatory excerpts are shown in Fig. 3.

The array sorting problem is specified by the bodyless **sort** method in the abstract module **Sorting**, resorting to auxiliary predicates. The frame condition "**modifies a**" indicates that an implementation may modify the contents referenced by **a**. In the postcondition, "old(a[...])" and "a[..]" give the array contents at the begin and end of method execution, respectively, as mathematical sequences. Dafny has some support for generic predicates, functions and methods, but, unfortunately, does not support type parameters that are subject to operations other than equality (==); so, for demo purposes, we declared the type of array elements with a specific **type** definition.

Sorting algorithms may be provided in concrete modules that refine the abstract module, as in the **InsertionSort** module, inheriting the method contract and providing the actual algorithm in the body (omitted here). In this case, we just had to provide the loop invariants for the verifier to successfully check the correctness of the insertion sort algorithm with respect to the specification.

The module **TestSorting** shows an example of a test case of the **sort** method. For the Dafny verifier to successfully check the test outcome in the last **assert** statement, we had to write an auxiliary lemma implying that the outcome of **sort** is unique. Surprisingly, for the code to be checked successfully, we also had to provide some further "proof helper" assertions (as the first assertion) stating trivial facts that we expected to be taken for granted.

```
abstract module Sorting {
  type T = int // generics limitation!
  method sort(a: array<T>)
    modifies a
    ensures isSorted(a[..]) && isPermutation(a[..], old(a[..]))
}
```

```
module InsertionSort refines Sorting {
  method sort(a: array<T>) {...}
}
```

```
abstract module TestSorting {
  import opened Sorting
  method testSort () {
    var a := new T[] [9, 3, 6, 9];
    assert a[..] == [9, 3, 6, 9]; // proof helper!
    sort(a);
    SortingUniquenessProp(a[..], [3, 6, 9, 9]); //proof helper!
    assert a[..] ==  [3, 6, 9, 9];
  }
  lemma SortingUniquenessProp(a: seq<T>, b: seq<T>)
    requires isSorted(a) && isSorted(b) && isPermutation(a, b)
    ensures a == b
  { /* handwritten proof by induction goes here*/}
}
```

Fig. 3. Organization of an array sorting program in Dafny using modules.

2.4 State Abstraction and Automatic Contracts (Priority Queue)

In this case study, we explore Dafny features for separating specification and implementation and handling class invariants in object-oriented programs, following design by contract (DbC) principles. Excerpts of the specification of a priority queue and its implementation with a binary heap are shown in Fig. 3.

The operations' pre and postconditions of the priority queue (top box in Fig. 3) are specified independently of the internal state representation (a binary heap in this case), by resorting to a *state abstraction function* (elems). This function gives the priority queue contents as a multiset (allowing repeated values), and serves only for specification and verification purposes (doesn't generate executable code); to keep the specification at a high level of abstraction, it doesn't tell the ordering of elements (which is given by deleteMax).

In a subsequent refinement (box at the center of Fig. 3), it is chosen an internal (concrete) state representation - a binary heap stored in an array. It is also provided an implementation (body) for each method (box at the bottom of Fig. 4). The definition and verification of class invariants, stating restrictions on the internal state to be respected at method boundaries, is facilitated in Dafny with so-called automatic contracts, using the ":autocontracts" attribute. The class invariant is specified in a predicate Valid; calls to that predicate, together with some frame conditions, are automatically injected in the preconditions of all methods and in the postconditions of all methods and constructors.

```
class {:autocontracts} PriorityQueue {
  function elems(): multiset<T> // State abstraction function
  constructor ()
    ensures isEmpty()
  predicate method isEmpty()
    ensures isEmpty() <==> elems() == multiset{}
  method insert(x : T)
    ensures elems() == old(elems()) + multiset{x}
  method deleteMax() returns (x: T)
    requires ! isEmpty()
    ensures isMax(x,old(elems())) && elems()==old(elems())-multiset{x}
}
```

```
// Concrete state representation
var heap: array<T>;
var size : nat;
// State abstraction function
function elems(): multiset<T> { multiset(heap[..size]) }
// Class invariant (heap invariant)
predicate Valid() {
  // valid size && each node is less or equal than its parent
  size<=heap.Length && forall i :: 1<=i<size ==> heap[i]<=heap[(i-1)/2]
}
```

```
// Inserts a value x in the heap.
method insert(x : T)
  ensures elems() == old(elems()) + multiset{x}
{
  // if needed, grows the array
  if size == heap.Length { grow(); }
  // Place at the bottom
  heap[size] := x;
  size := size + 1;
  // Move up as needed in the heap
  heapifyUp();
}
```

Fig. 4. Excerpts of a specification (top) of a priority queue and its implementation (center and bottom) with a binary heap in Dafny.

Thanks to the state abstraction function and the class invariant, the Dafny verifier is able to automatically check the conformity of the methods' implementation (defined in terms of the concrete state) against the methods' pre and postconditons (defined in terms of the abstract state), without further burden from the user! We only had to define an auxiliary lemma, showing that the heap invariant (indicated by the predicate Valid in Fig. 4) implies that the maximum is at the top (array index 0).

2.5 Proof Techniques (Topological Sorting, Eulerian Circuit)

Not surprisingly, simple algorithms may require complex proofs, as illustrated in the topological sorting case study. In fact, the Kahn's algorithm [17] can be encoded in just 6 lines of code (at a high level of abstraction), but, to prove its correctness, we had to write 7 auxiliary lemmas, sketched in Fig. 5. Fortunately, Dafny supports a rich variety of proof techniques and is able to fill in most (if not all) of the proof steps, so we only had to provide key intermediate steps, making the handwritten proof of each lemma rather short.

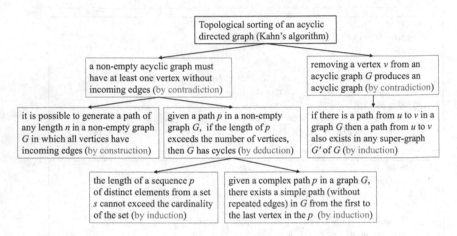

Fig. 5. Lemmas and proof techniques used to prove the correctness of Kahn's algorithm.

However, the way the proof steps are written may have a significant impact on the verification time. E.g., in the Eulerian circuit case study, approximately 20 s were spent in the verification of a lemma stating that, if an Euler trail r exists in a graph G (i.e., a path that traverses each edge of G exactly once), then each vertex of G has an even number of adjacent vertices, except for the first and last vertex in r in case they are different. The proof is done by induction. By rewriting the inductive step so that the first edge is removed from r and G instead of the last one (possibly better matching the structure of recursive definitions needed in the proof), the verification time was reduced to less than 1 s!

3 Results and Discussion

In this section, we summarize the metrics collected and lessons learned from the case studies conducted, and draw some conclusions regarding our research goal.

3.1   Metrics Collected

Table 2 summarizes the metrics collected in the case studies. Size of the code categories described in Table 3 is measured in physical lines of code (LOC), ignoring blank lines and comments.

The execution times were measured in an Intel(R) Core(TM) i7-8750H CPU @ 2.20 GHz laptop with 6 cores and 16 GB RAM running Windows 10 Enterprise. We used v2.1.1 of the Dafny extension for VS Code and version 3.3.0 of the Dafny server and, in some cases, version 2.3.0 due to a bug with Z3 and Dafny v3[4].

Table 2. Results of the case studies (size, time and proof obligations).

Program	Impl. LOC	Test LOC	Spec. LOC	Verif. LOC	Total LOC	(S+V)/ (I+T)	Proof Oblig.	Ver.Time (sec.)
Integer Division	10	5	2	2	19	0.27	15	0.5
Power of a Number	17	7	4	5	33	0.38	45	0.5
Binary Search	15	7	7	3	32	0.45	51	0.5
Insertion Sort	13	13	10	21	57	1.19	90	1
Priority Queue	74	13	30	35	152	0.75	483	3
Hash Set	86	16	57	38	197	0.93	656	16
Tree Set	**87**	13	39	38	177	0.77	**809**	18
Stable Marriage	50	**66**	54	10	180	0.55	209	7
Topological Sorting	19	18	21	94	152	3.11	157	3
Eulerian Circuit	32	10	**66**	**115**	**223**	**4.31**	407	**19**
Total	**403**	**168**	**290**	**361**	**1222**	**1.14**	**2922**	**69**

On average, the amount of code written for formal specification (S) and verification (V) purposes is of the same order of magnitude as the "traditional" code written for implementation (I) and testing (T) purposes – an "overhead" that certainly pays off, at least for high-integrity software. The average ratio is $(S+V)/(I+T) = 1.14$, ranging from 0.27 in the simplest case to 4.31 in the most complex case. The pie chart of Fig. 6 shows a balanced size distribution, on average, between the different code categories.

---

[4] https://github.com/dafny-lang/dafny/issues/1498.

Table 3. Code categories.

Category	Description
Implementation	"Traditional", compilable, implementation code (method signatures, method bodies, data definitions, etc.).
Test	Test code (checked statically or dynamically), including assertions.
Specification	Specification of contracts, including requires and ensures clauses, class invariants, frame conditions, and auxiliary definitions used in them.
Verification	Verification helper code, such as, lemmas and all non-compilable code inside method bodies (loop variants, loop invariants, assertions, invocation of lemmas, manipulation of ghost variables, etc.)

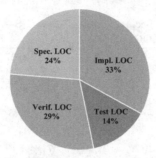

Fig. 6. Code size (LOC) distribution.

The overhead on user time is difficult to measure as it depends heavily on the user experience. A fair assessment should be done in a different context (in the case studies, the algorithms were known, but the verification strategies had to be discovered in many cases). We believe that, with proper training, in cases where new algorithms have to be designed, the specification and verification effort can be of the same order of magnitude as the design, implementation, and test effort.

The number of proof obligations (POs) generated and checked by the Dafny verifier is impressive, with 2.4 POs generated on average per LOC written (2922 POs/1222 LOC in Table 2), and 7.3 per implementation LOC (2922 POs/403 LOC in Table 2), in the case studies. The performance of the Dafny verifier was also impressive, with 24 ms spent on average per PO generated and verified (69 sec/292 POs in Table 2), in this set of case studies.

However, based on the experience of the case studies, it is important to note that the verification of some POs may be significantly higher, in the order of minutes, or not even terminate. When that happens, with careful debugging and refactoring (of assertions, verification code, etc.), one may usually reduce the verification time drastically (as illustrated in the Euler Circuit case study).

Table 4. Lessons learned from the case studies (Part I).

Category	Lessons learned (strengths and weaknesses)
Dafny Language	– **Integrated language** for writing **specifications** (methods' pre and postconditions), **implementations** (methods' bodies), and **verification helper code** (e.g., loop invariants)[ex: Integer Division]. – Rich set of **logical quantifiers** (`forall`, `exists`, etc.) and **mathematical collections** (sequences, sets, multisets, maps, etc.), for writing specifications and assertions and describing complex algorithms at a high level of abstraction [ex: Binary Search, Stable Marriage]. – **Inductive data types** and **pattern matching** expressions may be used to keep the code at a high level of abstraction [ex: Hash Set]. – **Null safety**: reference types are not nullable unless they are marked with the "?" suffix. [ex: Tree Set] – Constructs to specify **frame conditions** and **query the old object state**, when working with mutable objects [ex: Insertion Sort]. – **Modules** enable a clear separation between specification, implementation, and test code [ex: Insertion Sort]. – Limited support for **generics**: lack of support for type parameters that are subject to operations other than equality [ex: Binary Search]. – The support for explicitly separating specification and implementation and hiding implementation details in object-oriented programs has room for improvement (e.g., there are no visibility modifiers) [ex: Tree Set].
Dafny Compiler	– The Dafny compiler is able to generate executable code in **multiple target languages** (in this case, only C# is explored). – Assertions and other constructs used for specification & verification purposes are not compiled, so they imply **no runtime overhead**.
Dafny Verifier	– In many cases, the verifier is able to **automatically check that the implementation conforms to the specification**, with minimal user help (that may only have to write loop invariants) [ex: Integer Division]. – Dafny is frequently able to discover loop variants [ex: Binary Search]. – Outside of a method, the method body is opaque for verification purposes (only the pre and postconditions matter), making the verification process modular and scalable.
Manual Verification Work	– Dafny effectively supports a rich variety of **proof techniques** (by **deduction**, by **induction**, by **contradiction**, by **construction**, calculational [18]) [ex: Topological Sorting, Tree Set]. – Auxiliary properties may need to be defined by the user (as **lemmas**) to help the verifier, but the proof itself may be greatly or totally automated, with many details automatically filled in; discovering what properties need to be defined is not trivial, though [ex: Power, Top. Sort.]. – It is **difficult to predict when and what manual work will be needed** (beyond writing loop invariants) for a successful verification [ex: Insertion Sort, Topological Sorting].

3.2 Lessons Learned

The lessons learned from the case studies are summarized in Tables 4 and 5, using a color scheme to highlight strengths and weaknesses. Overall, the Dafny

Table 5. Lessons learned from the case studies (Part II).

Category	Lessons learned (strengths and weaknesses)
Automatic contracts	– Dafny supports the definition and enforcement of **class invariants**, especially using the ": autocontracts " attribute, also taking care of the generation of appropriate frame conditions [ex: Priority Queue]. – Automatic contracts have room for improvement; in some cases, the user may need to resort to lower level features [ex: Tree Set, Hash Set]. – Getting the contracts right in classes that represent self-referencing data structures may be rather tricky [ex: Tree Set]. – There are apparent conflicts between inheritance and automatic contracts [ex: Priority Queue].
State Abstraction	– **State abstraction functions** (ghost functions) allow specifying the semantics (pre/postconditions) of the services provided by a class independently from the implementation (method bodies and internal state representation) [ex: Priority Queue]. – State abstraction may also be accomplished through **abstract state variables** (ghost variables), whose abstraction relation to the concrete state variables is specified in the class invariant [ex: Hash Set].
Testing	– Testing is still relevant, but mainly for **statically testing the specification**, and not dynamically testing the implementation (proved to be correct with respect to the specification) [ex: Integer division, Ins. Sort]. – Test cases that allow multiple outputs can be easily specified and checked [ex: Insertion Sort].
Debugging and Profiling	– When verification fails, the Dafny language and the Dafny verifier provide several convenient features for debugging purposes, such as the assume statement and the "/tracePOs" option [ex: Eulerian Circuit]. – When the verification time is high, most of the time may be concentrated on one or two assertions. By identifying and rewriting such assertions, the verification time may be drastically reduced [ex: Eulerian Circuit].

language and verifier proved to be very powerful, automating most of the verification work, with minor language limitations (regarding generics, automatic contracts, and other aspects). Regarding our main research question, the major difficulty we found is that the manual verification work may be significant and difficult to predict and master in non-trivial programs.

3.3 Accessibility Assessment

We distinguish three levels of competencies required for the development of verified programs in Dafny, with decreasing accessibility:

– **basic**: writing implementation and test code;
– **intermediate**: writing specifications (pre/post-conditions, frame conditions, class invariants, and related predicates and functions), and loop variants and invariants;
– **advanced**: identifying and writing the needed verification code, besides loop variants and invariants (auxiliary lemmas, assertions, ghost variables, etc.).

The lessons learned and metrics collected in the case studies suggest that, even in seemingly simple problems, the user may need to be skilled in advanced verification techniques. Hence, despite the impressive improvements in automated program verification provided by Dafny, we claim that "we are very close to, but not there yet" regarding the goal of making the development of verified programs accessible for software engineering practitioners and students. Further automation and systematization of verification tasks (including reusable libraries of common properties and "how to" guides), and integration in mainstream languages, are possible directions for further work in the field.

Our assessment is corroborated by our experience in teaching a course on "Formal Methods in Software Engineering"[5] with 151 master students enrolled in the 2020/21 academic year, with a very positive students feedback (average score of 6 out of 7). Students with a high grade ($\geq 85\%$) in a midterm exam were invited to develop a project in Dafny, consisting in the development of a verified implementation of an algorithm or data structure of medium complexity (hash set, tree set, stable marriage, topological sorting, Eulerian circuit, and text compression). Out of 28 students eligible, 14 picked the challenge, but only 9 delivered, and none met the goals fully. We should note that the classes on formal specification and verification (4h per week during 6 weeks) only superficially addressed advanced verification techniques, and the students had a relatively short time to do the project (1 month). This experience led us to conclude that more advanced training is required to prepare interested students to handle nontrivial specification and verification problems using Dafny or similar systems.

4 Related Work

In [19], the authors report their experience of using Dafny at the VerifyThis 2021 program verification competition, which aims to evaluate the usability of logic-based program verification tools in a controlled experiment, challenging both the verification tools and the users of those tools. They tackled two of the proposed challenges, and, as a result, identify strengths and weaknesses of Dafny in the verification of relatively complex algorithms. Some strengths mentioned are: Dafny's ability to prove termination and memory safety with little input; built-in value types, such as sets, sequences, multisets, and maps; predicates and lemmas for more concise specifications; automatic induction; ghost variables and functions. They found it difficult to verify properties of possibly null objects, among other difficulties, impeding them from completing all the tasks on time.

In [20] the authors argue that formal verification tools are often developed by experts for experts; as a result, their usability by programmers with little formal methods experience may be severely limited. They present their experiences with AutoProof (a tool that can verify the functional correctness of object-oriented software in Eiffel) in two contexts representative of non-expert usage. First, they discuss its usability by students in a graduate course on software

---

[5] https://sigarra.up.pt/feup/en/UCURR_GERAL.FICHA_UC_VIEW? pv_ocorrencia_id=459493.

verification, who were tasked with verifying implementations of various sorting algorithms. Second, they evaluate its usability in verifying code developed for programming assignments of an undergraduate course. They report their experiences and lessons learned, from which they derive some suggestions for improving the usability of verification tools. They report an average 1.3 ratio between the number of tokens in specification and verification annotations and implementation code, in two small programs. In spite of the differences in context and measurement units, that ratio is of the same order of magnitude as ours.

In [21] the authors refer that formal methods are often resisted by students due to perceived difficulty, mathematicity, and practical irrelevance. They redeveloped their software correctness course by taking a programming intensive approach, using Dafny to provide instant formative feedback via automated assessment, which resulted in increased student retention and course evaluation. Although very positive overall, their students found Dafny difficult to learn and use, and the informal observations of the authors are that many of those difficulties stem from "accidental" complexity introduced by the Dafny tool. They propose some changes to Dafny's design to tackle some issues found related to program testing, verification debugging, and class invariants, among others.

5　Conclusions and Future Work

We conducted a set of case studies of developing verified implementations in Dafny of some real-world and well-known algorithms and data structures, with the goal of determining its accessibility for software engineering students, practitioners and researchers. We concluded that, despite the impressive improvements in automated program verification provided by Dafny, the manual work needed in writing auxiliary verification code may be significant and difficult to predict and master. Further automation and systematization of verification tasks (including reusable libraries of common properties and "how to" guides), and integration in mainstream languages, are possible directions for further work in the field. We also intend to conduct further studies with other verifiers and problems.

Acknowledgements. This work is financed by National Funds through the Portuguese funding agency, FCT—Fundação para a Ciência e a Tecnologia within project EXPL/CCI-COM/1637/2021.

References

1. Boehm, B.: Some future trends and implications for systems and software engineering processes. Syst. Eng. **9**(1), 1–19 (2006)
2. Dijkstra, E.W., et al.: Notes on structured programming (1970)
3. Humphrey, W.S.: Introduction to the Team Software Process (SM). Addison-Wesley Professional (2000)
4. Hoare, C.A.R.: An axiomatic basis for computer programming. Commun. ACM **12**(10), 576–580 (1969)

5. Vardi, M.Y.: The automated-reasoning revolution: from theory to practice and back. In: Distinguished Lecture at NSF CISE. Spring (2016)
6. de Moura, L., Bjørner, N.: Z3: an efficient SMT solver. In: Ramakrishnan, C.R., Rehof, J. (eds.) TACAS 2008. LNCS, vol. 4963, pp. 337–340. Springer, Heidelberg (2008). https://doi.org/10.1007/978-3-540-78800-3_24
7. Rustan, K., Leino, M.: Accessible software verification with Dafny. IEEE Softw. **34**(6), 94–97 (2017)
8. Cuoq, P., Kirchner, F., Kosmatov, N., Prevosto, V., Signoles, J., Yakobowski, B.: Frama-C. In: Eleftherakis, G., Hinchey, M., Holcombe, M. (eds.) SEFM 2012. LNCS, vol. 7504, pp. 233–247. Springer, Heidelberg (2012). https://doi.org/10.1007/978-3-642-33826-7_16
9. Filliâtre, J.-C., Paskevich, A.: Why3—where programs meet provers. In: Felleisen, M., Gardner, P. (eds.) ESOP 2013. LNCS, vol. 7792, pp. 125–128. Springer, Heidelberg (2013). https://doi.org/10.1007/978-3-642-37036-6_8
10. Abreu, R., et al.: Using constraints to diagnose faulty spreadsheets. Softw. Q. J. **23**(2), 297–322 (2015)
11. Rebello de Andrade, F., Faria, J.P., Lopes, A., Paiva, A.C.R.: Specification-driven unit test generation for Java generic classes. In: Derrick, J., Gnesi, S., Latella, D., Treharne, H. (eds.) IFM 2012. LNCS, vol. 7321, pp. 296–311. Springer, Heidelberg (2012). https://doi.org/10.1007/978-3-642-30729-4_21
12. Campos, J., Abreu, R.: Encoding test requirements as constraints for test suite minimization. In: 2013 10th International Conference on Information Technology: New Generations, pp. 317–322. IEEE (2013)
13. Diedrich, A., et al.: Applying simulated annealing to problems in model-based diagnosis. In: International Workshop on Principles of Diagnosis: DX-2016. ARC-E-DAA-TN35662. ebook DX Conference Series (2016)
14. Lima, B., Faria, J.P., Hierons, R.: Local observability and controllability analysis and enforcement in distributed testing with time constraints. IEEE Access **8**, 167172–167191 (2020)
15. Jackson, D.: Software Abstractions: Logic, Language, and Analysis. MIT Press, Cambridge (2012)
16. Faria, J.P., Abreu, R.: Case studies of development of verified programs with Dafny for accessibility assessment (2023). https://doi.org/10.48550/ARXIV.2301.03224. https://arxiv.org/abs/2301.03224
17. Kahn, A.B.: Topological sorting of large networks. Commun. ACM **5**(11), 558–562 (1962)
18. Leino, K.R.M., Polikarpova, N.: Verified calculations. In: Cohen, E., Rybalchenko, A. (eds.) VSTTE 2013. LNCS, vol. 8164, pp. 170–190. Springer, Heidelberg (2014). https://doi.org/10.1007/978-3-642-54108-7_9
19. Farrell, M., Reynolds, C., Monahan, R.: Using Dafny to solve the VerifyThis 2021 challenges. In: Proceedings of the 23rd ACM International Workshop on Formal Techniques for Java-like Programs, pp. 32–38 (2021)
20. Furia, C.A., Poskitt, C.M., Tschannen, J.: The auto-proof verifier: usability by non-experts and on standard code. arXiv preprint arXiv:1508.03895 (2015)
21. Noble, J., et al.: More programming than programming: teaching formal methods in a software engineering programme. In: Deshmukh, J.V., Havelund, K., Perez, I. (eds.) NASA Formal Methods Symposium, pp. 431–450. Springer, Cham (2022). https://doi.org/10.1007/978-3-031-06773-0_23

TPGen: A Self-stabilizing GPU-Based Method for Test and Prime Paths Generation

Ebrahim Fazli[1] and Ali Ebnenasir[2(✉)]

[1] Department of Computer Engineering, Zanjan Branch,
Islamic Azad University, Zanjan, Iran
efazli@znu.ac.ir

[2] Department of Computer Science, Michigan Technological University,
Houghton, MI 49931, USA
aebnenas@mtu.edu

Abstract. This paper presents a novel scalable GPU-based method for Test Paths (TPs) and Prime Paths (PPs) Generation, called TPGen, used in structural testing and in test data generation. TPGen outperforms existing methods for PPs and TPs generation in several orders of magnitude, both in time and space efficiency. Improving both time and space efficiency is made possible through devising a new non-contiguous and hierarchical memory allocation method, called Three-level Path Access Method (TPAM), that enables efficient storage of maximal simple paths in memory. In addition to its high time and space efficiency, a major significance of TPGen includes its self-stabilizing design where threads execute in a fully asynchronous and order-oblivious way without using any atomic instructions. TPGen can generate PPs and TPs of structurally complex programs that have an extremely high cyclomatic and/or Npath complexity.

Keywords: Prime Path · Test Path · GPU Programming

1 Introduction

This paper presents a scalable GPU-based method for the Generation of all Test Paths (TPs) and Prime Paths (PPs), called TPGen, for structural testing. Complete Path Coverage (CPC) is an ideal testing requirement where all execution paths in a program are tested. However, such coverage may be impossible because some execution paths may be infeasible, and the total number of program paths may be unbounded due to loops and recursion. Lowering expectations, one would resort to testing all simple paths, where no vertex is repeated in a simple path, but the Control Flow Graph (CFG) of even small programs may have an extremely large number of simple paths. Amman and Offutt [1] propose the notion of Prime Path Coverage (PPC), where a *prime path* is a *maximal* simple path; a simple path that is not included in any other simple

© IFIP International Federation for Information Processing 2023
Published by Springer Nature Switzerland AG 2023
H. Hojjat and E. Ábrahám (Eds.): FSEN 2023, LNCS 14155, pp. 40–54, 2023.
https://doi.org/10.1007/978-3-031-42441-0_4

path. PP coverage is an important testing requirement as it subsumes other coverage criteria (e.g., branch coverage) in structural testing. As such, finding the set of all PPs of a program (1) expands the scope of path coverage, and (2) enables the generation of Test Paths (TPs), which are very important in test data generation. This paper presents a scalable approach for the generation of PPs and TPs in structurally complex programs.

Despite the crucial role of PPC in structural testing, there are a limited number of methods that offer effective and efficient algorithms for generating PPs and TPs for complex real-world programs. Amman and Offutt [2] propose a dynamic programming solution for extracting all PPs. Dwarakanath and Jankiti [6] utilize Max-Flow/Min-Cut algorithms to generate minimum number of TPs that cover all PPs. Hoseini and Jalili [10] use genetic algorithms to generate PPs/TPs of CFGs extracted from sequential programs. Sayyari and Emadi [14] exploit ant colony algorithms to generate TPs covering PPs. Sirvastava *et al.* [15] extract a Markov chain model and produce an optimal test set. Bidgoli *et al.* [4] apply swarm intelligence algorithms using a normalized fitness function to ensure the coverage of PPs. Lin and Yeh [11] and also Bueno and Jino [5] present methods based on genetic algorithm to cover PPs. Our previous work [8] generates PPs and TPs in a compositional fashion where we separately extract the PPs of each Strongly Connected Component (SCC) in a CFG, and then merge them towards generating the PPs of the CFG. Most aforementioned methods are applicable to simple programs and cannot be utilized for PP coverage of programs that have a high structural complexity; i.e., very large number of PPs. This paper exploits the power of GPUs in order to provide a time and space efficient parallel algorithm for the generation of all PPs.

Contributions: The major contributions of this paper are multi-fold. First, we present a novel high-performance GPU-based algorithm for PPs and TPs generation that works in a self-stabilizing fashion. The TPGen algorithm first generates the component graph of the input CFG on the CPU and then processes each vertex of the component graph (each SCC) in parallel on a GPU. TPGen is vertex-based in that each GPU thread T_i is mapped to a vertex v_i and a list l_i of partial paths is associated with v_i. Each thread extends the paths in l_i while ensuring their simplicity. The execution of threads is completely asynchronous. Thread T_i updates l_i based on the extension of the paths in the predecessors of v_i, and removes all covered simple paths from l_i. The experimental evaluations of TPGen show that it can generate all PPs of programs with extremely large cyclomatic [12] and Npath complexity [13] in a time and space efficient way. Cyclomatic Complexity (CC) captures the number of linearly independent execution paths in a program [12]. Npath complexity is a metric for the number of execution paths in a program while limiting the loops to at most one iteration [13]. TPGen outperforms existing sequential methods up to 3.5 orders of magnitude in terms of time efficiency and up to 2 orders of magnitude in space efficiency for a given benchmark. TPGen achieves such efficiency while ensuring data race-freedom without using 'atomic' statements in its design. Moreover, TPGen is self-stabilizing in the sense that the GPU threads start in any order.

Our notion of self-stabilization provides robustness against arbitrary initialization of TPGen where the order of execution of threads is arbitrary. This is different from traditional understanding of self-stabilization where an algorithm recovers if perturbed by transient faults. TPGen threads generate PPs without any kind of synchronization with each other, or with the CPU. Such lack of synchronization significantly improves time efficiency but is hard to design due to the risk of thread interference. As a result, we consider the design of TPGen as a model for other GPU-based algorithms, which by itself is a novel contribution. Second, we propose a non-contiguous and hierarchical memory allocation method, called Three-level Path Access Method (TPAM), that enables efficient storage of maximal simple paths. We also put forward a benchmark of synthetic programs for evaluating the structural complexity of programs and for experimental evaluation of PPs/TPs generation methods.

Organization. Section 2 defines some basic concepts. Section 3 states the PPs generation problem. Subsequently, Sect. 4 presents the TPAM method of memory allocation. Section 5 puts forward a highly time and space-efficient parallel algorithm implemented on GPU for PPs generation. Section 6 presents our experimental results. Section 7 discusses related work. Finally, Sect. 8 makes concluding remarks and discusses future extensions of this work.

2   Preliminaries

This section presents some graph-theoretic concepts that we utilize throughout this paper. A *directed graph* $G = (V, E)$ includes a set of vertices V and a set of arcs $(v_i, v_j) \in E$, where $v_i, v_j \in V$. A *simple path* p in G is a sequence of vertices $v_1, \cdots, v_k$, where each arc (v_i, v_{i+1}) belongs to E for $1 \le i < k$ and $k > 0$, and no vertex appears more than once in p unless $v_1 = v_k$. A vertex v_j is *reachable* from another vertex v_i iff (if and only if) there is a simple path that emanates from v_i and terminates at v_j. A SCC in G is a sub-graph $G' = (V', E')$, where $V' \subseteq V$ and $E' \subseteq E$, and for any pair of vertices $v_i, v_j \in V'$, v_i and v_j are reachable from each other. Tarjan [16] presents a polynomial-time algorithm that finds the SCCs of the input graph and constructs its *component graph*. Each vertex of the input graph appears in exactly one of the SCCs. The result is a Directed Acyclic Graph (DAG) whose every vertex is an SCC. A Control Flow Graph (CFG) models the flow of execution control between the basic blocks in a program, where a *basic block* is a collection of program statements without any conditional or unconditional jumps. A CFG is a directed graph, $G = (V, E)$. Each vertex $v \in V$ corresponds to a basic block. Each edge/arc $e = (v_i, v_j) \in E$ corresponds to a possible transfer of control from block v_i to block v_j. A CFG often has a *start vertex* that captures the block of statement starting with the first instruction of the program, and has some *end vertices* representing the blocks of statements that end in a halt/exit/return instruction. (We use the terms 'arc' and 'edge' interchangeably throughout this paper.) Figure 1 illustrates an example method as well as its corresponding CFG (adopted from [3]) for a class in the Apache Commons library.

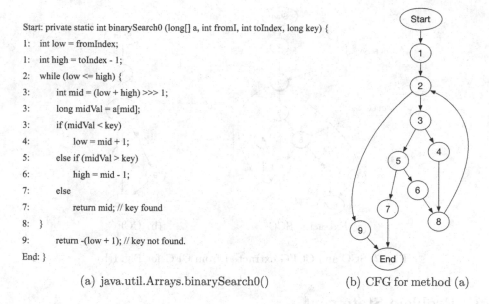

```
Start: private static int binarySearch0 (long[] a, int fromI, int toIndex, long key) {

1:    int low = fromIndex;

1:    int high = toIndex - 1;

2:    while (low <= high) {

3:        int mid = (low + high) >>> 1;

3:        long midVal = a[mid];

3:        if (midVal < key)

4:            low = mid + 1;

5:        else if (midVal > key)

6:            high = mid - 1;

7:        else

7:            return mid; // key found

8:    }

9:    return -(low + 1); // key not found.

End: }
```

(a) java.util.Arrays.binarySearch0()   (b) CFG for method (a)

Fig. 1. Example method and corresponding CFG

Definition 1 (PP). *A PP is a maximal simple path in a directed graph; i.e., a simple path that cannot be extended further without breaking its simplicity property (e.g., PP $\langle 2, 3, 4, 8, 2 \rangle$ in Fig. 1(b)).*

Definition 2 (TP). *A path p from v_s to v_t is a TP iff v_s is the Start vertex of G and v_t is an End vertex in G. (e.g., the path $\langle Start, 1, 2, 3, 4, 8, 2, 9, End \rangle$ in Fig. 1(b))*

Definition 3 (CompletePP). *A PP p from v_s to v_t is a CompletePP iff v_s is the Start vertex of G and v_t is an End vertex in G. (e.g., the PP $\langle Start, 1, 2, 3, 5, 7, End \rangle$ in Fig. 1(b))*

Definition 4 (Component Graph of CFGs). *The component graph of a CFG $G = (V, E)$, called CCFG, is a DAG whose vertices are the SCCs of G, and each arc $(v_i, v_j) \in E$ starts in an SCC_i and ends in a distinct SCC_j (see Fig. 2(b)).*

Since this paper presents a parallelized version of the method in [8], we represent a summary of the major steps of the algorithm of [8], illustrated in Fig. 3: (1) compute the component graph of the input CFG, denoted CCFG; (2) generate the set of PPs of CCFG and the set of PPs of each individual SCC in CCFG; (3) extract different types of intermediate paths of each SCC, and (4) merge the PPs of SCCs to generate all PPs of the original input CFG. Experimental evidence [8] indicates that the most time consuming step is the second one (i.e., PP generation) where we generate the internal PPs of each individual SCC. This is due to cyclic structure of SCCs. To resolve this bottleneck, we present an efficient parallel algorithm in Sect. 5.

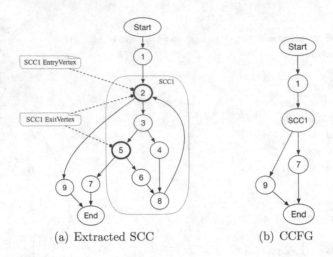

(a) Extracted SCC   (b) CCFG

Fig. 2. SCC and CCFG extracted from CFG for Fig. 1(b)

3   Problem Statement

Generating PPs and TPs of the control flow graphs related to real world programs with a large Npath complexity is an important problem in software structural testing. These types of graphs have a huge number of PPs and processing them under conventional algorithms on CPUs requires a lot of time. Thus, it is necessary to develop algorithms that address this problem and maintain the accuracy of the PP generation. In a graph-theoretic setting, the PPs generation problem can be formulated as follows:

Problem 1 (**PPs Generation**).

- **Input**: A graph $G = (V, E)$ that represents the CFG of a given program, a start vertex $s \in V$ and an end vertex $e \in V$.
- **Output**: The set of PPs finished at each vertex $v \in V$ and the set of TPs covering all PPs.

In principle, the number of PPs could be exponential. However, testers should ideally work with a minimum number of TPs that provide a complete PP coverage. Since finding the minimum number of TPs that provide complete PP coverage is hard, we focus on generating a small number of TPs, where each TP covers multiple PPs. For example, consider the second TP in the first column of Table 1 that covers six PPs in the second column of Table 1 (illustrated by the bold fonts). Notice that, this TP starts from the Start node (in Fig. 2(a)), iterates twice in the loop 2-3-4-8-2, and exits through the nodes 5, 7 and End. Figuring out that such a TP can cover six PPs by going through the loop 2-3-4-8-2 twice is non-trivial for human testers. Moreover, generating such TPs is impossible without extracting all PPs. Thus, it is important to efficiently solve Problem 1. We emphasize that testers generate test data only for TPs.

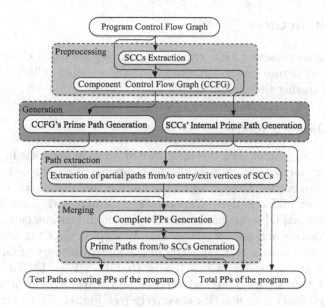

Fig. 3. Overview of the compositional method of [8].

Table 1. TPs and PPs generated for Fig. 1(b)

Test Paths	Prime Paths
{0,1,2,3,5,6,8,2,3,5,6,8,2,3,5,7,10}	**{8,2,3,4,8}{4,8,2,3,4}{2,3,4,8,2}**{4,8,2,3,5,6}
{0,1,2,3,4,8,2,3,4,8,2,3,5,7,10}	{5,6,8,2,3,5} {0,1,2,3,5,6,8} {3,5,6,8,2,9,10}
{0,1,2,3,5,6,8,2,3,4,8,2,9,10}	{2,3,5,6,8,2} **{4,8,2,3,5,7,10}** {3,4,8,2,9,10}
{0,1,2,3,4,8,2,3,5,6,8,2,9,10}	{6,8,2,3,5,7,10} {3,5,6,8,2,3} **{0,1,2,3,4,8}**
{0,1,2,3,5,7,10}	**{3,4,8,2,3}** {6,8,2,3,5,6} {8,2,3,5,6,8}
{0,1,2,9,10}	{5,6,8,2,3,4} {0,1,2,3,5,7,10} {0,1,2,9,10}

In practice, solving Problem 1 is more costly when the input graph is an SCC because every vertex is reachable from any other vertex in an SCC. For this reason, Sect. 5 proposes a parallel GPU-based algorithm that extracts the PPs of SCCs in a time and space efficient fashion. The in-degree of s is 0, and out-degree of e is 0. We focus on CFGs where all vertices $v \in V$ except e have a maximum out-degree of 2. Without loss of generality, we can convert a vertex v with an out-degree greater than 2 (i.e., switch-case structure) to vertices with out-degree 2 by adding some new intermediate vertices between v and its successor vertices. (See details in [9]).

4   Data Structures

In this section, we present a data structure for storing the input CFG (Sect. 4.1), a path data structure (Sect. 4.2), and a novel memory allocation method (Sect. 4.3) for storing the generated PPs.

4.1   CFG Data Structure

A matrix is usually stored as a two-dimensional array in memory. In the case of a sparse matrix, memory requirements can be significantly reduced by maintaining only non-zero entries. Depending on the number and distribution of non-zero entries, we can use different data structures. The Compressed Sparse Row (CSR, CRS or Yale format) [7] represents a matrix by a one-dimensional array that supports efficient access and matrix operations. We employ the CSR data structure (see Fig. 4) to maintain a directed graph in the global memory of GPUs, where vertices of the graph receive unique IDs in $\{0, 1, \cdots, |V| - 1\}$. To represent a graph in CSR format, we store end vertices and start vertices of arcs in two separate arrays $EndV$ and $StartV$ respectively (see Fig. 4). Each entry in EndV points to the starting index of its adjacency list in array $StartV$. We assign one thread to each vertex. That is, thread t is responsible for the vertex whose ID is stored in $EndV[t]$, where $\{0 \leq t < |V| - 1\}$ (see Fig. 4). For example, Fig. 4 illustrates the CSR representation of the graph of Fig. 1(b). Since the proposed algorithm computes all PPs ending in each vertex $v \in V$, maintaining the predecessor vertices is of particular importance. In CSR data structure, first the vertex itself and then its predecessor vertices are stored.

4.2   Path Structure

We utilize a set of flags to keep the status of each recorded path along with each vertex (see Fig. 5). Let v_i be a vertex and p be a path associated with v_i. The PathValidity flag ($p[0]$) indicates whether or not the recorded information represents a simple path. The PathExtension flag ($p[1]$) means that the current path is an extended path; hence not a PP. We assume each non-final vertex can have a maximum of two successor vertices. We use the LeftSuccessor ($p[2]$) and the RightSuccessor ($p[3]$) flags to indicate whether the thread of each corresponding successor has read the path ending in vertex v_i. Once one of those successor threads reads the path ending in v_i it will mark its flag. In each iteration of the algorithm, paths with marked extension and marked successor flags will be pruned. We set the CyclicPath flag ($p[4]$) if p is a cyclic path. If p is cyclic, then it will no longer be processed by the successor threads of v and is recorded as a PP at the v_i. (see Fig. 5).

   Note: Since there is a unique thread associated to each vertex, we use the terms "successor" and "predecessor" for both vertices and threads.

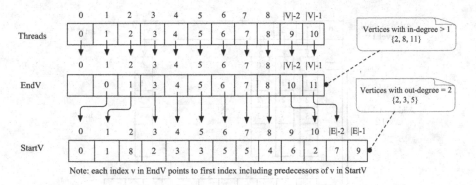

Note: each index v in EndV points to first index including predecessors of v in StartV

Fig. 4. Compressed Sparse Row (CSR) graph representation of Fig. 1(b)

Fig. 5. Path structure

4.3 Three-Level Path Accessing Method (TPAM)

In each CFG, the extraction of the PPs is based on the generation of the simple paths terminated in each vertex $v_i \in V$. There is a list associated to each vertex v_i, denoted $v_i.list$ to record all generated PPs ending in v_i. To implement this idea, all acyclic paths ending in predecessors of v_i must be copied to the list of the vertex v_i. For a large CFG, the number of such paths could be enormous, which would incur a significant space cost on the algorithm. To mitigate this space complexity, we introduce a non-contiguous memory allocation method with a pointer-based Three-level Path Accessing Method (TPAM). TPAM is a path accessing scheme which consists of three levels of address tables in a hierarchical manner. The entries of Level 1 address table with length $|V|$ are pointers to each $v_i.list$ at Level 2 address tables. Level 2 address tables contain addresses of all paths stored in each $v_i.list$. The entries of the last level tables are actual paths information in memory (see Fig. 6).

All activities such as compare, copy, extend and delete are applied to the paths of each vertex. Let v_i be a vertex in V and p be a path in $v_i.list$. To access path p, the start address of the $v_i.list$ is discovered from the first array (i.e., $Path[v_i]$). The start address of path p is stored in Level 2 address table in Fig. 6 (i.e., $Path[v_i][p]$). The list of vertices of path p is in Level 3 path table, which according to path structure mentioned in Fig. 5, all activities can be done on the elements of the path (i.e., $Path[v_i][p][5]$ shows the length of the path p).

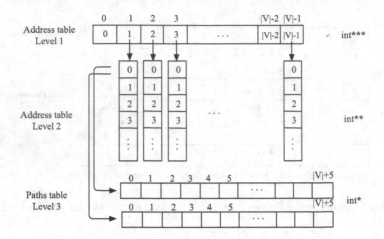

Fig. 6. Three-level Path Accessing Method (TPAM).

Instead of using malloc in allocating host memory, we call CUDA to create page-locked pinned host memory. Page-Locked Host Memory for CUDA (and other external hardware with DMA capability) is allocated on the physical memory of the host computer. This allocation is labeled as non-swappable (not-pageable) and non-transferable (locked, pinned). This memory can be accessed with the virtual address space of the kernel (device). This memory is also added to the virtual address space of the user process to allow the process to access it. Since the memory is directly accessible by the device (i.e., the GPU), the write and read speeds are high bandwidth. Excessive allocation of such memory can greatly reduce system performance as it reduces the amount of memory available for paging, but proper use of this memory allocation method provides a high performance data transfer scheme.

5 GPU-Based Prime Paths Generation

In order to scale up PPs generation, this section presents a parallel compositional method that provides better time efficiency in comparison with existing sequential methods for PPs generation. Specifically, we introduce a GPU-based PPs generation algorithm. The input of the PP generation algorithm (Algorithm 1) includes a CFG representing the Program Under Test (PUT). The output of Algorithm 1 is the set of all PPs finished at each vertex $v_i \in V$.

A GPU-based CUDA program has a CPU part and a GPU part. The CPU part is called the *host* and the GPU part is called the *kernel*, capturing an array of threads. The proposed algorithm includes one kernel. The host (i.e., CPU) initializes the $v_i.list$ of all v_i and an array of boolean flags, called *PublicFlag*, where $PublicFlag[v_i] = true$ indicates that the predecessors of vertex v_i have been updated and so the $v_i.list$ needs to be updated. One important objective is to design a self-stabilizing algorithm with no CPU-GPU communications, thus the host launches the kernel Update-Vertex (i.e., Algorithm 1) only once. The proposed algorithm is implemented in such a way that there is no need for repeated calls to synchronize different threads. One of the major challenges in parallel applications that drastically reduces their efficiency is the use of atomic instructions. Atomic instructions are executed without any interruption, but greatly reduce the efficiency of parallel processing. The self-stabilizing device (i.e., GPU) code in this section is implemented without using atomic instructions.

Algorithm 1 forms the core of the kernel, and performs three kinds of processing on each vertex $v_i \in V$: pruning the extended paths in $v_i.list$, extending acyclic simple paths in the lists of predecessors of v_i, and examining the termination of all backward reachable vertices from v_i. **Lines 2 to 8** in Algorithm 1 remove extra paths from $v_i.list$. A path $p \in v_i.list$ is *extra* if it is extended by one of the v_i's successor(s) or covered by another path $p' \in v_i.list$.

Lines 9 to 19 extend eligible acyclic simple paths in the lists of all predecessor vertices of v_i. Suppose that $v_j \in V$ is one of the v_i's predecessor. A path $q \in v_j.list$ is an eligible path if q is not a cyclic path, and v_i is the start vertex of q in case v_i already appeared in q. The thread assigned to v_i runs a function called *ExtendPath* (in Algorithm 2) to append the new eligible path to the $v_i.list$. In **Lines 21 to 33**, the thread of v_i cannot be terminated if the vertex v_i is not the final vertex and has any unread paths in $v_i.list$ (Lines 21 to 25). Thread of v_i then examines the termination of all its backward reachable vertices by examining their *PublicFlag*. If all the ancestor vertices of v_i are terminated, then the vertex v_i will also set its *PublicFlag* to false and exit the while loop (Lines 28 to 32). In fact, self-stabilization is achieved through localizing path extension to each thread, but making sure that any change in ancestors of a vertex will eventually propagate to it.

We devise Algorithm 2 to append a new simple path to the list of a given vertex. This algorithm takes a path p as well as a specified vertex v as inputs. Algorithm 2 first adds the vertex v at the end of the path p and increments the length of p (Lines 2 and 3). Then, it checks the occurrence of vertex v as the first vertex of p. This property causes the new path p to be considered as a cycle in vertex v (Lines 4 to 6). Finally, Algorithm 2 sets *PathValidity* flag of the new path p to true and appends it to the end of $v.list$ (Lines 7 and 8).

Theorem 1. *Algorithm 1 terminates, is data race free and finds all PPs.*

Proof. Due to space constraints, we present a proof sketch and refer the readers to the complete proof in [9]. To **prove the termination** of Algorithm 1, we show that at some finite point in time, $v_i.LocalFlag$ and $v_i.PublicFlag$ will become false for every $v_i \in V$ and will remain false. As such, when *PublicFlag* of all vertices in $v_i.ReachedFrom$ are set to false, the thread assigned to v_i will eventually stop. When no more extensions occur for any vertex, Algorithm 1 terminates. To **prove data race freedom**, we show that neighboring threads cannot perform read and write operations on the same path simultaneously. Consider two arcs (v_j, v_i) and (v_i, v_k) in the input CFG. A data race could arise when the thread of v_k reads a path p in $v_i.list$ in Line 12 and at the same time the thread of v_i

---

Algorithm 1. Update-Vertex($v_i, G = (V, E)$)

1: **while** ($v_i.PublicFlag = true$) **do**
2:      **for each** path $p \in v_i.list$ **do**
3:          **if** p has been read by both successors **then**
4:              **if** (p is an extended path) or (p is already included in some path $p' \in$ $v_i.list$) **then**
5:                      remove p;
6:              **end if**
7:          **end if**
8:      **end for**
9:      **for each** v_j where $(v_j, v_i) \in E$ **do** // Read from predecessors.
10:          **for each** path $q \in v_j.list$ **do** // PathValidity flag
11:              **if** q is not read by v_i **then**
12:                  Label q as read by v_i; // Left or Right Successor flag
13:                  **if** (q is not a cycle) **and** (v_i does not appear in q **or** v_i is the first vertex of q) **then**
14:                          ExtendPath (q, v_i);
15:                          Label q as an extended path; // PathExtension flag
16:                  **end if**
17:              **end if**
18:          **end for**
19:      **end for**
20:      $v_i.LocalFlag = false$;
21:      **for each** path $p \in v_i.list$ **do**
22:          **if** p is not read by both successors **then**
23:              $v_i.LocalFlag = true$;
24:          **end if**
25:      **end for**
26:      **if** $v_i.LocalFlag = false$ **then** // all paths in $v_i.list$ have been read by both $v_i's$ successors
27:          $v_i.PublicFlag = false$;
28:          **for each** v_k where v_i is Reachable from v_k **do**
29:              **if** $v_k.PublicFlag = true$ **then**
30:                  $v_i.PublicFlag = true$;
31:              **end if**
32:          **end for**
33:      **end if**
34: **end while**

Algorithm 2. ExtendPath(Path[] p, Vertex v)

1: Path[] $NewPath = p$;
2: $NewPath[5 + |p| + 1] = v$;
3: $NewPath[5] = p[5] + 1$;
4: **if** v is the first vertex of p **then**
5:      $NewPath[4] = 1$; // CyclicPath flag
6: **end if**
7: $NewPath[0] = 1$; // PathValidity flag
8: append $NewPath$ to $v.list$;

---

may be removing p in Line 5. However, this cannot occur because thread of v_i removes p if it has been read by both successors. That is, v_k must have read p before v_i can remove it. A similar conflict could occur when v_i extends a path p in $v_j.list$ in Line 14 and v_j wants to remove p in Line 5. This scenario is also impossible to occur because v_j can remove p only if it has already been read by v_i. We also show that if Algorithm 1 fails to find some prime path, then the list of some vertex must have been empty initially, which is contrary to initializing the list of every vertex with itself.

6 Experimental Results

This section presents the results of our experimental evaluations of the proposed GPU-based method for PPs and TPs generation compared to the CPU-based approach proposed in [8]. The experimental benchmark consists of a set of ten modified CFGs from [3] (which are taken from Apache Commons libraries). To increase the structural complexity of input CFGs, we synthetically include extra nested loops and a variety of conditional statements to create more SCCs. Our strategy for creating additional loops/SCCs is to include new arcs from the 'then' part of conditional statements back to their beginning. Table 2 presents the structure of these CFGs. Columns 3 to 9 of Table 2 provide the number of nodes, edges, and SCCs of each CFG. The total numbers of nodes and edges of all SCCs are mentioned as SccNodes and SccEdges, respectively. Columns 7 and 8 show the Cyclomatic Complexity (CC) [12] and Npath Complexity [13] of the input CFGs. The last column illustrates the number of prime paths produced with the GPU-based method. We compare the parallel and the sequential approaches with respect to their running time and memory consumption. The number of generated PPs for each CFG is provided in Column 9 of Table 2. We ran all the experiments on an Intel Core i7 machine with 3.6 GHz X 8 processors and 16 GB of memory running Ubuntu 17.01 with gcc version 5.4.1. The parallel approach is implemented on a Nvidia GTX graphical processing unit equipped with 4G RAM and 768 CUDA cores.

The bar graph of Fig. 7 illustrates the time efficiencies of the CPU-based and GPU-based approaches. (The reported timings for each approach is the average of twenty runs.) These values reflect the fact that the time costs of the CPU-based sequential method is less for smaller CFGs. Specifically, for the CFGs of the top five rows of Table 2, on average, the CPU-based method consumed 61% less time than the GPU-based method (due to the transfer overhead from CPU to GPU). However, for large CFGs at the bottom of Table 2, the parallel GPU-based method costs 39% less time than the sequential method. This time efficiency increases significantly with growing graph size. For example, the GPU-based time efficiency in the last graph is 71%. The recorded times indicate that by increasing the structural complexity, the GPU-based algorithm provides a better performance (assigning exactly one thread for each vertex). Thus, for real-world applications that have a large number of lines and complex structures, the GPU-based algorithm is expected to be highly efficient.

Table 2. Modified benchmark CFGs and their structural complexity

CFG	Original Functions	Graph structure after modification							PPs
		Nodes	Edges	SCC	SccNodes	SccEdges	CC	Npath	
1	AsmClassReaderAccept	180	214	18	78	83	35	2.1e7	35629
2	AsmClassWriterToByteArray	215	258	24	103	110	44	6.1e11	176481
3	SquareMesh2DcreateLinks	244	290	27	115	125	49	3.3e12	139684
4	PrivilizerAsmMethodWriter	355	431	38	160	173	68	4.5e22	253954
5	SingularValueDecomposition	486	567	47	223	244	104	1.1e23	643738
6	ListParserTokenManager	723	853	75	331	351	131	2.0e32	1016762
7	BOBYQAOptimizer	874	994	83	409	762	155	9.3e39	1477397
8	ParserParserTokenManager	963	1119	93	448	490	213	1.3e44	2573594
9	InternalXsltcCompilerCUP	1441	1713	149	626	712	273	4.1e68	4478382
10	XPathLexerNextToken	2160	2566	224	957	1073	404	8.4e97	9563583

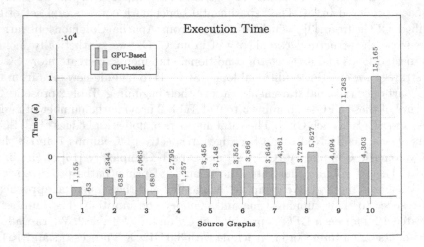

Fig. 7. Time cost of CPU-based vs. GPU-based method.

The bar graph of Fig. 8 illustrates the space efficiency of the CPU-based vs. the GPU-based approach. These values indicate that the GPU-based approach applying TPAM method has less memory costs than the CPU-based method. On average, the GPU-based approach consumes 62% less memory for the input CFGs. On the other hand, for more complex CFGs, the CPU-based method consumes a lot of memory due to the contiguous memory allocation.

7   Related Work

This section discusses related works on the prime and test paths coverage in model-based software testing context. There are two major categories of TPs generation/coverage. Static methods generate TPs of a given CFG. For example, Amman and Offutt [1] start with the longest PP and extend every PP to

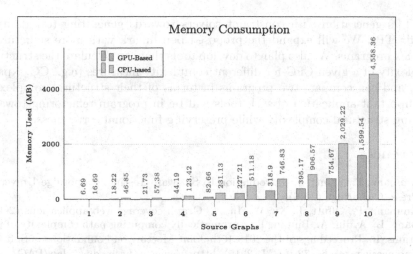

Fig. 8. Memory cost of CPU-based vs. GPU-based method.

visit the start and end vertices, thus forming a TPs. Their process continues with the remaining uncovered longest PPs. This algorithm does not attempt to minimize the number of TPs but is extremely simple. Fazli and Afsharchi [8] extract the set of SCC's entry-exit paths that cover all internal PPs of all SCCs. Then, they merge these paths using the complete paths of the component graph, thereby yielding complete TPs that cover all incomplete PPs. Dynamic methods instrument the PUT in order to analyze the coverage of a set of desired paths. For example, nature-inspired methods (e.g., genetic algorithms [10], ant colony [15], swarm intelligence [4]) provide dynamic methods for PPs and TPs coverage. TPGen, however, is a parallel self-stabilizing vertex-based algorithm that significantly scales up the PPs and TPs generation in a static fashion for structurally complex programs that are beyond the reach of existing methods.

8   Conclusions and Future Work

We presented a novel scalable GPU-based method, called TPGen, for the generation of all Test Paths (TPs) and Prime Paths (PPs) used in structural testing and in test data generation. TPGen outperforms existing methods for PPs and TPs generation in several orders of magnitude, both in time and space efficiency. To reduce TPGen's memory costs, we designed a non-contiguous and hierarchical memory allocation method, called Three-level Path Access Method (TPAM), that enables efficient storage of maximal simple paths in memory. TPGen does not use any synchronization primitives for the execution of the kernel threads on GPU, and starting from any execution order of threads, TPGen generates the PPs ending in any individual vertex; hence providing a fully asynchronous self-stabilizing GPU-based algorithm.

As an extension of this work, we plan to further improve the scalability of TPGen through execution on a network of GPUs. Moreover, we will integrate

PPs/TPs generation with constraint solvers towards generating test data for specific TPs. We will expand the proposed benchmark with more structurally complex programs. We also plan to develop tools that can calculate the structural complexity of a given CFG for different complexity measures (e.g., CC, Npath, PPs), and can compare two programs in terms of their structural complexity. An important application of such tools will be in program refactoring towards lowering structural complexity while preserving functional correctness.

References

1. Ammann, P., Offutt, J.: Introduction to Software Testing. Cambridge University Press, Cambridge (2016)
2. Ammann, P., Offutt, J., Xu, W., Li, N.: Graph coverage web applications (2008)
3. Bang, L., Aydin, A., Bultan, T.: Automatically computing path complexity of programs. In: Proceedings of the 2015 10th Joint Meeting on Foundations of Software Engineering, pp. 61–72. ACM (2015). http://www.cs.ucsb.edu/~vlab/PAC/
4. Monemi Bidgoli, A., Haghighi, H., Zohdi Nasab, T., Sabouri, H.: Using swarm intelligence to generate test data for covering prime paths. In: Dastani, M., Sirjani, M. (eds.) FSEN 2017. LNCS, vol. 10522, pp. 132–147. Springer, Cham (2017). https://doi.org/10.1007/978-3-319-68972-2_9
5. Bueno, P.M.S., Jino, M.: Automatic test data generation for program paths using genetic algorithms. Int. J. Software Eng. Knowl. Eng. **12**(06), 691–709 (2002)
6. Dwarakanath, A., Jankiti, A.: Minimum number of test paths for prime path and other structural coverage criteria. In: Merayo, M.G., de Oca, E.M. (eds.) ICTSS 2014. LNCS, vol. 8763, pp. 63–79. Springer, Heidelberg (2014). https://doi.org/10.1007/978-3-662-44857-1_5
7. Eisenstat, S.C., Schultz, M.H., Sherman, A.H.: Algorithms and data structures for sparse symmetric Gaussian elimination. SIAM J. Sci. Stat. Comput. **2**(2), 225–237 (1981)
8. Fazli, E., Afsharchi, M.: A time and space-efficient compositional method for prime and test paths generation. IEEE Access **7**, 134399–134410 (2019)
9. Fazli, E., Ebnenasir, A.: TPGen: a self-stabilizing GPU-based method for prime and test paths generation. arXiv preprint arXiv:2210.16998 (2022). https://arxiv.org/abs/2210.16998
10. Hoseini, B., Jalili, S.: Automatic test path generation from sequence diagram using genetic algorithm. In: 2014 7th International Symposium on Telecommunications (IST), pp. 106–111. IEEE (2014)
11. Lin, J.C., Yeh, P.L.: Automatic test data generation for path testing using gas. Inf. Sci. **131**(1–4), 47–64 (2001)
12. McCabe, T.J.: A complexity measure. IEEE Trans. Softw. Eng. **4**, 308–320 (1976)
13. Nejmeh, B.A.: NPATH: a measure of execution path complexity and its applications. Commun. ACM **31**(2), 188–200 (1988)
14. Sayyari, F., Emadi, S.: Automated generation of software testing path based on ant colony. In: 2015 International Congress on Technology, Communication and Knowledge (ICTCK), pp. 435–440. IEEE (2015)
15. Srivastava, P.R., Jose, N., Barade, S., Ghosh, D.: Optimized test sequence generation from usage models using ant colony optimization. Int. J. Softw. Eng. Appl. **2**(2), 14–28 (2010)
16. Tarjan, R.: Depth-first search and linear graph algorithms. SIAM J. Comput. **1**(2), 146–160 (1972)

An Optimised Complete Strategy
for Testing Symbolic Finite State Machines

Wen-ling Huang⬤, Niklas Krafczyk⬤, and Jan Peleska$^{(\boxtimes)}$⬤

Department of Mathematics and Computer Science,
University of Bremen, Bremen, Germany
{huang,niklas,peleska}@uni-bremen.de

Abstract. In this paper, we specialise a more general theory for testing symbolic finite state machines (SFSM) to an important sub-class of SFSMs. This specialisation allows for a significant reduction of test cases needed for proving language equivalence between an SFSM reference model and an implementation whose true behaviour is captured by another SFSM from a given fault domain.

Keywords: model-based testing · symbolic finite state machines · complete test suites

1 Introduction

Background and Motivation. In model-based (black-box) testing (MBT), test cases to be executed against a system under test (SUT) are derived from reference models specifying the expected behaviour of the SUT, as far as visible at its interfaces. MBT is often performed with the objective to show that the SUT fulfils a *conformance relation* to the reference model, such as language equivalence at the interface level. Alternatively, in *property-oriented testing*, MBT is applied to check whether an SUT fulfils just a set of selected properties that are fulfilled by the reference model [12].

In the context of safety-critical systems, so-called *complete* test suites are of special interest. A suite is complete, if it (1) accepts every SUT fulfilling the correctness criterion (*soundness*), and (2) rejects every SUT violating the correctness criterion (*exhaustiveness*). In black-box testing, completeness can only be guaranteed under certain hypotheses about the kind of errors that can occur in implementations. Therefore, the potential faulty behaviours are identified by so-called *fault domains*: these are models representing both correct and faulty behaviours, the latter to be uncovered by complete test suites. Without these constraints, it is impossible to guarantee that finite test suites will uncover *every* deviation of an implementation from a reference model: the existence of hidden internal states leading to faulty behaviour after a trace that is longer than the

Funded by the Deutsche Forschungsgemeinschaft (DFG, German Research Foundation) – project number 407708394.

H. Hojjat and E. Ábrahám (Eds.): FSEN 2023, LNCS 14155, pp. 55–71, 2023.
https://doi.org/10.1007/978-3-031-42441-0_5

ones considered in a finite test suite cannot be checked in black-box testing. The original work on complete test suites [3] was considered to be mainly of theoretical interest, but practically infeasible, due to the size of the test suites to be performed in order to prove conformance. Since then however, it has been shown that complete test suites can be generated with novel strategies leading to significantly smaller numbers of test cases [5], and complete test suites for complex systems can be generated with acceptable size, if equivalence class strategies are used [9]. Moreover, the possibility to generate and execute large test suites in a distributed manner on cloud server farms have pushed the limits of practically tractable test suite sizes in a considerable way.

While the original theories on complete test suites have been elaborated for finite states machines (FSM) with input and output alphabets (Mealy machines), FSMs are less suitable for modelling reactive systems with complex, conceptually infinite data structures. Therefore, complete strategies for MBT with different modelling formalisms have been elaborated over the years, such as extended finite state machines [11], timed automata [19], process algebras [13], variants of Kripke structures [9], and symbolic finite state machines [12,15].

Symbolic finite state machines (SFSM) offer a good compromise between semantic tractability and expressiveness: just like FSMs, they still operate on a finite state space, but they allow for typed input and output variables. Transitions are guarded by Boolean expressions (so-called symbolic inputs) over input variables. In the more general case of SFSMs investigated in this paper, symbolic outputs are Boolean first order expressions involving arithmetic expressions over input and output variables, so that nondeterministic outputs are admissible. This makes SFSMs well-suited for modelling control systems with inputs obtained from discrete or analogue sensors and outputs to likewise discrete or analogue actuators. The control decisions depend on the guard valuations for the given inputs and on a finite number of internal control states. Typical systems of this kind are airbag controllers, speed monitors [10], or train protection units for autonomous trains [4].

Objectives and Main Contributions. In this paper, we present a complete testing strategy for verifying language equivalence against a sub-class of SFSM reference models. The SFSMs in this class may be nondeterministic with respect to both transition guards and output expressions, but they are required to possess *separable alphabets*, as defined in Sect. 2. Intuitively speaking, their output expressions are pairwise distinguishable for every guard condition by selecting a specific input valuation for that the respective guard evaluates to true.

As fault domains, SFSMs of this class, with a bounded number of states, arbitrary transfer faults (misdirected transitions), interchanged guards or output expressions, and finitely many mutations of guards and outputs are accepted.

We consider the following results as the main contributions of this paper. (1) A new complete language equivalence testing strategy is presented for SFSMs with separable alphabets. The underlying mathematical theory is considerably simpler than the general theory providing complete strategies for unrestricted

SFSMs. (2) In contrast to competing approaches [14–16,20], the SFSMs considered here may use nondeterministic transitions and output expressions. (3) It is explained by means of a complexity argument and illustrated by an example that the complete test suites for SFSMs with separable alphabets are significantly shorter in general than those needed for SFSMs with arbitrary alphabets. (4) An open source tool is provided that creates test suites according to the strategy described in this paper and executes them against software SUTs.

Observe that we have chosen language equivalence as the desired conformance relation and not *reduction*, where the implementation language is a subset of the reference model's language. In principle, since reduction preserves the safety properties of the model, it would also be well-suited for testing safety-critical control systems. In the worst case, however, complete test suites for reduction testing require significantly more test cases than needed for equivalence testing [18, Sect. 5.8.3]. Practically, language equivalence testing requires that the reference model should be sufficiently detailed, so that the implementation is expected to realise *all* behaviours the model is capable of.

Overview. In Sect. 2, SFSMs are defined, and their basic semantic properties are introduced. The restricted family of SFSMs that are covered by the testing theory presented here is introduced. In Sect. 3, the generation of complete test suites for this SFSM sub-class is described, and the lemmas and theorems for proving the completeness property are presented. In Sect. 4, an open source tool implementing the test generation method presented here is introduced. The test suite generation is illustrated by means of an example in Sect. 5. Complexity considerations regarding test suite size are presented in Sect. 6. Section 7 presents the conclusion.

The complete underlying theory covering general SFSMs, conformance testing, and property-oriented testing, as well as the SFSM specialisations investigated in this paper are available in the technical report [8]. This paper focuses on the main contributions listed above, and it is self-contained, so that it can be understood without studying the report. The latter is intended for readers interested in the "big picture" of the general theory and further results beyond those presented here. Due to the usual space limitations, the full proofs of the lemmas and theorems discussed in this paper are only contained in the report [8, Appendix A]. The report also discusses comprehensive related work [8, Section 14]. In this paper, we refer to selected related work where appropriate.

2   Symbolic Finite State Machines

Definition. A *Symbolic Finite State Machine (SFSM)* is a tuple

$$\mathcal{S} = (S, s_0, R, I, O, D, \Sigma_I, \Sigma_O, \Sigma).$$

Finite set S denotes the state space, and $s_0 \in S$ is the initial state. Finite set I contains input variable symbols, and finite set O output variable symbols. The sets I and O must be disjoint. We use *Var* to abbreviate $I \cup O$. We assume that the variables are typed, and infinite domains like reals or unlimited integers are admissible. Set D denotes the union over all variable type domains. The *input alphabet* Σ_I consists of finitely many *guard conditions*, each guard condition being a predicate, that is, a Boolean quantifier-free first-order expression over input variables. The finite *output alphabet* Σ_O consists of *output expressions*; these are predicates over (optional) input variables and at least one output variable. We admit constants, function symbols, and arithmetic operators in these expressions, but require that they can be solved based on some decision theory, for example, by an SMT solver. The *symbolic alphabet* $\Sigma \subseteq \Sigma_I \times \Sigma_O$ consists of all non-equivalent pairs of guards and output expressions used by the SFSM. Set $R \subseteq S \times \Sigma \times S$ denotes the *transition relation*.

This definition of SFSMs is consistent with the definition of "symbolic input/output finite state machines (SIOFSM)" introduced by Petrenko [14], but slightly more general: SIOFSMs allow only assignments on output variables, while our definition admits general quantifier-free first-order expressions. This is useful for specifying nondeterministic outputs and for performing data abstraction.

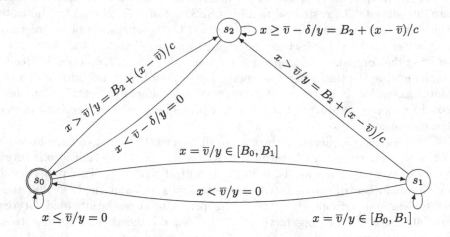

Constants. $\bar{v} = 200$, $\delta = 10$, $B_0 = 0.9$, $B_1 = 1.1$, $B_2 = 2$, $c = 100$

Fig. 1. Braking system BRAKE.

Example 1. Consider the SFSM BRAKE that is graphically represented in Fig. 1. It describes a (fictitious) braking assistance system to be deployed in modern vehicles. Input variable $x \in [0, 400]$ is the actual vehicle speed that should not exceed $\bar{v} = 200[\text{km/h}]$. As long as the speed limit is not violated, the system remains in state s_0 and does not interfere with the brakes: the brake force output[1]

---

[1] This output y is a scalar value, to be multiplied with a constant to obtain the braking force in physical unit Newton.

$y \in \mathbb{R}_{\geq 0}$ is set to 0. When the speed exceeds $\bar{v}$, guard condition $x > \bar{v}$ evaluates to true, and a transition $s_0 \longrightarrow s_2$ is performed. This transition sets the braking force y to

$$y = B_2 + (x - \bar{v})/c \tag{1}$$

with constants $B_2 = 2$ and $c = 100$. The resulting brake force y to be applied is greater than 2, and it is increased linearly according to the extent that x exceeds the allowed threshold $\bar{v}$. For the maximal speed $x = 400$ that is physically possible for this vehicle type, the maximal brake force $y = 4$ is applied. Note that the output expressions do not represent assignments, but quantifier free first-order expressions involving at least one output variable and optional input variables.

While in state s_2, the brake force is adapted according to the changing speed by means of Formula (1). To avoid repeated alternation between releasing and activating the brakes when the speed varies around $\bar{v}$, the system remains in state s_2 while $x \geq \bar{v} - \delta$ with constant $\delta = 10$. As a consequence, the braking force is decreased down to $B_2 - 0.1 = 1.9$ while the vehicle slows down to $x = \bar{v} - \delta$. As soon as the speed is below $\bar{v} - \delta$, the braking system releases the brakes ($y = 0$) and returns to state s_0.

When BRAKE is in state s_0 and the speed equals $\bar{v}$, a nondeterministic system reaction is admissible. Either the system stays in state s_0 without any braking intervention, or it transits to state s_1 while applying a low brake force $y \in [B_0, B_1]$ with $B_0 = 0.9$, $B_1 = 1.1$ (we allow nondeterministic output expressions). This nondeterminism could be due to an abstraction hiding implementation details. While in state s_1, this nondeterministic brake force in range $[B_0, B_1]$ is applied, until either the speed is increased above $\bar{v}$ (this triggers the same reaction as in state s_0), or the speed is decreased below $\bar{v}$, which results in a transition $s_1 \longrightarrow s_0$.

Computations, Valuation Functions, and Traces.

A *symbolic finite computation* of $\mathcal{S}$ is a sequence $\zeta = (s_0, (\varphi_1, \psi_1), s_1).(s_1, (\varphi_2, \psi_2), s_2) \cdots \in (S \times \Sigma \times S)^*$, such that $(s_{i-1}, (\varphi_i, \psi_i), s_i) \in R$ for all $i > 0$. Its projection $\xi = (\varphi_1, \psi_1).(\varphi_2, \psi_2) \cdots \in \Sigma^*$ is called a *symbolic trace*. The *symbolic language* $L_s(\mathcal{S})$ of an SFSM $\mathcal{S}$ is the set of all its symbolic traces.

A *valuation function* $\sigma : X \longrightarrow D$ with $X \in \{I, O, Var\}$ assigns values to variable symbols. In case $X = I$, values are only defined for input variables, in case $X = O$ only for output symbols; for $X = Var$, all variables are mapped to concrete values from their domain contained in D. Given any quantifier-free formula φ over variable symbols from X, we write $\sigma \models \varphi$ and say that σ *is a model for* φ, if and only if the Boolean expression $\varphi[v/\sigma(v) \mid v \in X]$ (this is the formula φ with every symbol $v \in X$ replaced by its valuation $\sigma(v)$) evaluates to true.

We assume that each SFSM is *completely specified*. This means that in every state, the union of all valuations that are models for at least one of the guards applicable in this state equals the whole set D^I of input valuations. Alternatively, this can be expressed by the fact that the disjunction over all guards of a state is always a tautology.

A *concrete finite computation* of $\mathcal{S}$ is a sequence $\zeta_c = (s_0, \sigma_1, s_1)(s_1, \sigma_2, s_2) \dots$ with valuation functions σ_i defined on Var, such that there exists a symbolic computation ζ traversing the same sequence of states and satisfying $\sigma_i \models \varphi_i \wedge \psi_i$ for all $i > 0$. The concrete computation ζ_c is called a *witness* of ζ, this is abbreviated by $\zeta_c \models \zeta$. This is the *synchronous interpretation* of the SFSM's visible input/output behaviour, as discussed by van de Pol [17]: inputs and outputs occur simultaneously, that is, in the same computation step σ_i.

The set of all valuations $\sigma : X \longrightarrow D$ is denoted by D^X. A *(concrete) trace* is a sequence $\kappa = \sigma_1 \dots \sigma_n \in \left(D^{Var}\right)^*$ of valuation functions, such that there exists a symbolic trace $\xi = (\varphi_1, \psi_1) \dots (\varphi_n, \psi_n) \in L_s(\mathcal{S})$ with $\kappa \models \xi$, i.e., $\sigma_i \models \varphi_i \wedge \psi_i$, for all $i = 1, \dots, n$. The set of all traces of $\mathcal{S}$ is called its *(concrete) language* and denoted by $L(\mathcal{S})$. For any $\alpha = (\varphi_1, \psi_1) \dots (\varphi_k, \psi_k) \in (\Sigma_I \times \Sigma_O)^*$, define $\alpha|_{\Sigma_I} = \varphi_1 \dots \varphi_k$. $\mathcal{S}$ is called *reduced* if its states are pairwise distinguishable by concrete input traces leading to different outputs when applied to these states. We can check this by trying to find a concrete trace $\kappa_s = \sigma_1 \dots \sigma_n \in \left(D^{Var}\right)^*$ for each state pair $(s, s') \in S$ with $s \neq s'$, where κ_s is a model for some concrete finite computation $\zeta_s = (s, \sigma_1, s_1) \dots (s_{n-1}, \sigma_n, s_n)$ starting in s, but where there is *no* concrete finite computation $\zeta_{s'} = (s', \sigma_1, s'_1) \dots (s'_{n-1}, \sigma_n, s'_n)$ for s'. If such a concrete trace κ_s exists for all distinct $s, s' \in S$, the states in S are pairwise distinguishable and $\mathcal{S}$ is reduced.

For the remainder of this paper, only *well-formed* SFSMs are considered. This means that all guard conditions and associated output expressions can be solved in the sense that every transition label $(\varphi, \psi) \in \Sigma$ has at least one model $\sigma \in D^{Var}$ satisfying $\sigma \models \varphi \wedge \psi$.

A Restricted Family of SFSMs – Separable Alphabets. As indicated in Sect. 1, we consider a slightly restricted class of SFSMs $\mathcal{S}$ in this paper that allows for considerably smaller complete test suites for language equivalence testing. All restrictions refer to the input alphabet Σ_I, output alphabet Σ_O, and alphabet $\Sigma \subseteq \Sigma_I \times \Sigma_O$ used by these SFSMs. The restrictions are specified as follows, and we call any alphabet tuple $(\Sigma_I, \Sigma_O, \Sigma)$ fulfilling them *separable*.

1. The alphabet $\Sigma \subseteq \Sigma_I \times \Sigma_O$ contains pairwise non-equivalent pairs of guards and output expressions: for every two elements $(\varphi, \psi) \neq (\varphi', \psi') \in \Sigma$, formulae $\varphi \wedge \psi$ and $\varphi' \wedge \psi'$ have differing sets of models.
2. The symbolic input alphabet Σ_I *partitions the set* D^I of input valuations, that is, for all $\sigma \in D^I$, there exists a uniquely determined $\varphi \in \Sigma_I$ such that $\sigma \models \varphi$.
3. *Separability of output expressions.* For any $(\varphi, \psi) \in \Sigma$, there exists at least one input valuation $\sigma_I \in D^I$ *distinguishing* (φ, ψ) from all other $(\varphi, \psi') \in \Sigma$ with $\psi' \neq \psi \in \Sigma_O$, in the sense that σ_I fulfils

$$(\exists \sigma_O \in D^O \centerdot \sigma_I \cup \sigma_O \models \varphi \wedge \psi) \wedge \hspace{3cm} (2)$$

$$(\forall \psi' \in \Sigma_O \setminus \{\psi\} \centerdot (\varphi, \psi') \in \Sigma \implies$$

$$(\forall \sigma_O' \in D^O \centerdot (\sigma_I \cup \sigma_O' \models \psi) \implies (\sigma_I \cup \sigma_O' \models \neg \psi')))$$

Restriction 1 is only syntactic: if $(\varphi, \psi) \neq (\varphi', \psi') \in \Sigma$ differ syntactically, but are equivalent first order expressions, one of these pairs, say (φ', ψ'), is removed from Σ. SFSM transitions $(s_1, \varphi', \psi', s_2) \in R$ are replaced by $(s_1, \varphi, \psi, s_2)$ without changing the language of the SFSM.

Likewise, Restriction 2 is only syntactic: by refining guard conditions, a new syntactic representation of the original SFSM is obtained that has the same language. The detailed refinement mechanism is described in [8], a simple case is shown below in Sect. 5.

Only Restriction 3 reduces the *semantic* domain of SFSMs that can be tested according to the strategy described here. Intuitively speaking, Formula (2) requires for each pair of guard φ and output expression ψ the existence of an input valuation $\sigma_I \in D^I$ such that a suitable output valuation $\sigma_O \in D^O$ satisfying $\sigma_I \cup \sigma_O \models \varphi \wedge \psi$ exists, and *every* possible output σ_O' that can occur for output expression ψ and the given inputs σ_I could *not* have been produced by any other output expression $\psi' \neq \psi$. In the example presented in Sect. 5, it is illustrated how the syntactic Requirements 1,2 can be established by a refining transformation, and how the third restriction is checked.

The airbag controllers, speed monitors, and train protection units mentioned in Sect. 1 can all be modelled as SFSMs with separable alphabets. A simple class of alphabet tuples that are *not* separable are those where the output expressions define nondeterministic, overlapping data ranges that do not depend on input values at all, such as, for example,

$$(\Sigma_I, \Sigma_O, \Sigma) = (\{x < 0, x \geq 0\}, \{y \in [0,2], y \in [1,3]\}, \Sigma_I \times \Sigma_O).$$

Here, the more general testing theory described in [8] needs to be applied.

The following lemma states the important property that separability of alphabets is preserved when an SFSM only uses a subset of the output expressions occurring in a separable alphabet.

Lemma 1. *Let $(\Sigma_I, \Sigma_O, \Sigma)$ be a separable alphabet. Then any alphabet $(\Sigma_I, \Sigma_O', \Sigma')$ satisfying $\Sigma_O' \subseteq \Sigma_O$, $\Sigma' \subseteq \Sigma_I \times \Sigma_O'$ and $\Sigma' \subseteq \Sigma$ is also separable.*

Complete Testing Assumptions. As is usual in black-box testing of nondeterministic systems, we adopt the *complete testing assumption* [7]. This requires the existence of some known $k \in \mathbb{N}$ such that, if an input sequence (i.e. a test case) is applied k times to the SUT, then all possible responses are observed, and, therefore, all states reachable by means of this sequence have been visited. Since we are dealing with possibly infinite input and output domains, *"all possible responses"* is interpreted in the way that all satisfiable symbolic traces of the system under test are visited when executing a test case k times.

In "real-world" test campaigns for safety-critical systems, code coverage and/or hardware address coverage measurements are performed during software tests and HW/SW integration tests, so that it can be determined whether all reactions to a given test case have been observed after its k-fold execution.

Finite State Machine Abstraction. Recall that a *finite state machine (FSM, Mealy Machine)* is a tuple $M = (S, s_0, R, \Sigma_I, \Sigma_O, \Sigma)$ with finite state space S, initial state $s_0 \in S$, finite input and output alphabets Σ_I, Σ_O, transition relation $R \subseteq S \times \Sigma \times S$.

Given a SFSM $\mathcal{S} = (S, s_0, R, I, O, D, \Sigma_I, \Sigma_O, \Sigma)$, simply deciding to leave guard conditions and output expressions uninterpreted yields an FSM $M = (S, s_0, R, \Sigma_I, \Sigma_O, \Sigma)$. The language $L(M)$ of FSM M is the set of all traces $\alpha = (\varphi_1, \psi_1) \ldots (\varphi_k, \psi_k) \in \Sigma^*$, such that there exists a sequence of states $s_0.s_1 \ldots s_k$ satisfying $\forall i \in \{1, \ldots, k\} \centerdot (s_{i-1}, \varphi_i, \psi_i, s_i) \in R$.

Since M uses the SFSM's transition relation and symbolic alphabets, and since the language of M is defined exactly as the symbolic language of $\mathcal{S}$, this abstraction of SFSM $\mathcal{S}$ to FSM M preserves the symbolic language, that is, $L(M) = L_s(\mathcal{S})$.

Fault Domains. In the context of this paper, a *fault domain* is an SFSM-set $\mathcal{F}(\Sigma_I, \Sigma_O, \Sigma, m)$, that is defined for any separable alphabet $(\Sigma_I, \Sigma_O, \Sigma)$. All SFSMs $\mathcal{S}' \in \mathcal{F}(\Sigma_I, \Sigma_O, \Sigma, m)$ have the following properties. (1) The alphabet $(\Sigma_I, \Sigma_O', \Sigma')$ of $\mathcal{S}'$ satisfies $\Sigma_O' \subseteq \Sigma_O$ and $\Sigma' \subseteq \Sigma$. (2) When represented in observable, reduced form[2], $\mathcal{S}'$ has at most m states. Moreover, (3) The reference model $\mathcal{S}$ is also contained in $\mathcal{F}(\Sigma_I, \Sigma_O, \Sigma, m)$ and has $n \leq m$ states, when represented in observable, reduced form.

Following the concept of mutation testing, a fault domain admits finitely many mutants of guard conditions and mutants of output expressions, these are contained in Σ_I and Σ_O, respectively. Since, as explained above, the input alphabet of any SFSM can always be transformed for a set of refined guard conditions without changing the language, it can always be assumed that all SFSMs in the fault domain operate on the same input alphabet. This is usually more fine-grained than the original alphabet used by the reference model, in order to accommodate for erroneous guard conditions. Erroneous implementations may use faulty combinations of guards φ and output expressions ψ, but these faulty combinations (φ, ψ) must be captured in Σ. Faulty SFSMs may possess up to $m - n$ additional states, and they may exhibit arbitrary *transfer faults*, that is, misdirected transitions. The fault domain construction principle is illustrated in the example discussed in Sect. 5.

---

[2] An SFSM is *observable* if every concrete trace leads to a uniquely determined target state. Every non-observable SFSM can be transformed into an observable one without changing its language [8]. An observable SFSM is *reduced* if its states are pairwise distinguishable.

3   Test Suite Generation

Throughout this section, SFSM $\mathcal{S}$ plays the role of a reference model, and $\mathcal{S}'$ is the representation of the true SUT behaviour as an SFSM. $\mathcal{S}'$ is supposed to be contained in the fault domain.

Symbolic and Concrete Test Cases, Test Suites. A *symbolic test case* is a sequence of (guard condition/output expression) pairs, that is, any sequence $\alpha \in \Sigma^*$. A *concrete test case* is a sequence τ of pairs of (input/output) valuation, that is $\tau \in (D^{Var})^*$.

Note that in other contexts, test cases represent just sequences of inputs [3]. In this paper, a test case is a sequence of symbolic or concrete input/response pairs, because this facilitates the investigation of language equivalence. Observe further, that it is not required for a test case to be in the language of the reference model: a test case can also contain responses to inputs that are erroneous from the reference model's perspective.

A *symbolic input test case* is a finite sequence of guard conditions $\xi_I \in \Sigma_I^*$. For concrete test executions, of course, only the input projections of concrete test cases are passed to the SUT, we denote these sequences as *concrete input test cases*. Given a concrete input test case $\tau_I = \sigma_I^1 \ldots \sigma_I^p \in (D^I)^*$ and a sequence of output valuations $\tau_O = \sigma_O^1 \ldots \sigma_O^p \in (D^O)^*$ of the same length as τ_I, we use the abbreviated notation $\tau_I/\tau_O = (\sigma_I^1 \cup \sigma_O^1) \ldots (\sigma_I^p \cup \sigma_O^p) \in (D^{Var})^*$.

Let $out_k(\mathcal{S}', \tau_I)$ denote the collection of output responses of $\mathcal{S}'$ to the concrete input test case τ_I obtained during k executions of this test case. Note that $out_k(\mathcal{S}', \tau_I)$ is a random collection: for repeated execution of k test case runs each, $out_k(\mathcal{S}', \tau_I)$ may contain different output traces in the nondeterministic case.

A *symbolic test suite* TS $\subseteq \Sigma^*$ is a set of symbolic test cases, a *concrete test suite* TS $\subseteq (D^{Var})^*$ is a set of concrete test cases.

Pass Relations

Definition 1 (Pass relation for symbolic test cases). *Let $\alpha \subseteq \Sigma^*$ be a symbolic test case. We say $\mathcal{S}'$ passes α (with respect to reference model $\mathcal{S}$) if and only if*

$$\alpha \in L_s(\mathcal{S}') \iff \alpha \in L_s(\mathcal{S}).$$

Definition 2 (Pass relation for concrete input test cases). *Let $\tau_I \in (D^I)^*$ be a concrete input test case. We say $\mathcal{S}'$ passes τ_I if and only if*

1. *for any $\tau_O \in out_k(\mathcal{S}', \tau_I)$, it holds that $\tau_I/\tau_O \in L(\mathcal{S})$, and*
2. *for any $\alpha \in L_s(\mathcal{S})$ with $\tau_I/\tau_O \models \alpha$, there exists $\tau_O' \in out_k(\mathcal{S}', \tau_I)$ satisfying $\tau_I/\tau_O' \models \alpha$.*

Condition 1 of this pass relation requires that all concrete outputs τ_O observable in k executions of input test case τ_I conform to $\mathcal{S}$ in the sense that τ_I/τ_O is contained in the language of $\mathcal{S}$.

Language Equivalence Testing. A symbolic test suite is called *complete*, if passing this suite is equivalent to proving equality of the symbolic languages of reference model and implementation.

Definition 3 (Complete test suites). *Let* TS $\subseteq \Sigma^*$ *be a symbolic test suite.* TS *is called* complete *for proving the equivalence of* $L_s(\mathcal{S})$ *and* $L_s(\mathcal{S}')$ *if and only if* $L_s(\mathcal{S}) \cap \text{TS} = L_s(\mathcal{S}') \cap \text{TS} \iff L_s(\mathcal{S}) = L_s(\mathcal{S}')$.

In the sense of Definition 1, this means that $\mathcal{S}'$ passes all test cases from TS with respect to reference model $\mathcal{S}$, because

$$L_s(\mathcal{S}) \cap \text{TS} = L_s(\mathcal{S}') \cap \text{TS} \equiv \forall \alpha \in \text{TS} \cdot \left(\alpha \in L_s(\mathcal{S}) \iff \alpha \in L_s(\mathcal{S}') \right)$$

A symbolic input test suite $\text{TS}_I \subseteq \Sigma_I^*$ *is called* complete for proving the equivalence of $L_s(\mathcal{S})$ and $L_s(\mathcal{S}')$ *if and only if the symbolic test suite* $\text{TS} = \{\alpha \in \Sigma^* \mid \alpha|_{\Sigma_I} \in \text{TS}_I\}$ *is complete for proving the equivalence of* $L_s(\mathcal{S})$ *and* $L_s(\mathcal{S}')$.

Definition 4 (Distinguishing Function). *A* distinguishing function $T : \Sigma^* \to (D^I)^*$ *is a function from sequences of the symbolic alphabet to sequences of input valuations, such that for any* $\alpha \in \Sigma^*$, $|T(\alpha)| = |\alpha|$, *and* $T(\alpha)(i) \in dis(\alpha(i))$, $\forall i = 1, \ldots, |\alpha|$, *where* $dis(\varphi, \psi') = \{\sigma_I \in D^I \mid \sigma_I$ *satisfies Formula (2)}.*

A function $T : \Sigma \to D^I$ is called a distinguishing function associated with Σ, if its natural extension $T : \Sigma^* \to (D^I)^*$ defined by $T((\varphi_1, \psi_1) \ldots (\varphi_k, \psi_k)) = T(\varphi_1, \psi_1) \ldots T(\varphi_k, \psi_k)$ is a distinguishing function.

A given distinguishing function T can be reduced to a function depending on symbolic input sequences only by defining $T(\alpha_I) = \{T(\alpha) \mid \alpha \in \Sigma^* \wedge \alpha|_{\Sigma_I} = \alpha_I\}$.

For the remainder of this paper, T always denotes a distinguishing function. The following lemma states that any sequence of input valuations obtained by a distinguishing function already determines the associated sequence of symbolic alphabet elements in a unique way.

Lemma 2. *Suppose* $\alpha, \beta \in \Sigma^*$, $\tau_I = T(\alpha) \in (D^I)^*$ *and* $\tau_O \in (D^O)^*$, *such that* $\tau_I/\tau_O \models \alpha$ *holds. Then* $\tau_I/\tau_O \models \beta$ *implies* $\alpha = \beta$.

Lemma 3. *Let* $\alpha \in \Sigma^*$ *be a symbolic test case. Suppose* $\mathcal{S}'$ *passes concrete input test case* $T(\alpha)$. *Then* $\mathcal{S}'$ *passes symbolic test* α, *i.e.,* $\alpha \in L_s(\mathcal{S}) \iff \alpha \in L_s(\mathcal{S}')$.

The following theorem shows that for the restricted class of SFSMs considered in this paper, concrete language equivalence already implies symbolic language equivalence.

Theorem 1. $L_s(\mathcal{S}) = L_s(\mathcal{S}') \iff L(\mathcal{S}) = L(\mathcal{S}')$.

Theorem 2. *Let* TS $\subseteq \Sigma^*$ *be a complete test suite for proving the equivalence of* $L_s(\mathcal{S})$ *and* $L_s(\mathcal{S}')$. *Then* $T(\text{TS})$ *is a complete concrete input test suite for proving the equivalence of* $L(\mathcal{S})$ *and* $L(\mathcal{S}')$.

We can now state the main theorem about complete test suites for SFSMs with separable alphabets: complete symbolic input test suites can be directly transformed into likewise complete concrete input test suites, using the distinguishing function.

Theorem 3. *Let* $\mathrm{TS}_I \subseteq \Sigma_I^*$ *be a complete symbolic input test suite for proving the equivalence of symbolic languages* $L_s(\mathcal{S})$ *and* $L_s(\mathcal{S}')$. *Then* $T(\mathrm{TS}_I)$ *is a complete concrete input test suite for proving the equivalence of* $L(\mathcal{S})$ *and* $L(\mathcal{S}')$.

For generating a complete test suite for testing language equivalence against some SFSM reference model $\mathcal{S}$, we can abstract $\mathcal{S}$ to an FSM M and use an arbitrary complete test generation method for testing language equivalence against M. A complete FSM test suite $\mathrm{TS}_{\mathrm{FSM}}$ consists of test cases that are input sequences α over the alphabet Σ_I. Each sequence α can be turned into a concrete SFSM input test case by applying a distinguishing function $T : \Sigma \longrightarrow D^I$ associated with $\mathcal{S}$. The resulting test suite generation method is specified in Algorithm 2 below. Algorithm 1 specifies how to calculate the distinguishing function T for a given SFSM $\mathcal{S}$.

Algorithm 1 Calculate Distinguishing Function T for alphabet $(\Sigma_I, \Sigma_O, \Sigma)$.

$T \leftarrow \varnothing$;
for all $(\varphi, \psi) \in \Sigma_I \times \Sigma_O$ **do**
  find solution $\sigma_I \in D^I$ for Formula (2) using an SMT solver supporting quantified satisfaction [2]:
  $(\exists \sigma_O \in D^O . \sigma_I \cup \sigma_O \models \varphi \wedge \psi) \wedge \big(\forall \psi' \in \Sigma_O \setminus \{\psi\} . (\varphi, \psi') \in \Sigma \implies$
  $\qquad\qquad\qquad (\forall \sigma_O' \in D^O . (\sigma_I \cup \sigma_O' \models \psi) \implies (\sigma_I \cup \sigma_O' \models \neg\psi')))$
  if solution σ_I exists **then**
    $T \leftarrow T \cup \{(\varphi, \psi) \mapsto \sigma_I\}$;
  else
    terminate with error *"Alphabet does not fulfil separability condition"*;
  end if
end for
return T.

---

4   Tool Support

Essential for creating a complete concrete input test suite is the calculation of the distinguishing function $T : \Sigma \longrightarrow D^I$ according to Definition 4. This can be performed using Algorithm 1. The crucial step in this algorithm is the calculation of a valuation function σ_I satisfying Formula (2) for given $(\varphi, \psi) \in \Sigma$. To solve this formula, an SMT solver supporting *quantified satisfaction (QS)* is required [2]. Several tools are available for this purpose, we have integrated Z3[3] into our test generator for this purpose.

---

[3] https://github.com/Z3Prover/z3.

Algorithm 2 Generate test suite for proving language equivalence against SFSM
$S = (S, s_0, R, I, O, D, \Sigma_I, \Sigma'_O, \Sigma')$ and fault domain $\mathcal{F}(\Sigma_I, \Sigma_O, \Sigma, m)$

Require: $(\Sigma_I, \Sigma_O, \Sigma)$ is separable, $\Sigma'_O \subseteq \Sigma_O$, $\Sigma' \subseteq \Sigma$;
  Calculate distinguishing function $T : \Sigma \longrightarrow D^I$ using Algorithm 1;
  if calculation of T returns an error **then**
      return error message *"Test suite cannot be generated, since alphabet does not
      fulfil separability condition"*
  end if
  Define FSM $M = (S, s_0, R, \Sigma_I, \Sigma'_O, \Sigma')$ abstracting S as described in Section 2;
  Calculate complete input test suite $\text{TS}_{\text{FSM}} \subseteq \Sigma_I^*$ for checking FSM language equivalence against M and fault domain $\mathcal{F}_{\text{FSM}}(\Sigma_I, \Sigma_O, m)$;
  return $T(\text{TS}_{\text{FSM}})$.

The complete test suite generation is specified in Algorithm 2. As shown in Theorem 4, this algorithm yields a complete test suite for the SFSM reference model S, when applying the distinguishing function T to a complete test suite from the FSM obtained by abstracting S. For calculating a complete test suite for a given reference FSM and fault domain $\mathcal{F}(\Sigma_I, \Sigma_O, \Sigma, m)_{\text{FSM}}$ the tool makes use of the library `libfsmtest` [1] that contains many of the well-established test generation algorithms for testing against FSM models.

Theorem 4. *Algorithm 2 generates a test suite* TS *that is complete for proving language equivalence against reference model* $S = (S, s_0, R, I, O, D, \Sigma_I, \Sigma_O, \Sigma)$ *and fault domain* $\mathcal{F}(\Sigma_I, \Sigma_O, \Sigma, m)$.

Note that a value of m can be obtained by static analysis of the SUT state variables occurring in the source code. The potential mutations of guards and output expressions can be obtained by identifying the condition expressions and the right-hand sides of assignments, respectively. These techniques have been manually applied by Gleirscher et al. [6], but automated static analysers for these purposes are not yet available.

A demonstration instance of the tool with a web interface exists at http://fsmtestcloud.informatik.uni-bremen.de.

5 Application of the Test Method: Example

In this section, we use the SFSM BRAKE introduced in Example 1 to illustrate the transformations needed to incorporate the fault hypotheses and to obtain the required syntactic representation that is necessary to apply the testing method presented in Sect. 3. Then a test suite is produced according to the algorithms described in Sect. 4.

Step 1 – define input and output alphabet mutations. Initially, the possible mutations of the reference model's alphabet that may occur in erroneous implementations are identified. To keep this example readable, we only add one guard mutation $x \leq \overline{v} - \delta$ to the set of guards actually used by SFSM BRAKE. Additionally, one mutated output expression $y = B_2 + (x - \overline{v})^2/c$ is added.

Step 2 – input alphabet refinement. Next, the input alphabet including guard mutations is refined to ensure that Restriction 2 (input alphabet partitions D^I) is fulfilled. The original input alphabet of BRAKE extended by the above guard mutation does *not* fulfil this condition. Therefore, a refined alphabet $\Sigma_I = \{\varphi_1, \varphi_2, \varphi_3, \varphi_4, \varphi_5\}$ with

$$\begin{aligned}
&\varphi_1 \equiv x \in [0, \overline{v} - \delta) \quad \varphi_2 \equiv x = \overline{v} - \delta \quad \varphi_3 \equiv x \in (\overline{v} - \delta, \overline{v}) \\
&\varphi_4 \equiv x = \overline{v} \qquad\qquad \varphi_5 \equiv x \in (\overline{v}, 400]
\end{aligned} \tag{3}$$

is introduced, and SFSM BRAKE is transformed accordingly. This leads to the new representation BRAKE' that is shown in tabular form in Table 1. Obviously, BRAKE' and BRAKE are language-equivalent. Moreover, it is easy to see that the states s_0, s_1, s_2 of BRAKE' are still distinguishable, so $n = 3$ for the reference model BRAKE' of this example.

Table 1. Refined SFSM BRAKE' fulfilling assumptions 1 — 3 specified in Sect. 2. Left column lists source states, starting with initial state. First row lists guard conditions from Σ_I. Inner table cells c_{ij} list 'next state/output expression', applicable when guard condition φ_j is triggered in source state s_i. Guards φ_i are specified in Eq. (3), and output expressions ψ_j are defined in Eq. (4).

	φ_1	φ_2	φ_3	φ_4	φ_5
s_0	s_0/ψ_1	s_0/ψ_1	s_0/ψ_1	s_0/ψ_1 s_1/ψ_2	s_2/ψ_3
s_1	s_0/ψ_1	s_0/ψ_1	s_0/ψ_1	s_1/ψ_2	s_2/ψ_3
s_2	s_0/ψ_1	s_2/ψ_3	s_2/ψ_3	s_2/ψ_3	s_2/ψ_3

Step 3 – specify the fault domain. For the fault domain $\mathcal{F}(\Sigma_I, \Sigma_O, \Sigma, m)$, the input alphabet Σ_I is already defined by Eq. (3). For specifying Σ_O, the output alphabet of BRAKE is extended by the output mutation identified in Step 1. This results in $\Sigma_O = \{\psi_1, \psi_2, \psi_3, \psi_4\}$ with

$$\psi_1 \equiv y = 0, \ \psi_2 \equiv y \in [B_0, B_1], \ \psi_3 \equiv y = B_2 + (x - \overline{v})/c, \ \psi_4 \equiv y = B_2 + (x - \overline{v})^2/c \tag{4}$$

for our example. Since $\varphi_4 \wedge \psi_4$ is equivalent to $\varphi_4 \wedge \psi_3$, the alphabet is specified by $\Sigma = (\Sigma_I \times \Sigma_O) \setminus \{(\varphi_4, \psi_4)\}$ to ensure separability.

As an estimate for the maximal number $m \geq n$ of states for SFSM behaviours captured by $\mathcal{F}(\Sigma_I, \Sigma_O, \Sigma, m)$, we choose $m = 4$ for this example.

Step 4 – calculate distinguishing function T. The distinguishing function $T : \Sigma \longrightarrow D^I$ is calculated according to Algorithm 1 in Sect. 4. For our example, T results in the function specified in Table 2.

It is easy to see that the separability condition for output expressions is fulfilled. Observe that for BRAKE′, the distinguishing function T does not depend on the second argument $\psi \in \Sigma_O$. In the general case, the image value of T depends on both guard condition and output expression.

Table 2. Function table $T : \Sigma \longrightarrow D^I$ for transformed SFSM BRAKE′. Guards φ_i are specified in Eq. (3), output expressions ψ_j in Eq. (4).

$T(\varphi_1, \psi_i) = \{x \mapsto 180\}$, $T(\varphi_2, \psi_i) = \{x \mapsto 190\}$, $T(\varphi_3, \psi_i) = \{x \mapsto 195\}$, $i = 1, 2, 3, 4$
$T(\varphi_4, \psi_i) = \{x \mapsto 200\}$, $i = 1, 2, 3$, $T(\varphi_5, \psi_i) = \{x \mapsto 210\}$, $i = 1, 2, 3, 4$

Step 5 – calculate complete test suite on FSM abstraction. We now abstract BRAKE′ to an FSM as described in Sect. 2 with $\mathcal{F}(\Sigma_I, \Sigma_O, \Sigma, m)_{\mathrm{FSM}}$ as fault domain. To generate a complete test suite for FSM language equivalence testing, we apply the well-known W-method [3] for this example, since this method is simple to introduce and to apply without tool support. From Theorem 3 follows that any complete *input* test suite $\mathcal{W}$ for the FSM abstraction will directly yield a complete input test suite for the SFSM BRAKE′ by applying the distinguishing function T to $\mathcal{W}$.

For fault domain $\mathcal{F}(\Sigma_I, \Sigma_O, \Sigma, m)_{\mathrm{FSM}}$, a complete input test suite according to the W-method is given by the set of input sequences

$$\mathcal{W} = V.\left(\bigcup_{i=0}^{m-n+1} \Sigma_I^i \right).W,$$

where V is a state cover consisting of input traces leading from the initial state to every state in the reference model, Σ_I^i is the set of all input traces of length i (Σ_I^0 just contains the empty trace ε), and W is a characterisation set, distinguishing all states of the reference model. The ".".-operator concatenates all traces in the first operand with all traces in the second operand. For our example, $m-n+1 = 2$ and

$$V = \{\varepsilon, \varphi_4, \varphi_5\}, \quad W = \{\varphi_4\}, \quad \bigcup_{i=0}^{2} \Sigma_I^i = \{\varepsilon, \varphi_j, \varphi_j.\varphi_k \mid j, k \in \{1, 2, 3, 4, 5\}\}.$$

Applying T to this FSM test suite results in the SFSM input test suite

$$\mathrm{TS}_{\mathrm{in}} = A.B.C, \quad A = \{\varepsilon, T(\varphi_4, \cdot), T(\varphi_5, \cdot)\}$$
$$B = \{\varepsilon, T(\varphi_j, \cdot), T(\varphi_j, \cdot).T(\varphi_k, \cdot) \mid j, k \in \{1, 2, 3, 4, 5\}\}, \quad C = \{T(\varphi_4, \cdot)\}$$

Consider, for example, a faulty implementation IBRAKE, that differs from BRAKE′ by a transfer fault: the correct BRAKE-transition $s_2 \xrightarrow{\varphi_2/\psi_3} s_2$ has been replaced by the faulty transition $s_2 \xrightarrow{\varphi_2/\psi_3} s_1$. This faulty transition is detected by the input test case $tc_1 = \{x \mapsto 210\}.\{x \mapsto 190\}.\{x \mapsto 200\} \in A.B.C$: execution of this test case against IBRAKE will result in witnesses for symbolic trace $\xi_1 = (\varphi_5, \psi_3).(\varphi_2, \psi_3).(\varphi_4, \psi_2)$. The reference model BRAKE', however, will produce only a witness for symbolic trace $\xi'_1 = (\varphi_5, \psi_3).(\varphi_2, \psi_3).(\varphi_4, \psi_3)$, and $\varphi_4 \wedge \psi_3$ has $y = B_2$ as the only solution, while $\varphi_4 \wedge \psi_2$ has solutions $y \in [B_0, B_1]$.

6   Complexity Considerations

After discarding input traces that are prefixes of longer ones, the test suite specified in the previous section results in 65 test cases. Using the general theory for testing language equivalence of arbitrary SFSMs would result in 176 test cases [8]. The reason for this significant difference can be understood from the general theory [8]: every complete test suite has to contain a "core set" $V.(\bigcup_{i=0}^{m-n+1} A^i)$ of test cases that are suitable for (a) reaching every state s in the SUT, and (b) exercising the relevant inputs from a set $A \subseteq D^I$ in every state s. In the general case, the number of elements in A depends on the number of *input/output equivalence classes*, each class constructed by conjunctions of positive and negated guards *and* output expressions. For our example, this leads to 8 concrete representatives of these input/output classes. The specialised theory presented in this paper, however, only needs one representative for every guard in Σ_I, after having previously ensured that Σ_I partitions D^I. This leads to 5 representatives only. For worst case estimates, the input set A has a cardinality of order $O(2^{(|\Sigma_I| + |\Sigma_O|)})$ in the general theory, whereas the cardinality of A is of order $O(2^{|\Sigma_I|})$ in the specialised cases presented here, due to the separability of alphabets.

7   Conclusion

We have presented a testing strategy for checking input/output language equivalence against a restricted class of nondeterministic symbolic finite state machines and proven its completeness. The restricted class of admissible SFSM models is characterised by separable alphabets. This means that output expressions are pairwise distinguishable for each transition guard, by choosing appropriate input valuations fulfilling the respective guard conditions. If a reference model conforms to this restriction, the resulting test suites proving language equivalence are significantly smaller than those needed for the general case, for which a complete theory exists as well.

It should be emphasised that for grey-box software testing, the check whether an implementation is really contained in a given fault domain can be performed by means of static analysis of the source code. Applying these analyses, the complete tests described here represent an alternative to code verification by model checking.

References

1. Bergenthal, M., Krafczyk, N., Peleska, J., Sachtleben, R.: libfsmtest an open source library for FSM-based testing. In: Clark, D., Menendez, H., Cavalli, A.R. (eds.) Testing Software and Systems, pp. 3–19. Springer International Publishing, Cham (2022)
2. Bjørner, N.S., Janota, M.: Playing with quantified satisfaction. In: Fehnker, A., McIver, A., Sutcliffe, G., Voronkov, A. (eds.) 20th International Conferences on Logic for Programming, Artificial Intelligence and Reasoning - Short Presentations, LPAR 2015, Suva, Fiji, November 24–28, 2015. EPiC Series in Computing, vol. 35, pp. 15–27. EasyChair (2015). https://doi.org/10.29007/vv21
3. Chow, T.S.: Testing software design modeled by finite-state machines. IEEE Trans. Softw. Eng. SE. **4**(3), 178–186 (1978)
4. Eder, K.I., Huang, W., Peleska, J.: Complete agent-driven model-based system testing for autonomous systems. In: Farrell, M., Luckcuck, M. (eds.) Proceedings Third Workshop on Formal Methods for Autonomous Systems, FMAS 2021, Virtual, 21st-22nd of October 2021. EPTCS, vol. 348, pp. 54–72 (2021). https://doi.org/10.4204/EPTCS.348.4
5. Endo, A.T., da Silva Simão, A.: Experimental comparison of test case generation methods for finite state machines. In: Antoniol, G., Bertolino, A., Labiche, Y. (eds.) Fifth IEEE International Conference on Software Testing, Verification and Validation, ICST 2012, Montreal, QC, Canada, April 17–21, 2012, pp. 549–558. IEEE Computer Society (2012). https://doi.org/10.1109/ICST.2012.140
6. Gleirscher, M., Peleska, J.: Complete test of synthesised safety supervisors for robots and autonomous systems. In: Farrell, M., Luckcuck, M. (eds.) Proceedings Third Workshop on Formal Methods for Autonomous Systems, FMAS 2021, Virtual, 21st-22nd of October 2021. EPTCS, vol. 348, pp. 101–109 (2021). https://doi.org/10.4204/EPTCS.348.7
7. Hierons, R.M.: Testing from a nondeterministic finite state machine using adaptive state counting. IEEE Trans. Comput. **53**(10), 1330–1342 (2004). https://doi.org/10.1109/TC.2004.85
8. Huang, W., Krafczyk, N., Peleska, J.: Model-Based Conformance Testing and Property Testing With Symbolic Finite State Machines. Technical report, Zenodo (2022). https://doi.org/10.5281/zenodo.7267975
9. Huang, W., Peleska, J.: Complete model-based equivalence class testing for nondeterministic systems. Formal Aspects Comput. **29**(2), 335–364 (2016). https://doi.org/10.1007/s00165-016-0402-2
10. Hübner, F., Huang, W., Peleska, J.: Experimental evaluation of a novel equivalence class partition testing strategy. Softw. Syst. Modeling **18**(1), 423–443 (2017). https://doi.org/10.1007/s10270-017-0595-8
11. Kalaji, A.S., Hierons, R.M., Swift, S.: Generating feasible transition paths for testing from an extended finite state machine (EFSM). In: ICST, pp. 230–239. IEEE Computer Society (2009)
12. Krafczyk, N., Peleska, J.: Exhaustive property oriented model-based testing with symbolic finite state machines. In: Calinescu, R., Păsăreanu, C.S. (eds.) SEFM 2021. LNCS, vol. 13085, pp. 84–102. Springer, Cham (2021). https://doi.org/10.1007/978-3-030-92124-8_5
13. Peleska, J., Huang, W., Cavalcanti, A.: Finite complete suites for CSP refinement testing. Sci. Comput. Program. **179**, 1–23 (2019). https://doi.org/10.1016/j.scico.2019.04.004

14. Petrenko, A.: Checking experiments for symbolic input/output finite state machines. In: 2016 IEEE Ninth International Conference on Software Testing, Verification and Validation Workshops (ICSTW), pp. 229–237 (2016). https://doi.org/10.1109/ICSTW.2016.9

15. Petrenko, A.: Toward testing from finite state machines with symbolic inputs and outputs. Softw. Syst. Modeling 18(2), 825–835 (2017). https://doi.org/10.1007/s10270-017-0613-x

16. Petrenko, A., Simao, A.: Checking experiments for finite state machines with symbolic inputs. In: El-Fakih, K., Barlas, G., Yevtushenko, N. (eds.) ICTSS 2015. LNCS, vol. 9447, pp. 3–18. Springer, Cham (2015). https://doi.org/10.1007/978-3-319-25945-1_1

17. van de Pol, J., Meijer, J.: Synchronous or alternating? In: Margaria, T., Graf, S., Larsen, K.G. (eds.) Models, Mindsets, Meta: The What, the How, and the Why Not? LNCS, vol. 11200, pp. 417–430. Springer, Cham (2019). https://doi.org/10.1007/978-3-030-22348-9_24

18. Sachtleben, R., Peleska, J.: Effective grey-box testing with partial FSM models. Softw. Test. Verification Reliab. 32(2) (2022). https://doi.org/10.1002/stvr.1806

19. Springintveld, J., Vaandrager, F., D'Argenio, P.: Testing timed automata. Theoret. Comput. Sci. 254(1–2), 225–257 (2001)

20. Timo, O.N., Petrenko, A., Ramesh, S.: Fault model-driven testing from FSM with symbolic inputs. Softw. Qual. J. 27(2), 501–527 (2019). https://doi.org/10.1007/s11219-019-9440-3

Afra: An Eclipse-Based Tool with Extensible Architecture for Modeling and Model Checking of Rebeca Family Models

Ehsan Khamespanah[1,2](✉), Marjan Sirjani[2,3], and Ramtin Khosravi[1]

[1] School of Electrical and Computer Engineering, University of Tehran, Tehran, Iran
[2] School of Computer Science, Reykjavik University, Reykjavik, Iceland
e.khamespanah@ut.ac.ir
[3] School of Innovation, Design, and Engineering,
Mälardalen University, Västerås, Sweden

Abstract. Afra is an *Eclipse*-based tool for the modeling and model checking of *Rebeca* family models. Together with the standard enriched editor, easy to trace counter-example viewer, modular temporal property definition, exporting a model and its transition system to some other formats facilities are features of Afra. Rebeca family provides actor-based modeling languages which are designed to bridge the gap between formal methods and software engineering. Faithfulness to the system being modeled, and the usability of Rebeca family languages help in ease of modeling and analysis of the model, together with the synthesis of the system based on the model. In this paper, architectural decisions and design strategies we made in the development of Afra are presented. This makes Afra an extensible and reusable application for the modeling and analysis of Rebeca family models. Here, we show how different compilers can be developed for the family of languages which are the same in general language constructs but have some minor differences. Then we show how the model checking engine for these different languages is designed. Despite the fact that Afra has a layered object-oriented design and is developed in Java technology, we use C++ codes for developing its model checking for the performance purposes. This decision made the design of the application even harder.

Keywords: Actors · Rebeca · Afra · Model Checking · Eclipse

1 Introduction

The actor model is a well-known model for the development of highly available and high-performance applications. It benefits from the universal primitives of concurrent computation [1], called actors, which are distributed, autonomous objects that interact by asynchronous message passing. Each actor provides a number of services, and other actors send messages to it to run the services.

© IFIP International Federation for Information Processing 2023
Published by Springer Nature Switzerland AG 2023
H. Hojjat and E. Ábrahám (Eds.): FSEN 2023, LNCS 14155, pp. 72–87, 2023.
https://doi.org/10.1007/978-3-031-42441-0_6

Messages are put in the mailbox of the receiver, the receiver takes a message from the mailbox and executes its corresponding service. Hewitt introduced the actor model as an agent-based language [2] and is later developed by Agha as a mathematical model of concurrent computation [1].

Rebeca is an operational interpretation of the actor model with formal semantics. Rebeca is designed to bridge the gap between formal methods and software engineering. The formal semantics of Rebeca is a solid basis for its formal verification [3]. Compositional and modular verification, abstraction, symmetry and partial-order reduction have been investigated for verifying Rebeca models [4]. The theory underlying these verification methods is already established and is embodied in verification tools [5, 6]. Different extensions have been provided for modeling and analyzing of different aspects of actor systems. Timed Rebeca is an extension on Rebeca with time features for modeling and verification of time-critical systems [7]. Probabilistic Rebeca is another extension of Rebeca which is developed to consider the probabilistic behavior of actor systems [8]. Probabilistic Timed Rebeca (PTRebeca) is an extension of Rebeca which benefits from modeling features of Timed Rebeca and Probabilistic Rebeca, combining the syntax of both languages [9]. More details about these extensions are provided in Sect. 2. RebecaSys is another extension of Rebeca which is developed to support hardware/software co-design (i.e. system-level design) [10]. In Broadcasting Rebeca [11] and Wireless Rebeca [12] the Core Rebeca is extended from a different dimension to provide broadcasting and multi-casting among actors which is crucial for modeling and verification of network protocols.

Afra is a toolset which is developed for the purpose of providing modeling and analysis facilities for the Rebeca family languages. As the same as many other Eclipse plugins, Afra contains a set of Eclipse views and editors together with a set of Java components for implementing models and analyzing them. In addition to the syntax-highlighting editor, Afra provides easy to use counterexample browser which made debugging of models easier. The focus of these futures is in improving the usability of the developed toolset. Beside the essence of providing usability, there is a need for considering extensibility and maintainability of the model checking toolset. This need becomes more important for the case of Afra as it has to support a set of modeling languages which require different compilers and model checking algorithms.

In this paper, we show how Afra is designed to make it extensible and maintainable for different languages of the Rebeca family. Starting from the architectural view (Sect. 3) we make clear how the main functional requirements of Afra are placed in a set of Java components. Then, we describe the techniques which are used for the implementation of compilers of the Rebeca family languages from syntax and semantics points of view (Sect. 4). To this end, we discussed techniques which can be used to develop the hierarchy of compilers using ANTLR [13] toolset. Then, we introduce the class diagram of the semantics-checker which we developed for performing semantical analysis of the Rebeca family models and make it clear that how it can be extended to consider the future extension on Rebeca.

To increase the performance of model checking, Afra transforms models into a set of C++ source codes. Running these codes results in generating the transition system of the model and performs property checking. This approach is very similar to the development approach of SPIN [14]. Decisions which are made in the design of C++ classes and how third-party template generators help in code reuse are issues which we address in Sects. 5 and 5.2.

2   Rebeca Family Modeling Languages

A Rebeca model is similar to the actor model as reactive objects without shared variables are its only computation units. Objects in Rebeca are reactive, self-contained, and each of them is called a *rebec* (reactive object). Note that in this paper we use rebec and actor interchangeably. Each actor has an unbounded buffer, called message *queue*, for its arriving messages. Communication among actors takes place by asynchronous message passing with no blocking send and no explicit receive. Computation is event-driven, meaning that each actor takes a message that can be considered as an event from the top of its message queue and executes the corresponding message server (also called a method). In Rebeca, the execution of a message server is atomic, i.e. there is no way to preempt the execution of a message server of an actor and start executing another message server of that actor. Note that we call the basic extension of Rebeca as Core Rebeca to avoid misunderstanding.

2.1   Core Rebeca

A Core Rebeca model consists of a set of reactive classes definitions and the main block. In the main block, actors which are instances of the reactive classes are declared. The body of the reactive class includes the declaration of its known actors, state variables, and message servers. Message servers consist of the declaration of local variables and the body of the message server. The statements in the body can be assignments, conditional statements, enumerated loops, non-deterministic assignment, and method calls. Method calls are sending asynchronous messages to other actors (or to itself). A reactive class has an argument of type integer denoting the maximum size of its message queue. Although message queues are unbounded in the semantics of Rebeca, to ensure that the state space is finite, we need a user-specified upper bound for the queue size. The operational semantics of Rebeca has been introduced in [15] in more detail. In comparison with the standard actor model, dynamic creation and dynamic topology are not supported by Core Rebeca. Also, actors in Core Rebeca are single-threaded.

We illustrate the Core Rebeca language with an example. Listing 1.1 shows the Core Rebeca model of the ticket service system. The model consists of three reactive classes: TicketService, Agent, and Customer. In this model, Customer sends the requestTicket message to Agent (line 32) and Agent forwards the message to TicketService (line 18). TicketService replies to Agent by sending a `ticketIssued` message (line 8) and `Agent` responds to `Customer` by sending the issued ticket (21). Upon receiving a ticket, `Customer` tries for another ticket (line 37).

Listing 1.1. The Rebeca model of Ticket Service System

```
1  reactiveclass TicketService (3) {
2      knownrebecs {Agent a;}
3      statevars {int nextId;}
4      TicketService() {
5          nextId = 0;
6      }
7      msgsrv requestTicket() {
8          a.ticketIssued(nextId);
9          nextId = nextId + 1;
10     }
11 }
12 reactiveclass Agent (3) {
13     knownrebecs {
14         TicketService ts;
15         Customer c;
16     }
17     msgsrv requestTicket() {
18         ts.requestTicket();
19     }
20     msgsrv ticketIssued(byte id) {
21         c.ticketIssued(id);
22     }
23 }
24 reactiveclass Customer (2) {
25     knownrebecs {Agent a;}
26     statevars {boolean sent;}
27     Customer() {
28         self.try();
29         sent = false;
30     }
31     msgsrv try() {
32         a.requestTicket();
33         sent = true;
34     }
35     msgsrv ticketIssued(byte id) {
36         sent = false;
37         self.try();
38     }
39 }
40 main {
41     Agent a(ts, c):();
42     TicketService ts(a):(3);
43     Customer c(a):();
44 }
```

For a given Core Rebeca model, a modeler can specify the correctness properties of the model as a set of assertions or LTL formula. As shown in Listing 1.2, a property specification has three parts. In the first part the atomic propositions of the properties are defined. An atomic proposition is defined by its name and a boolean expression as its value. `cIsSent` and `idCounter` are two atomic propositions in Listing 1.2.

Listing 1.2. Correctness property specification of Ticket Service System

```
1  property {
2      define {
3          cIsSent = c.sent;
4          idCounter = ts.nextId;
5      }
6      Assertion {
7          MaxNumberOfTickets: idCounter < 10;
8      }
9      LTL {
10         NoStarvation: G(cIsSent -> F(!cIsSent));
11     }
12 }
```

The assertions of models are defined in the second part of property specifications. An assertion is defined by its name and a boolean expression as its value, which its terms are the labels of atomic propositions. `MaxNumberOfTickets` is the only assertion of this model which makes sure that the number of issued tickets in this model is less than 10. Note that this model does not satisfy `MaxNumberOfTickets` as there is no limitation on the number of issued tickets. The last part of the property specification contains LTL formula. An LTL formula is defined by its name and combination of logical expressions and LTL modalities as its value, which its terms are the labels of atomic propositions. $G(\phi)$, $f(\phi)$, and $U(\phi, \psi)$ are used to specify $\Box\,\phi$ (*always*), $\Diamond\,\phi$ (*eventually*), and $\phi\,\mathbf{U}\,\psi$ (*until*) respectively. `NoStarvation` is the only LTL property of this model which makes sure that each request for ticket will be served in the future.

2.2 Timed Rebeca

Timed Rebeca is an extension on Rebeca with time features for modeling and verification of time-critical systems [7]. To this end, three primitives are added to Rebeca to address *computation time*, *message delivery time*, *message expiration*, and *period of occurrence of events*. In a Timed Rebeca model, each actor has its own local clock and the local clocks evolve uniformly. Methods are still executed atomically, however passing time while executing a method can be modeled. In addition, instead of a queue for messages, there is a bag of messages for each actor.

In comparison to the syntax of Rebeca, three timing primitives are defined in Timed Rebeca which are `delay`, `deadline` and `after`. The `delay` statement models the passing of time for an actor during the execution of a message server. The keywords `after` and `deadline` can only be used in conjunction with a method call. The value of the argument of *after* shows how long it takes for the message to be delivered to its receiver. The `deadline` shows the timeout for the message, i.e., how long it will stay valid. We illustrate the application of these keywords using the Timed Rebeca version of the ticket service system in Listing 1.3. Note that this source code only contains the parts of the model which are different in the Rebeca and Timed Rebeca models. As shown in line 3 of the model, issuing a ticket takes two or three time units (modeled by a non-deterministic expression). At line 10 the actor instantiated from `Agent` sends a message `requestTicket` to actor `ts` instantiated from `TicketService`, and gives a deadline of five to the receiver to take this message and start serving it. The periodic task of retrying for a new ticket is modeled in line 15 by the customer sending a `try` message to itself and letting the receiver to take it from its bag only after 30 units of time (by stating `after(30)`).

Listing 1.3. The Timed Rebeca model of ticket service system

```
1  reactiveclass TicketService {
2      msgsrv requestTicket() {
3          delay(?(2, 3));
4          a.ticketIssued(nextId);
5          nextId = nextId + 1;
6      }
7  }
8  reactiveclass Agent {
9      msgsrv requestTicket() {
10         ts.requestTicket()
               deadline(5);
11     }
```

```
12 }                              15        self.try() after(30);
13 reactiveclass Customer {      16      }
14    msgsrv ticketIssued(byte id) {   17 }
```

For a given Timed Rebeca model, a modeler can specify the correctness properties of the model as a set of assertions or TCTL formula. The structure of property specifications for Timed Rebeca models is the same as the property specification of Core Rebeca models except that there is TCTL part instead of LTL part. In TCTL specifications $AU(time <= c, \phi, \psi)$, $EU(time <= c, \phi, \psi)$, $AF(time <= c, \phi)$, $AG(time <= c, \phi)$ are used to specify $\forall \phi\, U^{\leq c}\, \psi$, $\exists \phi\, U^{\leq c}\, \psi$, $\forall \Diamond^{\leq c}\, \phi$, $\forall \Box^{\leq c}\, \phi$ respectively. The same formula can be used to express modalities with $\geq c$ time constraint.

2.3 Probabilistic and Probabilistic Timed Rebeca

Probabilistic Rebeca is an extension of Rebeca for modeling actor-based systems with probabilistic and nondeterministic behavior [8]. In order to provide a concise syntax for Probabilistic Rebeca, different possibilities of probabilistic aspects that could exist in an actor based system are investigated and two keywords together with one expression definition are added to Rebeca. The first keyword is **pAlt** which models probabilistic alternative behavior in the **switch-case** style. In a pAlt structure, each block of statements may be executed by its associated probabilities. The second keyword is **probloss** which can only be used in conjunction with a method call. The value of the argument of **probloss** shows the probability of losing this message in the communication among actors. They only new expression definition of Probabilistic Rebeca is the *probabilistic expression* which its definition is like nondeterministic expressions such that a real number is associated with each choice of it. We illustrate the application of these features using the Probabilistic Rebeca version of the ticket service system in Listing 1.4. As shown in line 3, there is a probability of 0.4 percent for the computation delay of 2 and 0.6 for 3. Finally, a customer may decide to not to ask for a new ticket with the probability of 0.5 as shown in line 10.

Listing 1.4. The Probabilistic Rebeca model of Ticket Service System

```
1 reactiveclass TicketService {      7 }
2    msgsrv requestTicket() {        8 reactiveclass Customer (2) {
3       delay(?(0.4:2, 0.6:3));      9    msgsrv try() {
4       a.ticketIssued(nextId);     10       pAlt{
5       nextId = nextId + 1;        11          0.5: a.requestTicket();
6    }                              12          0.5: self.try();
                                    13       }
                                    14    }
                                    15 }
```

Probabilistic Timed Rebeca (PTRebeca) is an extension of Rebeca which benefits from modeling features of Timed Rebeca and Probabilistic Rebeca, combining the syntax of both languages [9]. This aims at enhancing modeling abilities in order to cover performance evaluation of probabilistic real-time actors.

Although there is no new feature in the syntax of PTRebeca a new semantics is defined for it to support timing, probabilistic, and nondeterministic features [16]. PTRebeca is the first actor-based language which supports time, probability, and nondeterminism in modeling distributed systems with asynchronous message passing.

3   Afra Architecture

Afra is the modeling and analysis IDE of the Rebeca family models[1]. It is developed as an Eclipse plugin and released as a standalone Eclipse product. It contains a set of Eclipse views and editors together with three Java components for implementing models and analyzing them. As shown in Fig. 1, the Afra plugin contains compiler component for compiling its given models, RMC component for generating model checking codes for models, and model transformer component to transform the Rebeca family models to some other well-known models and programs.

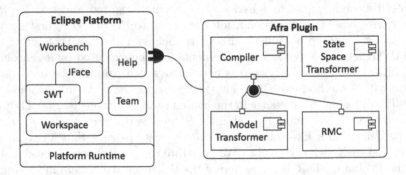

Fig. 1. Components and connectors view of Afra

Using Afra, the compiler component makes sure that a given model is syntactically and semantically correct. At the second step, the transition system of the given model has to be generated and it has to be analyzed against given correctness properties. To this aim, the given model is transformed to a set of C++ source. Running the generated C++ codes provides the model checking result by generating the transition system of the model. The summary of the user activities to this end is shown in the Activity Diagram of Fig. 2.

The first release of the Afra benefits from the model checking engine which was developed in 2006 for Core Rebeca models [17], called Modere. Modere has an object-oriented design and the next model checking engines for the other members of the Rebeca family are developed by extending Modere classes. The overview of the design of model checking classes of Afra is presented in Fig. 3. We

---

[1] Afra can be downloaded from http://rebeca-lang.org/alltools/Afra.

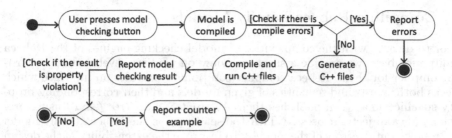

Fig. 2. The main activities of a user with Afra for the model checking of a model

will provide more details about the classes of this diagram in Sects. 5 and 5.2. As illustrated in Fig. 3, `AbstractModelChecker` and `AbstractActor` are two core classes of this design. For the case of Core Rebeca, there is `AbstractCore RebecaAnalyzer` class which deals with actors of models, produces states based on the behavior of actors, and stores them in the state spaces storage (i.e. `CoreRebecaDFSHashmap` in the figure). As the model checker of Core Rebeca has to consider actor classes and model checking algorithm, it is inherited from both of `AbstractModelChecker` and `AbstractCoreRebecaAnalyzer`. The figure illustrates that `AbstractCoreRebecaAnalyzer` is also used for simulating Core Rebeca models[2]. The detailed description of this part of the diagram is provided in Sect. 5. The same condition is valid for the case of Timed Rebeca models. For the case of PTRebeca, inheritance takes place from the classes of Timed Rebeca classes as both the model checking and actors behaviors are developed based on the timed model checker. The detailed description of this part is provided in Sect. 5.2. The extensible hierarchy of Fig. 3 illustrates it can be easily extended to combine/modify actor behaviors and model checking algorithms to support future members of the Rebeca family.

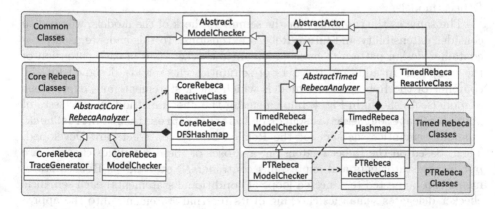

Fig. 3. The UML class diagram of model checkers in Afra

---

[2] This feature is excluded from the current release of Afra.

4   Compiling Rebeca Family Models

Prior to dealing with the complexities of model checking engines of the Rebeca family members, we provide a short overview on how we developed an extensible compiler for them. Rebeca compiler component provides an interface which checks both syntax and semantics of given models and their corresponding property specifications, then publishes their *Abstract Syntax Tree (AST)* using predefined Java objects. It uses ANTLR toolset to parse the Rebeca family model and report syntax errors of the models. To improve the extensibility of the design compiler, we developed two grammar specifications for Core Rebeca: 1) expressions of Rebeca which also includes method calls and sending messages and 2) Rebeca constructs. Then, using the inheritance mechanism of ANTLR for parser specifications, we developed parser specifications of the other Rebeca family extensions. For example, there is a rule for specifying primary terms of expressions which can be an identifier or message sending:

```
primary : IDENTIFIER (LPAREN expressionList RPAREN)?
```

To develop the grammar specification of Timed Rebeca, we explicitly specified that the new grammar is an extension of the Core Rebeca grammar. Then, we overwrite the **primary** rule with the following, as a sending message may be followed by **after** or **deadline** specifiers in Timed Rebeca:

```
primary : IDENTIFIER (LPAREN expressionList RPAREN)? (AFTER LPAREN
    expression RPAREN)? (DEADLINE LPAREN expression RPAREN)?)?
```

For the case of Probabilistic Rebeca, both of the parser specifications are extended to add probabilistic expressions in the expression parser and **pAlt** in the language constructs. The compiler of Probabilistic Timed Rebeca is developed by inheriting from the parsers of both Timed Rebeca and Probabilistic Rebeca and no modification in parsing rules is needed. Compilers of property specifications are developed using the same approach for Core Rebeca and Timed Rebeca models.

The same as the compilers, for the semantic check of the models, we need to consider extensibility and future Rebeca extensions. To this end, we used picocontainer design pattern to manage semantic checker rules of each extension of the language. In addition, two sets of semantics checker are designed for the compiler of the Rebeca family models which check statements and expressions of models, As shown in Fig. 4. Implementing the **check** method in subclasses of **AbstractStatementSemanticsCheck** or **AbstractExpressionSemanticsCheck**, different semantics checkers for the Rebeca family constructs are Developed. Then, based on the Rebeca extension, a subset of these semantics checkers are put in the statements and expressions containers. Note that as Rebeca statements can be nested (e.g. nested loops of conditional statements) each semantic checker delegates semantics checking of its internal statements into the appropriate semantics checker object, which is accessible from the containers. In addition, for considering dynamic scoping of Rebeca variables **ScopeHandler** class in defined which keeps track of activation records, shown in Fig. 4.

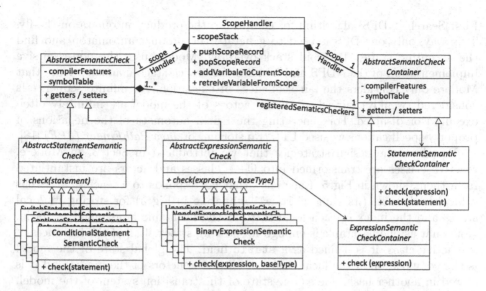

Fig. 4. The UML class diagram of the semantics checker of the Rebeca family

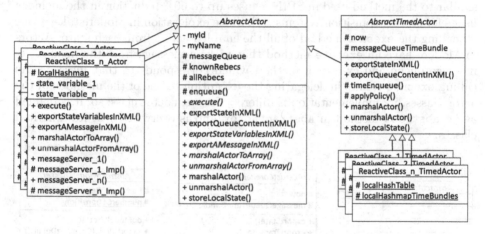

Fig. 5. The UML class diagram of actors classes in Modere

5   Model Checking of Rebeca Family Models

5.1   Model Checking of Core Rebeca

As mentioned before, the correctness properties of Core Rebeca models can be specified by assertions and LTL formulas. In Modere, the model and the negation of the correctness property are generated as two Büchi automata. The model satisfies the correctness property if and only if the synchronous product of these two automata does not accept any word. Otherwise, the accepted word has to be reported as the counterexample of the model. Modere uses Nested Depth

First Search (NDFS) algorithm for computing the product automata on-the-fly. This way, only one DFS is used to generate the product automaton and find the accepting states. To avoid stack overflow, Modere uses the non-recursive implementation of the NDFS and handles the search stack manually. Note that Modere only considers the fair sequences of execution. An infinite sequence is considered (weakly) fair when all the actors of the model are infinitely often executed or disabled. For generating the Büchi automata of the negations of property specifications we used LTL transformer of *Java PathFinder (JPF)* [18].

Based on the design strategies that we introduced in Sect. 3, in Modere, reactive classes are transformed into C++ classes and actors are instantiated from them, shown in Fig. 5. Each class that corresponds to a reactive class has a local hash table (its name if `localHashtable` in Fig. 5) for storing its local states and the index of each local state in the hashtable is assumed as its id. Note that as one hashtable is enough for storing states of all of the instances of a reactive class, it is defined as a `static` field. The global state of the model is the composition of the local states of all of the actors of the model and it is stored in another hashtable as one state of the transition system of the model. Dividing state of the system into inter-process and intra-process hashtables is similar to the method used in SPIN, causes up to 60% reduction in the memory usage for storing transition systems [17]. State exploration in Modere takes place by calling the `execute` method of all the enabled actors from each state. Actors in Modere have an `execute` method that picks a message from the head of its message queue and execute a method which corresponds to that message. As calling `execute` results in delegating the execution to one of the methods of the actor classes, its implementation is different for each actor class; so, it is defined as an `abstract` method in `AbstractActor` and is overwritten in its inherited classes.

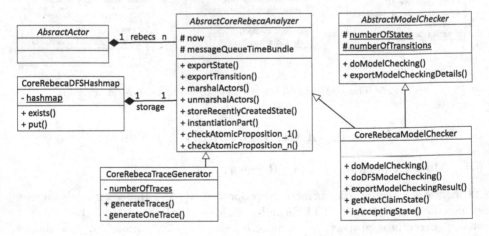

Fig. 6. The UML class diagram of Modere

As shown in Figs. 5, `AbstractActor` provides methods `marshalActor` and `unmarshalActor` for putting/restoring the state of an actor into/from its local hashtable, including the values of state variables and the queue content. But, as different actors have a different set of state variables, the implementation of these two methods are actor dependent. To break this dependency, we defined two abstract helper methods in `AbstractActor`, i.e. `marshalActorToArray` and `unmarshalActorFromArray`, which put/restore the state of an actor into/from a byte array. The actor classes implement these two methods based on their state variables and queues configuration. So, `marshalActor` and `unmarshalActor` methods consider dealing with the local hashtable and use the helper methods to deal with the actor state variables and queues contents. As we will discuss later, this strategy made the implementation of actor classes which correspond to Timed and Probabilistic Rebeca easier. The same strategy is followed in implementing methods which correspond to exporting the state of actors in XML. As shown in Fig. 5, `exportStateInXML` and `exportQueueContentInXML` methods are implemented in `AbstractActor`; but, `exportStateVariablesInXML` and `exportAMessageInXML` are defined as abstract methods and are implemented in the actor classes to consider state variables and message structure of actors.

To implement the provided services of reactive classes, two types of methods are defined in `ReactiveClass_x_Actor` classes, as shown in Fig. 5 (note that x in the name of classes are replaced with the name of reactive classes which are defined in the given model). The public methods are called by the other actors and put a message in the queue of actors. The protected methods (which have `_Imp` suffix) are called by the `execute` method of the actors to perform the expected behavior of executing message server.

Using these classes, the model checker of Core Rebeca can be implemented using the classes of Fig. 6. The common behavior of model checking and simulation are put in `AbsractCoreRebecaAnalyzer`. This class is able to handle instantiation of actors (as described in the `main` part), marshal or unmarshal the global state of the system, export the global state of the system in XML, and check atomic propositions in a global state. `CoreRebecaModelChecker` uses these methods to implement the model checking algorithm. The NDFS algorithm of Modere is implemented in `doDFSModelChecking` and two methods `getNextClaimState` and `isAcceptingState` are used to traverse the property Büchi automata and check its accepting states respectively.

As mentioned in [17], Modere has been used for the model checking of models from networking, distributed systems, an some other models from different domains and handles state spaces of up to 10 million states. Also, two reduction techniques have been implemented for it which made it applicable for the analysis of more complicated models.

5.2   Model Checking of Timed and PTRebeca Models

As depicted in Fig. 3, the structure of the Timed Rebeca model checking classes is the same that of in Core Rebeca. Two major semantics have been proposed considered for Timed Rebeca: coarse-grained semantics which is a natural event-based semantics for actors, and fine-grained semantics which is a standard state-based semantics [19]. Using the coarse-grained semantics, in each state, the local time of each actor can be different from the others, i.e., the execution of actors is not synchronized over their local times. The state space which is generated using this semantics is called Floating Time Transition System (FTTS). In contrast, using the fine-grained semantics, the local time of all actors is the same. Note that when we talk about synchronized local clocks we are explaining the concept of time in the model, while fine-grained semantics respects this synchrony, in the coarse-grained we relax the time synchronization constraint. Comparing to the fine-grained semantics, using FTTS can be considered as a reduced state transition system where the event-based properties are preserved.

In addition to differences in the semantics, the mechanism of detecting repeated states in Core Rebeca and Timed Rebeca are different. In Core Rebeca, two states are the same if the valuation of state variables of all actors are the same, together with the content of their message queues. In Timed Rebeca this condition is needed but progress in time does not allow states to be the same as it goes to infinity. It because of the fact that there is no explicit time reset operator in Timed Rebeca. However, reactive systems which generally show periodic or recurrent behaviors are modeled using Timed Rebeca. In other words, they perform periodic behaviors over infinite time. Based on this fact, in [20] we proposed a new notion for equivalence relation between two states to make the transition systems finite, called *shift equivalence relation*. Intuitively, in shift equivalence relation two states are equivalent if and only if they are the same except for the parts related to the time and shifting the times of those parts in one state makes it the same as the other one. To make detecting the shift equivalence relation possible, we divided the content of states into two parts in Timed Rebeca. The first part contains values of state variables and untimed part of the message bag. This part is stored in the local hashtable of actors the same as what we described for Core Rebeca actors. A list of time-bundles is associated with the states of the local hashtable of actors which stores the second part, i.e. the local time of the actor and timed specifier of messages of its message bag. This way, a newly generated state is repeated if it corresponds to an existing item in the local hashtable and shifting the values of its time-bundle make it equal to one of the existing time-bundles associated to that item. These changes require inheriting `AbstractTimedActor` from `AbstractActor` to deco-rate methods which are responsible for marshaling, unmarshaling, and storing the state of timed actors. In addition, methods which export the state of the timed actors have to be overwritten to put timing specification of actors and its received messages in exported data. As mentioned in [16], behaviors of actors and generating the state space of PTRebeca is very similar to that of in Timed Rebeca. So, `PTRebecaReactiveClass` and `PTRebecaModelChecker` are directly inherited from their corresponding classes in Timed Rebeca.

Combining the mentioned techniques, Timed Rebeca and PTRebeca is used in modeling, model checking, and performance evaluation of NoC designs, WSAN applications, network protocols, and transportation planning, which results in state spaces of up to 10 million states.

6 Conclusion and Future Work

In this paper, we addressed the problem of designing an extensible toolset for modeling and model checking of a family of languages. We showed that how Rebeca family models are defined and how an extensible compiler can be developed for the existing and future extensions of it, in Afra. Using the proposed approach, developing syntax and semantics checkers of the future extension of Rebeca only requires rewriting the compiler specification rules of the modified parts and their semantics checker observers. At the second step, we proposed an extensible design for developing the model checkers of a subset of Rebeca family extensions. Separating actors behavior from the state space generation mechanism, we illustrated that how a new model checker can be developed for a new extension of Rebeca.

We have used the proposed approaches for developing model checkers for Core Rebeca, Timed Rebeca, and Probabilistic Timed Rebeca and integrate them in Afra as an *Eclipse*-based standalone toolset. Afra provides an enriched editor, easy to trace counter-example viewer, and exports models and their transition systems to some other formats. As a future work, we planned to integrate compilers and model checkers of more members of Rebeca family in Afra to benefit from the mentioned facilities. We also want to enrich transformation from models and state spaces to other formalism to allow modelers to use them for analyzing their actor models.

Acknowledgments. The work on this paper has been supported in part by the project "Self-Adaptive Actors: SEADA" (nr. 163205-051) of the Icelandic Research Fund.

A   Graphical User Interface of Afra

An overview of Afra user interface is depicted in Fig. 7. Afra user interface consists five main sections which are, projects browser, model and property editor, model-checking result view, and counter example and its details views. The demo of how to work with the toolset is available from the address http://rebeca-lang. org/assets/tools/Afra/Afra-3.0-Demo.mov.

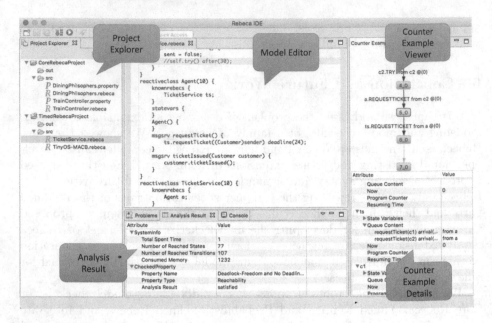

Fig. 7. Afra graphical user interface

References

1. Agha, G.A.: ACTORS - A Model of Concurrent Computation in Distributed Systems. Artificial Intelligence, MIT Press, Cambridge (1990)
2. Hewitt, C.: Description and Theoretical Analysis (Using Schemata) of PLANNER: A Language for Proving Theorems and Manipulating Models in a Robot. MIT Artificial Intelligence Technical report 258, Department of Computer Science, MIT, April 1972
3. Sirjani, M., Jaghoori, M.M.: Ten years of analyzing actors: Rebeca experience. In: Formal Modeling: Actors, Open Systems, Biological Systems, pp. 20–56 (2011)
4. Jaghoori, M.M., Sirjani, M., Mousavi, M.R., Khamespanah, E., Movaghar, A.: Symmetry and partial order reduction techniques in model checking Rebeca. Acta Inf. **47**(1), 33–66 (2010)
5. Sabouri, H., Sirjani, M.: Slicing-based reductions for Rebeca. Electr. Notes Theor. Comput. Sci. **260**, 209–224 (2010)
6. Sirjani, M., de Boer, F.S., Movaghar-Rahimabadi, A.: Modular verification of a component-based actor language. J. UCS **11**(10), 1695–1717 (2005)
7. Reynisson, A.H., et al.: Modelling and simulation of asynchronous real-time systems using timed Rebeca. Sci. Comput. Program. **89**, 41–68 (2014)
8. Varshosaz, M., Khosravi, R.: Modeling and verification of probabilistic actor systems using pRebeca. In: Aoki, T., Taguchi, K. (eds.) ICFEM 2012. LNCS, vol. 7635, pp. 135–150. Springer, Heidelberg (2012). https://doi.org/10.1007/978-3-642-34281-3_12
9. Jafari, A., Khamespanah, E., Sirjani, M., Hermanns, H.: Performance analysis of distributed and asynchronous systems using probabilistic timed actors. In: ECE-ASST 70 (2014)

10. Razavi, N., Behjati, R., Sabouri, H., Khamespanah, E., Shali, A., Sirjani, M.: Sysfier: Actor-based formal verification of systemc. ACM Trans. Embedded Comput. Syst. **10**(2), 19:1–19:35 (2010)
11. Yousefi, B., Ghassemi, F., Khosravi, R.: Modeling and efficient verification of broadcasting actors. In: Dastani, M., Sirjani, M. (eds.) FSEN 2015. LNCS, vol. 9392, pp. 69–83. Springer, Cham (2015). https://doi.org/10.1007/978-3-319-24644-4_5
12. Yousefi, B., Ghassemi, F., Khosravi, R.: Modeling and efficient verification of wireless ad hoc networks. CoRR abs/1604.07179 (2016)
13. Parr, T.J., Quong, R.W.: ANTLR: a predicated-LL(k) parser generator. Softw. Pract. Exp. **25**(7), 789–810 (1995)
14. Holzmann, G.J.: The model checker SPIN. IEEE Trans. Softw. Eng. **23**(5), 279–295 (1997)
15. Sirjani, M., Movaghar, A., Shali, A., de Boer, F.S.: Modeling and verification of reactive systems using Rebeca. Fundam. Inform. **63**(4), 385–410 (2004)
16. Jafari, A., Khamespanah, E., Sirjani, M., Hermanns, H., Cimini, M.: PTRebeca: modeling and analysis of distributed and asynchronous systems. Sci. Comput. Program. **128**, 22–50 (2016)
17. Jaghoori, M.M., Movaghar, A., Sirjani, M.: Modere: the model-checking engine of Rebeca. In: Haddad, H. (ed.) Proceedings of the 2006 ACM Symposium on Applied Computing (SAC), Dijon, France, April 23–27, 2006, pp. 1810–1815. ACM (2006)
18. Visser, W., Havelund, K., Brat, G.P., Park, S., Lerda, F.: Model checking programs. Autom. Softw. Eng. **10**(2), 203–232 (2003)
19. Khamespanah, E., Sirjani, M., Viswanathan, M., Khosravi, R.: Floating time transition system: more efficient analysis of timed actors. In: Braga, C., Ölveczky, P.C. (eds.) FACS 2015. LNCS, vol. 9539, pp. 237–255. Springer, Cham (2016). https://doi.org/10.1007/978-3-319-28934-2_13
20. Khamespanah, E., Sirjani, M., Sabahi-Kaviani, Z., Khosravi, R., Izadi, M.: Timed Rebeca schedulability and deadlock freedom analysis using bounded floating time transition system. Sci. Comput. Program. **98**, 184–204 (2015)

Interaction-Based Offline Runtime Verification of Distributed Systems

Erwan Mahe[1]([⊠])[iD], Boutheina Bannour[1][iD], Christophe Gaston[1][iD], Arnault Lapitre[1][iD], and Pascale Le Gall[2][iD]

[1] Université Paris -Saclay, CEA, List, 91120 Palaiseau, France
{erwan.mahe,Boutheina.Bannour,Christophe.Gaston,arnault.lapitre}@cea.fr
[2] Université Paris-Saclay, CentraleSupélec, 91192 Gif-sur-Yvette, France
pascale.legall@centralesupelec.fr

Abstract. Interactions are formal models describing asynchronous communications within a distributed system. They can be drawn in the fashion of sequence diagrams and associated with an operational semantics in the style of process algebras. In this paper, we propose an algorithm for offline runtime verification against interactions. Our algorithm deals with observability issues e.g. that some subsystems may not be observed or that some events may not be observed when the end of monitoring on different subsystems cannot be synchronized. We prove the algorithm's correctness and assess the performance of an implementation.

Keywords: distributed systems · offline runtime verification · interaction · multitrace semantics · partial observability

1 Introduction

Context. Distributed Systems (DS) have been identified in the recent survey [26] as one of the most challenging application domains for Runtime Verification (RV). An important bottleneck is that the formal references against which system executions are analyzed are specified using formalisms or logics usually equipped with trace semantics. Indeed, because DS are composed of subsystems deployed on different computers and communicating via message passing, their executions are more naturally represented as collections of traces observed at the level of the different subsystems' interfaces rather than as single global traces [7,24]. Those collections can be gathered using a distributed observation architecture involving several local observation devices, each one dedicated to a subsystem, and deployed on the same computer as the subsystem it is dedicated to. An approach to confront such collections of local execution traces to formal references with a trace semantics might consist in identifying the global traces that result from all possible temporal orderings of the events occurring in the local traces. If none of those global traces conforms to the formal reference, then we might conclude that an error is observed [24]. However, the absence of a global clock implies that, in all generality, it is not possible to synchronize the endings of the different local observation processes. Therefore, in the process of

© IFIP International Federation for Information Processing 2023
Published by Springer Nature Switzerland AG 2023
H. Hojjat and E. Ábrahám (Eds.): FSEN 2023, LNCS 14155, pp. 88–103, 2023.
https://doi.org/10.1007/978-3-031-42441-0_7

reconstructing global traces, some events might be missing in local traces. Such problems occur whenever, for technical or legal reasons, it is not possible to observe some subsystems or else the observation has been interrupted too early.

Contributions. In this paper, we propose a Runtime Verification approach dedicated to DS with an emphasis on overcoming issues of *partial observability*, whether due to the absence of a global clock, or to the impossibility of observing some subsystem executions. Our approach belongs to the family of offline RV techniques in which traces are logged prior to their analysis. As for formal references, we inherit the framework of *interaction* models from earlier works [18,20]. Interactions describe actor-oriented scenarios and can be represented graphically in the fashion of UML Sequence Diagrams (UML-SD) [25] or Message Sequence Charts (MSC) [14]. We designed in [18] an algorithm to decide whether or not a collection of local traces is accepted by an interaction. However, this algorithm cannot cope with partial observability. The core contribution of this paper is then to define an algorithm to tackle those limitations, i.e. to deal with collections of local traces with missing or incomplete ones. Theorem 1 will enable us to relate collections of local traces reflecting partially observed executions to those of the original reference interaction. The key operator in our algorithm is a removal operator (Definition 5) discarding parts of the interaction relative to unobserved subsystems. We prove the correctness of our algorithm and argue how the use of the removal operations allows us to solve partial observability (Theorem 2). All proofs are available in [19]. Finally, we present some experiments using an implementation of our algorithm, given as an extension of the HIBOU tool [17].

Related Work. Solutions to the oracle problem (offline RV) for DS using local logs often rely on a preliminary reordering of events using either timestamps [24] or some happened-before relations (of Lamport [15]) [7,16,23]. In [9,11,12] such solutions rely on a set of discrete and local behavioral models. DS behaviors are modeled by Input/Output Transition Systems (IOTS) [11,12] or by Communicating Sequential Processes (CSP) [9] and local observations are intertwined to associate them with global traces that can be analyzed w.r.t. models. Those approaches however require to synchronize local observations, based on the states in which each of the logging processes terminates (e.g., based on quiescence states in [11], termination/deadlocks in [9] or pre-specified synchronization points in [12]). The works [8,10,13,24] focus on verifying distributed executions against models of interaction (while [10,13] concern MSC, [24] considers choreographic languages, [8] session types, and [4] trace expressions). [10,24] propose offline RV that relies on synchronization hypotheses and on reconstructing a global trace by ordering events occurring at the distributed interfaces (by exploiting the observational power of testers [10] or timestamp information assuming clock synchronization [24]). Our RV approach for multitraces does not require synchronization prerequisites on DS logging. Thus, unlike previous works on offline RV, we can analyze DS executions without needing a synchronization hypothesis on the ending of local observations. For online RV, the work [13] depends on a global component (network sniffer) while the work [8] proposes local RV against projections of interactions satisfying conditions that enforce intended global behaviors. In contrast to these works, we process collections of local logs against interactions. The work [4] focuses on how distributed monitors can be adapted for partial observation. Yet, our notion of partial observation is distinct from that of [4] where messages are exchanged via channels which are associated to an observability likelihood. [4] proposes specification transformations by removing or making optional several identified unobservable events. We instead deal with partial observability from the perspective of analyzing truncated multitraces due to synchronization issues.

Paper Outline. Sect. 2 discusses the nature of DS, their modelling with interactions and the challenge of applying RV to DS. Section 3 defines multitraces, interactions and associated removal operations. Section 4 defines and proves the correctness of our RV algorithm. Section 5 reports experimental results.

2   Preliminaries

Notations. Given a set A, A^* is the set of words on A, with ε the empty word and the "." concatenation law. For any word $w \in A^*$, $|w|$ is the length of w and any word w' is a prefix of w if there exists a word w'', possibly empty, such that $w = w'.w''$. Let us note $\overline{w}$ the set of prefixes of a word $w \in A^*$ and $\overline{W}$ the set of prefixes of all words of a set $W \subseteq A^*$. Given a set A, $|A|$ designates its cardinal and $\mathcal{P}(A)$ is the set of all subsets of A.

Distributed Systems. From a black box perspective, the atomic concept to describe the executions of DS is that of communication *actions* occurring on a subsystem's interface. Here a subsystem refers to a software system deployed on a single machine. Anticipating the use of interactions as models in Sect. 3.2, a subsystem interface is called a *lifeline* and corresponds to an interaction point on which the subsystem can receive or send some messages. Lifelines are elements of a set $\mathcal{L}$ denoting the universe of lifelines. An action occurring on a lifeline is defined by its kind (emission or reception, identified resp. by the symbols ! and ?) and by the message which it carries. We introduce the universe $\mathcal{M}$ of messages. Executions observed on a lifeline l can be modelled as execution *traces* i.e. sequences of actions. For $l \in \mathcal{L}$, the set $\mathbb{A}_l$ of *actions over l* is $\{l\Delta m \mid \Delta \in \{!, ?\},\ m \in \mathcal{M}\}$ and the set $\mathbb{T}_l$ of *traces over l* is $\mathbb{A}_l^*$. For any $a \in \mathbb{A}_l$ of the form $l?m$ or $l!m$, $\theta(a)$ refers to l.

Figure 1 sketches out an example of DS composed of three remote subsystems, assimilated to their interface bro, pub and sub. This DS implements a simplified publish/subscribe scheme of communications (an alternative to client-server architecture). The publisher pub may publish messages on the broker bro which may then forward them to the subscriber sub if it is already subscribed. Figure 1c depicts an interaction defined between the three lifelines. Each lifeline is depicted by a vertical line labelled by its name at the top. By default, the top to bottom direction represents time passing. A communication action depicted above another one on the same lifeline occurs beforehand. Communication actions are represented by horizontal arrows labelled with the action's message. Whenever an arrow exits (resp. enters) a lifeline, there is a corresponding emission (resp. reception) action at that point on the line. For example,

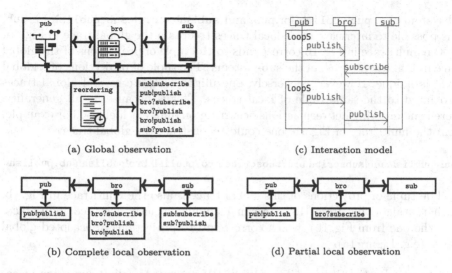

(a) Global observation

(c) Interaction model

(b) Complete local observation

(d) Partial local observation

Fig. 1. A simple publish/subscribe example: architectures & interaction model

the horizontal arrow from the lifeline sub to the lifeline bro indicates that the subsystem sub sends the message subscribe, denoted as sub!subscribe, which is then received by the lifeline bro, denoted as bro?subscribe. More complex behaviors can be introduced through operators (similar to combined fragments in UML-SD) drawn in the shape of boxes that frame sub-behaviors of interest. For instance, in Fig. 1c, $loop_S$ corresponds to a sequential loop. From the perspective of the bro lifeline, this implies that it can observe words of the form (bro?publish)*bro?subscribe(bro?publish.bro!publish)* i.e. it can receive an arbitrary number of instances of the publish message then one instance of subscribe and then it can receive and transmit an arbitrary number of publish. A representative global trace specified by the interaction in Fig. 1c is (see Fig. 1a):

sub!subscribe.pub!publish.bro?subscribe.bro?publish.bro!publish.sub?publish

This trace illustrates that the pub and sub lifelines can send their respective messages publish and subscribe in any order since there are no constraints on their ordering. In contrast, the reception of a message necessarily takes place after its emission. Since the reception of the message subscribe takes place before that of the publish message, this last message necessarily corresponds to the one occurring in the bottom loop. The global trace in Fig. 1a is a typical example of a trace *accepted* by the interaction in Fig. 1c. Indeed, this trace realizes one of the behaviors specified by the interaction which corresponds to: unfolding zero times the first loop; realizing the passing of the message subscribe between lifelines sub and bro; unfolding one time the second loop. None of the prefixes of this accepted trace is an accepted trace.

Accepted Multitraces. Following the terminology of [7,18], we call *multitrace* a collection of local traces, one per remote subsystem. Figure 1b depicts a multitrace involving 3 local traces: bro?subscribe.bro?publish.bro!publish for subsystem bro, pub!publish for pub, and sub!subscribe.sub?publish for sub. It is possible to interleave these local traces to obtain the global trace in Fig. 1a, i.e. the multitrace in Fig. 1b corresponds to the tuple of projections of the global trace in Fig. 1a onto each of the sub-systems. The tuple of projections of a global trace is unique. However, conversely, one might compute several global traces associated to the same tuple of local traces. This is because, in all generality, there is no ordering between actions occurring on different lifelines. For example, from the multitrace of Fig. 1b, one could reconstruct the global trace:

pub!publish.sub!subscribe.bro?subscribe.bro?publish.bro!publish.sub?publish

The tuple of projections of this global trace is also the multitrace in Fig. 1b. With the algorithm from [18] one can recognize exactly accepted multitraces (e.g. the one from Fig. 1b), which correspond to projections of accepted global traces (e.g. Figure 1a).

Logging and Partial Observability. Offline RV requires to collect execution traces prior to their analyses. In this process, it might be so that some subsystems cannot be equipped with observation devices. Moreover, due to the absence of synchronization between the local observations, the different logging processes might cease at uncorrelated moments. For example, let us consider the multitrace in Fig. 1d as an observed execution of the system considered in Fig. 1, where, by hypothesis, the subsystem sub is not observed. Remark that this multitrace corresponds to a partial observation of the multitrace in Fig. 1b. Indeed, each trace corresponding to a given subsystem in Fig. 1d is a prefix of the trace corresponding to the same sub-system in Fig. 1b. Thus, if sub executions were also observed and with longer observation times for each local observation processes, it may well be that one would have observed the multitrace in Fig. 1b rather than the one in Fig. 1d. when analyzing the multitrace in Fig. 1d against the interaction in Fig. 1c, we need the RV process not to conclude on the occurrence of an error. Hence, we want to be able to recognize multitraces in which each of the local traces can be extended to reconstruct a multitrace accepted by the interaction. Concretely, this means recognizing *multi-prefixes* of accepted multitraces. Let us remark that a projection of a prefix of an accepted global trace is a multi-prefix of an accepted multitrace. However the reverse is not true. For example, there exists no prefix of a global trace accepted by the interaction in Fig. 1c that projects on the multitrace in Fig. 1d. This is because the emission of subscribe by sub would precede its reception by bro in any accepted global trace. However, this emission is not observed in the multitrace in Fig. 1d. Therefore, dealing with partial observability does not boil down to a simple adaptation of the algorithm in [18]. In this paper, the aforementioned two types of partial observation (unobserved subsystems and early interruption of observation) will be approached in the same manner, noting in particular that an empty local trace can be seen both as missing and incomplete. The key mathematical operator used for that purpose consists in the removal of a lifeline from both interactions and multitraces. This operator allows us to define an algorithm for recognizing multi-prefixes of accepted multitraces while avoiding the complex search for a matching global execution, taking into account potential missing actions.

3 Multitraces, Interactions, and Removal Operations

3.1 Multitraces

As outlined in Sect. 2, a DS is a collection of communicating subsystems, each having a lifeline as local interface. A DS is characterized by a finite set of lifelines $L \subseteq \mathcal{L}$, called a *signature*. For $L \subseteq \mathcal{L}$, $\mathbb{A}(L)$ denotes the set $\cup_{l \in L} \mathbb{A}_l$. Executions of a DS are associated to *multitraces*, i.e. collections of traces, one per lifeline:

Definition 1. *Given $L \subseteq \mathcal{L}$, the set $\mathbb{M}(L)$ of* multitraces *over L is[1] $\prod_{l \in L} \mathbb{T}_l$. For $\mu = (t_l)_{l \in L}$ in $\mathbb{M}(L)$, we denote by $\mu_{|l}$ the trace component $t_l \in \mathbb{T}_l$ and by $\bar{\mu} = \{\mu' \mid \mu' \in \mathbb{M}(L), \forall l \in L, \mu'_{|l} \in \overline{\mu_{|l}}\}$ the set of its* multi-prefixes.

Multi-prefixes are extended to sets: $\overline{M}$ is the set of all multi-prefixes of all multitraces in $M \subseteq \mathbb{M}(L)$. We denote by ε_L the empty multitrace in $\mathbb{M}(L)$ defined by $\forall l \in L, \varepsilon_{L|l} = \varepsilon$. Additionally, for any $\mu \in \mathbb{M}(L)$, we use the notations $\mu[t]_l$ to designate the multitrace μ in which the component on l has been replaced by $t \in \mathbb{T}_l$ and $|\mu|$ to designate the cumulative length $|\mu| = \sum_{l \in L} |\mu_{|l}|$ of μ.

As discussed in Sect. 2, two communication actions occurring on different traces of a multitrace cannot be temporally ordered. Likewise, when several subsystems are observed concurrently, there is no way to synchronize the endings of their observations. So, any multitrace $\mu' \in \bar{\mu}$ can be understood as a partial observation of the execution characterized by μ. An edge case of this partial observation occurs when some of the subsystems are not observed at all, i.e. when some lifelines are missing. The rmv_h function of Definition 2 simply removes the trace concerning the lifeline h from a multitrace.

Definition 2. *For $L \subseteq \mathcal{L}$, the function $\mathsf{rmv}_h : \mathbb{M}(L) \to \mathbb{M}(L \setminus \{h\})$ is s.t.: $\forall \mu \in \mathbb{M}(L), \mathsf{rmv}_h(\mu) = (\mu_{|l})_{l \in L \setminus \{h\}}$*

The function rmv_h is canonically extended to sets. We introduce operations to add an action to the left (resp. right) of a multitrace. For the sake of simplicity, we use the same symbol ^ for these left- and right-concatenation operations:

$$\forall a \in \mathbb{A}(L), \forall \mu \in \mathbb{M}(L), \ a \hat{\ } \mu = \mu[a.\mu_{|\theta(a)}]_{\theta(a)} \quad \text{and} \quad \mu \hat{\ } a = \mu[\mu_{|\theta(a)}.a]_{\theta(a)}$$

Note that for any μ and a, we have $|\mu \hat{\ } a| = |a \hat{\ } \mu| = |\mu| + 1$. We extend ^ to sets of multitraces as follows: $a \hat{\ } T = \{a \hat{\ } \mu \mid \mu \in T\}$ and $T \hat{\ } a = \{\mu \hat{\ } a \mid \mu \in T\}$.

For two multitraces μ_1 and μ_2 in $\mathbb{M}(L)$:

- $\mu_1 \cup \mu_2$ denotes the alternative defined as follows: $\mu_1 \cup \mu_2 = \{\mu_1, \mu_2\}$;

---

[1] Given a family $(A_i)_{i \in I}$ of sets indexed by a finite set I, $\prod_{i \in I} A_i$ is the set of tuples $(a_1, \ldots, a_i, \ldots)$ with $\forall i \in I, a_i \in A_i$.

- $\mu_1; \mu_2$ denotes their sequencing defined as follows: if $\mu_2 = \varepsilon_L$ then $\mu_1; \mu_2 = \mu_1$ else, μ_2 can be written as $a\hat{\ }\mu_2'$ and $\mu_1; \mu_2 = (\mu_1\hat{\ }a); \mu_2'$;
- $\mu_1 \| \mu_2$ denotes their interleaving and is defined as the set of multitraces describing parallel compositions of μ_1 and μ_2:

$$\varepsilon_L \| \mu_2 = \{\mu_2\} \qquad\qquad \mu_1 \| \varepsilon_L = \{\mu_1\}$$
$$(a_1\hat{\ }\mu_1) \| (a_2\hat{\ }\mu_2) = (a_1\hat{\ }(\mu_1 \| (a_2\hat{\ }\mu_2))) \cup (a_2\hat{\ }((a_1\hat{\ }\mu_1) \| \mu_2)))$$

Let us remark that μ' is a prefix of a multitrace μ (i.e. $\mu' \in \overline{\mu}$) iff there exists μ'' verifying $\mu'; \mu'' = \mu$. Operations $\cup$, ; and $\|$ are extended to sets of multitraces as $\diamond : \mathcal{P}(\mathbb{M}(L))^2 \to \mathcal{P}(\mathbb{M}(L))$ for $\diamond \in \{\cup, ;, \|\}$. Operators ; and $\|$ being associative, this allows for the definition of repetition operators in the same manner as the Kleene star is defined over the classical concatenation. Given $\diamond \in \{;, \|\}$, the Kleene closure $\diamond^*$ is s.t. for any set of multitraces $T \subseteq \mathbb{M}(L)$ we have:

$$T^{\diamond *} = \bigcup_{j \in \mathbb{N}} T^{\diamond j} \text{ with } T^{\diamond 0} = \{\varepsilon_L\} \text{ and } T^{\diamond j} = T \diamond T^{\diamond(j-1)} \text{ for } j > 0$$

$\mathbb{M}(L)$ fitted with the set of algebraic operators $\mathcal{F} = \{\cup, ;, \|, ;^*, \|^*\}$ is an $\mathcal{F}$-algebra. The operation rmv_h preserves the algebraic structures between the $\mathcal{F}$-algebras of signatures L and $L \setminus \{h\}$.

Property 1 (Elimination preserves operators). For any μ_1 and μ_2 in $\mathbb{M}(L)$, for any $\diamond \in \{\cup, ;, \|\}$, $\mathsf{rmv}_h(\mu_1 \diamond \mu_2) = \mathsf{rmv}_h(\mu_1) \diamond \mathsf{rmv}_h(\mu_2)$.

Property 1 is obtained directly for the union and by induction for the other cases. Those results can be extended to sets of multitraces and imply that repetitions of those scheduling algebraic operators (with their Kleene closures) are also preserved by the elimination operator rmv_h.

3.2   Interactions

Interaction models, such as the one in Fig. 1c, can be formalized as terms of an inductive language. [18,20] consider an expressive language with two sequencing operators, weak and strict, for ordering actions globally. Here, as only collections of remote local traces are considered, weak and strict sequencing can no longer be distinguished. This explains why we only consider a unique sequencing operator *seq*. Following the syntax from Definition 3, the interaction term of Fig. 1c is:

$$\begin{aligned}
&(\{(\mathbf{pub!publish}, \epsilon, \epsilon)\}; \{(\epsilon, \mathbf{bro?publish}, \epsilon)\})^{;^*} \\
&; (\{(\epsilon, \epsilon, \mathbf{sub!subscribe})\}; \{(\epsilon, \mathbf{bro?subscribe}, \epsilon)\}) \\
&; \left(\begin{array}{c} (\{(\mathbf{pub!publish}, \epsilon, \epsilon)\}; \{(\epsilon, \mathbf{bro?publish}, \epsilon)\}) \\ ; (\{(\epsilon, \mathbf{bro!publish}, \epsilon)\}; \{(\epsilon, \epsilon, \mathbf{sub?publish})\}) \end{array} \right)^{;^*}
\end{aligned}$$

$$=$$

$$\left\{ \begin{array}{c} (\varepsilon, \mathbf{bro?subscribe}, \mathbf{sub!subscribe}) \\ \left(\mathbf{pub!publish}, \begin{array}{c} \mathbf{bro?publish} \\ \mathbf{bro?subscribe} \end{array}, \mathbf{sub!subscribe} \right) \\ \left(\mathbf{pub!publish}, \begin{array}{c} \mathbf{bro?subscribe} \\ \mathbf{bro?publish} \\ \mathbf{bro!publish} \end{array}, \begin{array}{c} \mathbf{sub!subscribe} \\ \mathbf{sub?publish} \end{array} \right) \\ \cdots \end{array} \right\}$$

Fig. 2. Semantics of example from Fig. 1c

$seq(\,loops(seq(\text{pub!publish}, \text{bro?publish})),\quad seq(seq(\text{sub!subscribe}, \text{bro?subscr}$
$\text{ibe}), loops(seq(seq(\text{pub!publish}, \text{bro?publish}), seq(\text{bro!publish}, \text{sub?publish}))))).$

Definition 3. *Given signature L, the set $\mathbb{I}(L)$ of interactions over L is the set of ground terms built over the following symbols provided with arities in $\mathbb{N}$:*
- *the empty interaction $\varnothing$ and any action a in $\mathbb{A}(L)$ of arity 0;*
- *the two loop operators $loops$ and $loop_P$ of arity 1;*
- *and the three operators seq, par and alt of arity 2.*

The semantics of interactions can be defined as a set of multitraces in a denotational style by associating each syntactic operator with an algebraic counterpart. This is sketched out in Fig. 2 in which the semantics of the interaction given in Fig. 1c is given. The denotational formulation, which is compositional, is defined in Definition 4 and illustrated in Fig. 1c.

Definition 4 (M-semantics). *Given $L \subseteq \mathcal{L}$, the multitrace semantics $\sigma_{|L}$: $\mathbb{I}(L) \to \mathcal{P}(\mathbb{M}(L))$ is defined inductively using the following interpretations:*
- *$\{\varepsilon_L\}$ for $\varnothing$ and $\{a\,\hat{}\,\varepsilon_L\}$ for a in $\mathbb{A}_L$;*
- *;* (resp. ||*) for loop operator $loops$ (resp. $loop_P$);*
- *; (resp. || and $\cup$) for binary operator seq (resp. par and alt).*

Interactions can also be associated with operational semantics in the style of Plotkin [21]. Its definition relies on two predicates denoted by $\downarrow$ and $\to$: for an interaction i, $i \downarrow$ states that $\varepsilon_L \in \sigma_{|L}(i)$ and $i \xrightarrow{a} i'$ states that all multitraces of the form $a\,\hat{}\,\mu'$ with $\mu' \in \sigma_{|L}(i')$ are multitraces of $\sigma_{|L}(i)$. This operational semantics is equivalent to the denotational formulation.

Property 2 (Operational semantics). There exist a predicate $\downarrow \subseteq \mathbb{I}(L)$ and a relation $\to \subseteq \mathbb{I}(L) \times \mathbb{A}(L) \times \mathbb{I}(L)$ such that, for any $i \in \mathbb{I}(L)$ and $\mu \in \mathbb{M}(L)$, the statement $\mu \in \sigma_{|L}(i)$ holds iff it can be proven using the following two rules:

$$\frac{i \downarrow}{\varepsilon_L \in \sigma_{|L}(i)} \qquad \frac{\mu \in \sigma_{|L}(i') \quad i \xrightarrow{a} i'}{a\,\hat{}\,\mu \in \sigma_{|L}(i)}$$

The proof is a transposition for multitrace semantics of the proof in [21] given for global traces. The algebraic characterisation of Definition 4 underpins results involving the use of the rmv_h function while the operational characterisation of Property 2 is required in the definition and proof of the RV algorithm. In this paper, we do not need the inductive

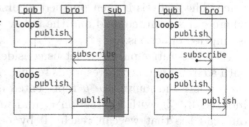

Fig. 3. Removing lifeline **sub**

definitions of $\downarrow$ and $\to$. It suffices to consider their existence (Property 2). In addition, we will use the notation $i \xrightarrow{a}$ (resp. $i \not\xrightarrow{a}$) when there exists (resp. does not exist) an interaction i' s.t. $i \xrightarrow{a} i'$.

The removal of lifelines for multitraces (cf. Definition 2) has a counterpart for interactions. On the left of Fig. 3 we draw our previous example while highlighting lifeline sub which we remove to obtain the interaction on the right. Whenever we remove a lifeline l, the resulting interaction does not contain any action occurring on l. Removal, as defined in[2] Definition 5 in a functional style, preserves the term structure, replacing actions on the removed lifeline with the empty interaction.

Definition 5. *For a signature $L \subseteq \mathcal{L}$ and a lifeline $h \in L$ we define rmv_h :*
$\mathbb{I}(L) \to \mathbb{I}(L \setminus \{h\})$ *s.t. for any interaction $i \in \mathbb{I}(L)$:*
$\mathsf{rmv}_h(i) = $ ***match*** *i* ***with***
$| \ \varnothing \qquad\quad \to \varnothing$
$| \ a \in \mathbb{A}(L) \to $ ***if*** *$\theta(a) = h$* ***then*** *$\varnothing$* ***else*** *a*
$| \ f(i_1, i_2) \ \to f(\mathsf{rmv}_h(i_1), \mathsf{rmv}_h(i_2))$ ***for*** *$f \in \{seq, alt, par\}$*
$| \ loop_k(i_1) \to loop_k(\mathsf{rmv}_h(i_1))$ ***for*** *$k \in \{S, P\}$*

Theorem 1 relates the removal operations on multitraces and interactions with one another. The semantics of an interaction i in which we remove lifeline h can be obtained by removing lifeline h from all the multitraces of the semantics of i. This result is obtained reasoning by induction on interaction terms.

Theorem 1. *For any signature L, any $i \in \mathbb{I}(L)$ and any $h \in L$:*

$$\sigma_{|L\setminus\{h\}}(\mathsf{rmv}_h(i)) = \mathsf{rmv}_h(\sigma_{|L}(i))$$

4   Offline RV for Multitraces

We aim to define a process to analyze a multitrace μ against a reference interaction i, both defined on a common signature L. To check whether or not a multitrace μ is accepted by i, i.e. $\mu \in \sigma_{|L}(i)$, the key principle given in [18] was to find a globally ordered behavior specified by i (via the $\to$ execution relation) that matches μ, i.e. an accepted global trace that can be projected into μ. To do so, it relies on a general rule $(i, a\hat{\ }\mu') \rightsquigarrow (i', \mu')$ s.t. $i \xrightarrow{a} i'$, i.e. it explores all the actions a directly executable from i and that match the head of a local trace. The analysis is then pursued recursively from (i', μ'), i.e. the multitrace where a has been removed and the follow-up interaction i', until the multitrace is emptied of actions.

For illustrative purposes, let us consider Fig. 4 where each square annotated with a circled number corresponds to such a tuple (i, μ), with interaction i drawn on the left and multitrace μ represented on the right. Starting from the tuple indexed by ③, with interaction i_3 and multitrace $\mu_3 = (\varepsilon, \texttt{bro?subscribe})$, one can see that we can reach ④ by both consuming $\texttt{bro?subscribe}$ from μ_3 and executing it in i_3, leading to the tuple (i_4, μ_4) in ④. This transition $(i_3, \texttt{bro?subscribe}\hat{\ }(\varepsilon, \varepsilon)) \rightsquigarrow (i_4, (\varepsilon, \varepsilon))$ is based on having $i_3 \xrightarrow{\texttt{bro?subscribe}} i_4$. Thus, Fig. 4 sketches the construction of a graph whose nodes are pairs of interactions and multitraces and whose arcs are built using the $\rightsquigarrow$ relation.

---

[2] We overload the notation rmv_h which applies to both multitraces and interactions.

While in [18], we were interested in solving the membership problem "$\mu \in \sigma_{|L}(i)$", we are now interested in defining an offline RV algorithm. In line with the discussion of Sect. 2 about partial observability, μ reveals an error if μ is neither in $\sigma_{|L}(i)$ nor can be extended into an element of $\sigma_{|L}(i)$ i.e. μ diverges from i iff $\mu \notin \overline{\sigma_{|L}(i)}$. We introduce a rule involving the removal operation to accommodate the need to identify multi-prefixes of multitraces. Indeed, as the execution relation $\rightarrow$ only allows executing actions in the global order in which they are intended to occur, we may reach cases in which the next action which may be consumed in the multitrace cannot be executed due to having a preceding action missing in the multitrace.

Let us illustrate this with node ⓪ of Fig. 4. `bro?subscribe` is the first action that occurs on lifeline `bro` in the multitrace. However, it cannot be executed because it must be preceded by `sub!subscribe`. Yet, either because the behavior on lifeline `sub` is not observed or because the logging process ceased too early on `sub`, it might well be that `sub!subscribe` occurred in the actual execution although it was not logged. With our new algorithm, because the condition that $\mu_{|sub} = \varepsilon$ is satisfied, from node ⓪, we apply a rule yielding the transformation $(i, \mu) \rightsquigarrow (\text{rmv}_{sub}(i), \text{rmv}_{sub}(\mu))$, removing lifeline `sub`, which allows us to pursue the analysis from node ①. To summarize, Fig. 4 illustrates (part of) the graph that can be constructed from a pair (i_0, μ_0) using the relation $\rightsquigarrow$. We have 5

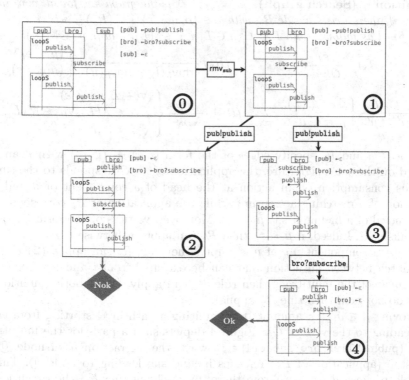

Fig. 4. An exploration s.t. $\omega_L(i, \mu) = Pass$

nodes numbered from 0 (the initial node of the analysis) to 4. Arcs correspond to the consumption of an action, the application of the rmv operator, or the emission of a verdict. The empty multitrace in node ④ allows us to conclude $\mu_0 \in \overline{\sigma_{|L}}(i_0)$.

4.1 The Algorithm

As the rmv operator has the effect of changing the signature, we introduce the set $\mathbb{I}_{\mathcal{L}}$ (resp. $\mathbb{M}_{\mathcal{L}}$) to denote the set of all interactions (resp. multitraces) defined on a signature of $\mathcal{L}$. Let us define a directed search graph with vertices either of the form $(i, \mu) \in \mathbb{I}_{\mathcal{L}} \times \mathbb{M}_{\mathcal{L}}$ or one of two specific verdicts Ok and Nok.

We denote by $\mathbb{V}$ the set of all vertices:

$$\mathbb{V} = \{Ok, Nok\} \cup \left(\bigcup_{L \subseteq \mathcal{L}} \mathbb{I}(L) \times \mathbb{M}(L) \right)$$

The arcs of $\mathbb{G}$ are defined by 4 rules: R_o, R_n leading to respectively the sink vertices Ok and Nok, R_e (for "execute") for consuming actions of the multitrace according to the $\rightarrow$ predicate of the operational formulation (cf. Property 2), and R_r (for "removal"), for removing a lifeline from the interaction and multitrace.

Definition 6 (Search graph). $\mathbb{G} = (\mathbb{V}, \rightsquigarrow)$ *is the graph s.t. for all v, v' in $\mathbb{V}$, $v \rightsquigarrow v'$ iff there exists a rule R_x with $x \in \{o, n, e, r\}$ s.t. $(R_x) \frac{v}{v'}$ where rules R_x are defined as follows, with $L \subseteq \mathcal{L}$, $h \in L$, $i, i' \in \mathbb{I}(L)$, and $\mu, \mu' \in \mathbb{M}(L)$:*

$$(R_o) \frac{i \quad \varepsilon_L}{Ok} \qquad (R_r) \frac{i \quad \mu}{\mathrm{rmv}_h(i) \quad \mathrm{rmv}_h(\mu)} \begin{cases} (\mu \neq \varepsilon_L) \wedge \\ (\mu_{|h} = \varepsilon) \end{cases}$$

$$(R_e) \frac{i \quad \mu}{i' \quad \mu'} \begin{cases} \exists a \in \mathbb{A}(L), \\ \mu = a\hat{\ }\mu' \wedge i \xrightarrow{a} i' \end{cases} (R_n) \frac{i \quad \mu}{Nok} \begin{cases} (\forall l \in L, \mu_{|l} \neq \varepsilon) \wedge \\ \left(\begin{matrix} \forall a \in \mathbb{A}(L), \forall \mu' \in \mathbb{M}(L), \\ \mu = a\hat{\ }\mu' \Rightarrow i \xrightarrow{a} \not{\ } \end{matrix} \right) \end{cases}$$

Rules R_e and R_r specify edges of the form $(i, \mu) \rightsquigarrow (i', \mu')$ with i' and μ' defined on the same signature: the application of R_e corresponds to the simultaneous consumption of an action at the head of a component of μ and the execution of a matching action in i while the application of R_r corresponds to the removal of a lifeline h s.t. $\mu_{|h} = \varepsilon$. Moreover, vertices of the form (i, μ) are not sinks of $\mathbb{G}$. Indeed, if $\mu = \varepsilon_L$ then R_o can apply, otherwise $\mu \neq \varepsilon_L$ and: **(1)** if at least a component $\mu_{|h}$ of μ is empty, then rule R_r can apply. **(2)** if there is a match between an action that can be executed from i and the head of a component of the multitrace then rule R_e can apply. **(3)** if both conditions 1 and 2 do not hold then rule R_n applies.

Proving $\mu \in \overline{\sigma_{|L}}(i)$, amounts to exhibiting a path in $\mathbb{G}$ starting from (i, μ) and leading to the verdict Ok. Figure 4 depicts such a path for the multitrace $\mu_0 = (\mathtt{pub!publish}, \mathtt{bro?subscribe}, \varepsilon)$ w.r.t. the interaction i_0 of node ⓪. A first step (application of R_r) removes lifeline $\mathtt{sub}$ leading to node ①. This is possible because $\mu_{|\mathtt{sub}} = \varepsilon$. From there, by applying rule R_e, the execution of $\mathtt{pub?publish}$ allows to reach either node ② or node ③ depending on the loop used. From node ③, the previous removal of lifeline sub has unlocked the execution of bro?subscribe (application of R_e). What remains is ε_L, and hence we can apply rule R_o. From the existence of this path leading to Ok we conclude that μ_0 is a multi-prefix of a multitrace of the interaction depicted in Fig. 1c.

Property 3 (Finite search space). Let $L \subseteq \mathcal{L}$, $\mu \in \mathbb{M}(L)$ and $i \in \mathbb{I}(L)$. The sub-graph of $\mathbb{G}$ of all vertices reachable from (i, μ) is finite.

We establish this property by using a measure $|v|$ defined on the vertices v in $\mathbb{V}$ by $|v| = 0$ if $v \in \{Ok, Nok\}$ and $|v| = |\mu| + |L| + 1$ if $s = (i, \mu) \in \mathbb{I}(L) \times \mathbb{M}(L)$.

Definition 7 (Multitrace analysis). *For any $L \subset \mathcal{L}$, we define $\omega_L : \mathbb{I}(L) \times \mathbb{M}(L) \rightarrow \{Pass, Fail\}$ s.t. for any $i \in \mathbb{I}(L)$ and $\mu \in \mathbb{M}(L)$:*
- *$\omega_L(i, \mu) = Pass$ iff there exists a path in $\mathbb{G}$ from (i, μ) to Ok*
- *$\omega_L(i, \mu) = Fail$ otherwise*

Given Property 3, Definition 7 is well founded insofar as the sub-graph of $\mathbb{G}$ issued from any pair (i, μ) of $\mathbb{V}$ is finite and all paths from (i, μ) can be extended until reaching a verdict (Ok or Nok). Then, we need to prove that the existence of a path from (i, μ) to Ok guarantees that μ is a prefix of a multitrace of i, and that the non-existence of such a path guarantees that μ is not such a prefix. By reasoning by induction on the measure of the vertices of $\mathbb{G}$, we can establish:

Theorem 2. *For any $i \in \mathbb{I}(L)$ and any $\mu \in \mathbb{M}(L)$:*

$$\left(\mu \in \overline{\sigma_{|L}(i)} \right) \Leftrightarrow \left(\omega_L(i, \mu) = Pass \right)$$

4.2 Considerations on Implementation

Using a reduction of the 3 SAT problem inspired by [3,18], we can state that the problem of recognizing correct multi-prefixes w.r.t. interactions is NP-hard:

Property 4. The problem of determining whether or not $\mu \in \overline{\sigma_{|L}(i)}$ is NP-hard.

Given the NP-hardness of the underlying problem, the implementation of our algorithm, which relies on the exploration of a graph $\mathbb{G}$, uses additional techniques to reduce the average complexity. Such techniques may include means to cut parts of the graph, the use of pertinent search strategies and priorities for the application of the rules. For instance, if R_r is applicable from a node (i, μ), we can apply rmv on all lifelines which can be removed simultaneously. Also, if both R_r and R_e are applicable from that same node, we can choose not to apply R_e. Those two points are respectively justified by a property of commutativity for rmv (i.e. $\mathrm{rmv}_h \circ \mathrm{rmv}_{h'} = \mathrm{rmv}_{h'} \circ \mathrm{rmv}_h$) and a confluence property for $\rightsquigarrow$ (i.e. if $(i, \mu) \overset{*}{\rightsquigarrow} Ok$ and $(i, \mu) \rightsquigarrow (\mathrm{rmv}_h(i), \mathrm{rmv}_h(\mu))$ then $(\mathrm{rmv}_h(i), \mathrm{rmv}_h(\mu)) \overset{*}{\rightsquigarrow} Ok$).

5   Experimental Assessment

5.1   3 SAT Benchmarks

We have implemented our approach as an extension of the tool HIBOU [17]. In light of Property 4, we have compared the results HIBOU obtained on translated three SAT problems against those of an SAT solver (Varisat [2]). We have used three sets of problems: two custom benchmarks with randomly generated problems and the UF20 benchmark [1]. Figure 5 provides details on 2 benchmarks with, on the top left, information about the input problems (numbers of variables, clauses, instances), on the bottom left statistical information about the time required for the analysis using each tool, and, on the right a corresponding scatter plot. In the plot, each point corresponds to a given 3-SAT problem,

# variables	3-10
# clauses	4-50
# instances	663
# SAT	376
# UNSAT	287

	varisat	hibou
min	0.01699	0.0002379
q1	0.01792	0.0012984
Mdn	0.01806	0.0027920
M	0.01833	0.0043448
q3	0.01848	0.0053158
max	0.02892	0.0267174
σ	0.001017846	0.004637261

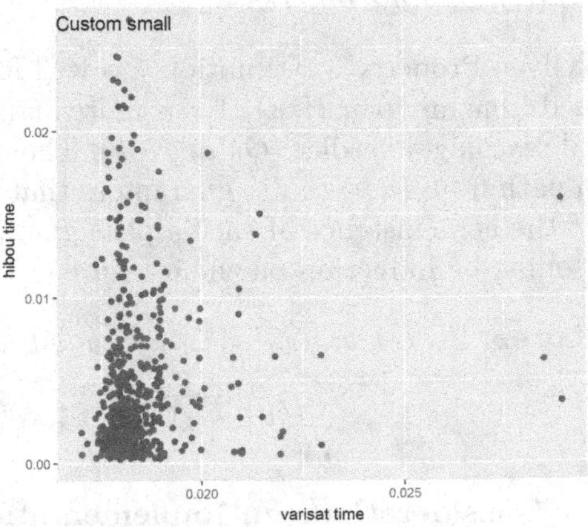

(a) Input problems and output results for 'small' custom benchmark

# variables	20
# clauses	91
# instances	1000
# SAT	1000
# UNSAT	0

	varisat	hibou
min	0.01559	0.007638
q1	0.01667	0.091421
Mdn	0.01833	0.229745
M	0.01847	0.313901
q3	0.01929	0.462385
max	0.03989	1.666777
σ	0.00255181	0.2865485

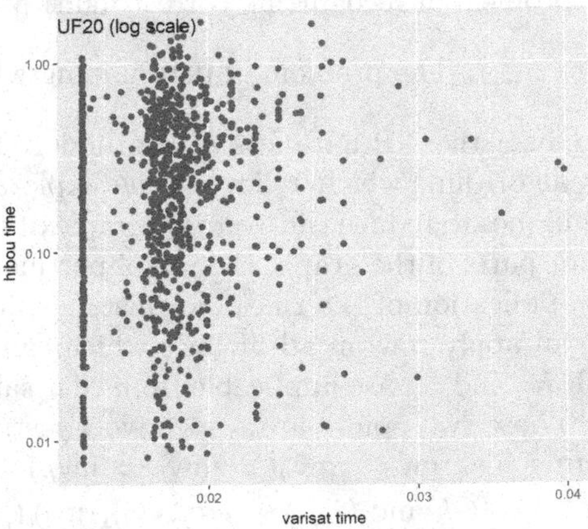

(b) Input problems and output results for UF-20 benchmark

Fig. 5. Experiments on 3SAT benchmarks (times in seconds)

with its position corresponding to the time required to solve it. Points in red are unsatisfiable problems while those in blue are satisfiable.

5.2 Use Cases Experiments

To consider concrete and varied interactions, we experiment with four examples: a protocol for purchasing books [4], a system for querying complex sensor data [5], the Alternating Bit Protocol [22] and a network for uploading data to a server [6]. Figure 6 partially reports on those experiments. For each example, we generated randomly accepted multitraces (ACPT) up to some depth, for which we then randomly selected prefixes (PREF). For each such prefix, we then performed mutations of three kinds: swapping actions (SACT), swapping trace components (SCMP) and inserting noise (NOIS). We report for each category of multitraces times to compute verdicts in Fig. 6. As expected, running the algorithm on those multitraces recognizes prefixes and mutants which go out of specification.

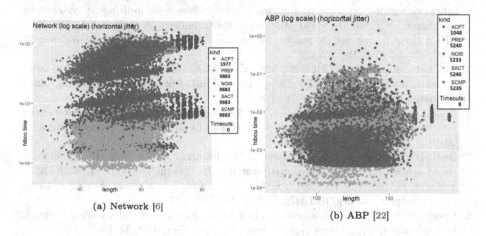

(a) Network [6]

(b) ABP [22]

Fig. 6. Experimental data on a selection of use cases (times in seconds)

6 Conclusion

We have proposed an algorithm for offline RV from multitraces (sets of local execution logs collected on the DS) against interaction models (formal specifications akin to UML-SD/MSC). These multitraces can be partial views of DS executions because some components may either not be observed at all or their observation may have ceased too early. We have proved the correctness of our algorithm which boils down to a graph search. This search is based on two principles, either we match actions of the interaction against those of the input multitrace, or we apply a removal operation on multitraces and interactions. Removal steps allow dealing with observability via disregarding components which are no longer observed parts of the interaction. Future works include other uses of the removal operator (e.g. for performance improvements on RV).

Acknowledgements. The research leading to these results has received funding from the European Union's Horizon Europe programme under grant agreement No 101069748 - SELFY project.

References

1. SATLIB - Benchmark. https://www.cs.ubc.ca/~hoos/SATLIB/benchm.html
2. Varisat CDCL solver. https://docs.rs/varisat/latest/varisat/
3. Alur, R., Etessami, K., Yannakakis, M.: Realizability and verification of MSC graphs. In: Orejas, F., Spirakis, P.G., van Leeuwen, J. (eds.) ICALP 2001. LNCS, vol. 2076, pp. 797–808. Springer, Heidelberg (2001). https://doi.org/10.1007/3-540-48224-5_65
4. Ancona, D., Ferrando, A., Franceschini, L., Mascardi, V.: Coping with bad agent interaction protocols when monitoring partially observable multiagent systems. In: Demazeau, Y., An, B., Bajo, J., Fernández-Caballero, A. (eds.) PAAMS 2018. LNCS (LNAI), vol. 10978, pp. 59–71. Springer, Cham (2018). https://doi.org/10.1007/978-3-319-94580-4_5
5. Bakillah, M., Liang, S., Zipf, A., Mostafavi, M.A.: A dynamic and context-aware semantic mediation service for discovering and fusion of heterogeneous sensor data. J. Spatial Inform. Sci. **6**, 155–185 (06 2013)
6. Bejleri, A., Domnori, E., Viering, M., Eugster, P., Mezini, M.: Comprehensive multiparty session types. The Art, Science, and Engineering of Programming 3 (02 2019)
7. Benharrat, N., Gaston, C., Hierons, R.M., Lapitre, A., Le Gall, P.: Constraint-based oracles for timed distributed systems. In: Yevtushenko, N., Cavalli, A.R., Yenigün, H. (eds.) ICTSS 2017. LNCS, vol. 10533, pp. 276–292. Springer, Cham (2017). https://doi.org/10.1007/978-3-319-67549-7_17
8. Bocchi, L., Chen, T., Demangeon, R., Honda, K., Yoshida, N.: Monitoring networks through multiparty session types. Theor. Comput. Sci. **669**, 33–58 (2017)
9. Cavalcanti, A., Gaudel, M.-C., Hierons, R.M.: Conformance relations for distributed testing based on CSP. In: Wolff, B., Zaïdi, F. (eds.) ICTSS 2011. LNCS, vol. 7019, pp. 48–63. Springer, Heidelberg (2011). https://doi.org/10.1007/978-3-642-24580-0_5
10. Dan, H., Hierons, R.M.: The oracle problem when testing from MSCs. Comput. J. **57**(7), 987–1001 (2014)
11. Hierons, R.M., Merayo, M.G., Núñez, M.: Controllable test cases for the distributed test architecture. In: Cha, S.S., Choi, J.-Y., Kim, M., Lee, I., Viswanathan, M. (eds.) ATVA 2008. LNCS, vol. 5311, pp. 201–215. Springer, Heidelberg (2008). https://doi.org/10.1007/978-3-540-88387-6_16
12. Hierons, R.M., Merayo, M.G., Núñez, M.: Scenarios-based testing of systems with distributed ports. Softw. Pract. Exp. **41**(10), 999–1026 (2011)
13. Inçki, K., Ari, I.: A novel runtime verification solution for IoT Systems. IEEE Access **6**, 13501–13512 (2018)
14. ITU: Message Sequence Chart (MSC). http://www.itu.int/rec/T-REC-Z.120

15. Lamport, L.: Time, clocks, and the ordering of events in a distributed system. In: Concurrency: the Works of Leslie Lamport, pp. 179–196. ACM (2019)
16. Mace, J., Roelke, R., Fonseca, R.: Pivot tracing: dynamic causal monitoring for distributed systems. In: SOSP, pp. 378–393. ACM (2015)
17. Mahé, E.: Hibou tool. http://www.github.com/erwanM974/hibou_label (2022)
18. Mahé, E., Bannour, B., Gaston, C., Lapitre, A., Le Gall, P.: A small-step approach to multi-trace checking against interactions, pp. 1815–1822. SAC '21, ACM (2021)
19. Mahé, E., Bannour, B., Gaston, C., Lapitre, A., Le Gall, P.: Dealing with observability in interaction-based offline runtime verification of distributed systems. CoRR (2022). https://arxiv.org/abs/2212.09324
20. Mahé, E., Gaston, C., Le Gall, P.: Revisiting Semantics of Interactions for Trace Validity Analysis. In: FASE 2020. LNCS, vol. 5311, pp. 482–501. Springer, Cham (2020). https://doi.org/10.1007/978-3-030-45234-6_24
21. Mahé, E., Gaston, C., Le Gall, P.: Equivalence of denotational and operational semantics for interaction languages. In: TASE. pp. 113–130. Springer (2022). https://doi.org/10.1007/978-3-031-10363-6_8
22. Mauw, S., Reniers, M.A.: High-level message sequence charts. In: SDL Forum. pp. 291–306. Elsevier (1997)
23. Neves, F., Machado, N., Pereira, J.: Falcon: A practical log-based analysis tool for distributed systems. In: DSN, pp. 534–541. IEEE Computer Society (2018)
24. Nguyen, H.N., Poizat, P., Zaïdi, F.: Passive conformance testing of service choreographies. In: ACM SAC 2012, pp. 1528–1535 (2012)
25. OMG: Unified Modeling Language, http://www.uml.org
26. Sánchez, C., et al.: A survey of challenges for runtime verification from advanced application domains (beyond software). Formal Methods in System Design , pp. 1–57 (2019). https://doi.org/10.1007/s10703-019-00337-w

Genetic Algorithm for Program Synthesis

Yutaka Nagashima[✉][iD]

Cambridge, UK
united.reasoning@gmail.com

Abstract. A deductive program synthesis tool takes a specification as input and derives a program that satisfies the specification. The drawback of this approach is that search spaces for such correct programs tend to be enormous, making it difficult to derive correct programs within a realistic timeout. To speed up such program derivation, we improve the search strategy of a deductive program synthesis tool, SuSLik, using evolutionary computation. Our cross-validation shows that the improvement brought by evolutionary computation generalises to unforeseen problems.

1 Introduction

A far-fetched goal of artificial intelligence research is to build a system that writes computer programs for humans. To achieve this goal, researchers take two distinct approaches: deductive program synthesis and inductive program synthesis. Both approaches attempt to produce programs requested by human users. The difference lies how they produce programs: deductive synthesis tries to *deduce* programs that satisfy specifications, while inductive program synthesis tries to *induce* programs from examples.

While such inductive synthesis alleviates the burden of implementation by guessing programs from given input-output examples, in inductive synthesis resulting programs are not trustworthy. Deductive synthesis overcomes this limitation with formal specifications: it allows users to formalise *what* they want as specifications, whereas inductive synthesis tools guess *how* programs should behave from examples provided by users. Thus, in deductive synthesis providing formal specifications remains as users' responsibility. The upside of deductive synthesis is, however, users can obtain *correct* programs upon success.

SuSLik [19], for example, is one of such deductive synthesis tools. It takes a specification provided by humans and attempts to produce heap-manipulating programs satisfying the specification in a language that resembles the C language. Internally, this derivation process is formulated as proof search: SuSLik composes a heap-manipulating program by conducting a best-first search for a proof goal presented as specification. The drawback is that the search algorithm often fails to find a proof within a realistic timeout. That is, even we

---

Y. Nagashima—Independent.

We would like to thank Andreea Costea for preparing additional SuSLik problems for cross-validations.

H. Hojjat and E. Ábrahám (Eds.): FSEN 2023, LNCS 14155, pp. 104–111, 2023.
https://doi.org/10.1007/978-3-031-42441-0_8

pass a specification to SuSLik, SuSLik may not produce a program satisfying the specification. According to Itzhaky *et al.* [5], *different synthesis tasks benefit from different search parameters, and that we might need a mechanism to tune SuSLik's search strategy for a given synthesis task.*

2   SuSLik's Search Strategy

SuSLik synthesises a program by searching for a corresponding proof. We can see SuSLik's proof search as an exploration of an OR-tree, nodes of the tree represent (intermediate) synthesis goals, while edges of the tree represent rule applications. The shape of such search tree is not known in advance, and the task of SuSLik is to identify a solved node, in which a proof is complete.

Since such OR-trees can be too large to find proofs within a realistic timeout, SuSLik narrows the search space using a *proof strategy*. Essentially, proof strategy in SuSLik is a function that takes a synthesis goal and returns an ordered list of rules to apply next. Itzhaky *et al.* developed the default strategy by manually encoding human expertise. For exam-

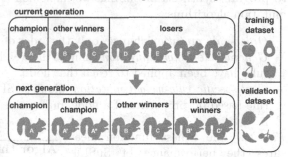

Fig. 1. Mutation and Elitist Selection

ple, the default strategy precludes the application of a rule called CALL when another rule CLOSE has been applied before reaching the current node. This way, the SuSLik rules are grouped into 10 ordered lists, and the order of these rules define how SuSLik explores the corresponding OR-tree.

Another decision SuSLik has to make for an effective search is to select the next node to expand. The current version of SuSLik make this decision using a cost function, manually developed and tuned by Itzhaky *et al.* [5].

Both the weights of the cost function and orders of derivation rules are manually tuned for the benchmark used in their evaluation [5]; however, as we show in Sect. 4, our evolutionary framework finds better strategies through evolution.

3   Evolutionary Computation for SuSLik

The aim of our evolutionary computation is to optimise the order of each group of derivation rules and the weights of the cost function, which is used to implement best-first search.

Algorithm 1 summarises the genetic algorithm we used in our framework to improve the search strategy of SuSLik. Firstly, the algorithm takes a set of training problems an inputs, using which we evolve SuSLik instances over 40 generations. Line 1 defines the initial population. Each individual in a population is evaluated according to the fitness function described in Sect. 3.

For each generation, we copy individuals from the previous iteration (Line 6), mutate them (Line 7), evaluate individuals (Line 8). Then, we sort all individuals in the current generation based on their performance (Line 9–10). And we continue to the next generation using the best 20 individuals from the current pool. In the following, we explain the mutation algorithm, the fitness function, and our selection algorithm.

Mutation. As we explained in Sect. 2, by default a search strategy of SuSLik is defined by two factors: the order of rule application and weights of each node in the search tree. To determine an effective way to apply genetic algorithms to program synthesis in SuSLik, we implemented the following three different mutation algorithms:

- *Order-only mutation* changes only the order of rule application for each node.
- *General rule-weight mutation* changes the weights of each node based on what rules have been applied to reach that node.
- *Goal-specific rule-weight mutation* allows SuSLik to choose a weight for each rule based on properties of a node during a search.

Fitness. The fitness function measures the performance of SuSLik instances. More specifically, it measures how many derivation problems each SuSLik instance solves within the timeout of 2.5 s for each problem. When multiple SuSLik instances solve the same number of derivation problems, the fitness function uses the numbers of rules fired by the instances as a tie-breaker: it considers that the instance that solves a certain number of problems with a smaller number of rule applications is better than another instance that solves the same number of problems with a larger number of rule applications.

Algorithm 1 Evolutionary Computation for SuSLik

Input: synthesis problems for SuSLik
Output: a SuSLik search strategy

1: Let *old_pop* be the initial population.
2: fitness(*old_pop*)
3: *generation* ← 1
4: **while** *generation* ≤ 40 **do**
5:    *generation* ← *generation* + 1
6:    *new_pop* ← *old_pop*
7:    mutate(*new_pop*)
8:    fitness(*new_pop*)
9:    *whole_pop* ← *old_pop* + *new_pop*
10:   sort (*whole_pop*)
11:   *old_pop* ← take (*whole_pop*, 20)
12: **end while**

Selection. We adopt a version of *elitist selection* as our selection method: we pass individuals from the current generation to the next generation. By copying them and mutating them if they show better performance in the current generation. Figure 1 provides the schematic view of our elitist selection. Unlike the standard elitist selection algorithm, ours prioritizes the best individual in each generation to speed up the evolution: the best individual in each generation, called *champion*, is entitled with three children, one original copy without mutation and two mutated children, whereas each of other 19 winners has one original copy and only one mutated child in the next generation.

Note that each individual has two kinds of properties to mutate: the order of derivation rules, and weights used in the cost function. While we represent the weights as floating point numbers, we adopt permutation encoding for the orders of derivation rules.

For each permutation encoding, each individual has the probability of 0.1 to be moved, while we change weights by multiplying a random number between 0.8 and 1.2. In our framework, we do not apply crossover to permutation encoding: since our sequences denoting rule orders tend to be short, we are not sure if crossovers would result in a better performance of evolution.

Our evolutionary computation for program synthesis differs from genetic programming [9] or evolutionary programming [1]: we did not directly apply simulated evolution to programs, but our framework improves the search mechanism for deriving correct programs through evolution. We take this approach to take the best of both worlds: the correctness of resulting programs guaranteed by the deductive synthesis and its certification tool, and the search heuristics enhanced through evolutionary computation.

4   Evaluation

We conducted cross-validations to evaluate what improvements our evolutionary computation framework brought to SuSLik. We measured how many synthesis problems SuSLik failed to solve with in 2.5 s of timeout. For this evaluation, we used a consumer laptop running Ubuntu 20.04.3 LTS on a machine with 16 CPUs of AMD Ryzen 7 4,800H with Radeon Graphics and 15,854 MB of main memory.

As SuSLik is a new tool, we have only 65 problems available in our benchmark: problems from a preceding work on SuSLik [5] and new problems prepared for this project. These problems include tasks on various data-structures such as integers, singly linked lists, sorted lists, doubly linked lists, lists of lists, binary trees, and packed trees.

Firstly, we randomly split our benchmarks into two groups: the validation dataset and training dataset. Then, using the training dataset we apply our evolutionary computation described in Algorithm 1 to evolve SuSLik's search strategy. As explained in Sect. 3, the output of our evolutionary computation is just one search strategy produced after 40 generations. However, in this experiment we conducted cross-validations using the best individual from the training set for each generation to see how our framework produces transferable improvement over generations.

To reduce the influence from a specific random split, we conducted this experiment four times, and the result of each experiment is illustrated from Fig. 2 to Fig. 5. In these figures, the horizontal axes represent the number of generations, while the vertical axes represent the number of synthesis problems SuSLik did *not* solve within the timeout.

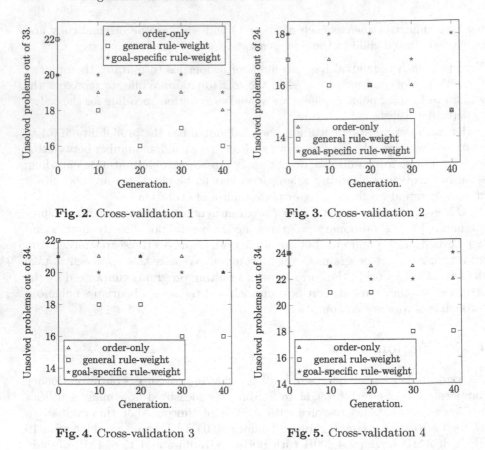

Fig. 2. Cross-validation 1   **Fig. 3.** Cross-validation 2

Fig. 4. Cross-validation 3   **Fig. 5.** Cross-validation 4

These figures show that when adopting the general rule-weight mutation, our evolutionary framework managed to improve SuSLik's capability to find solutions in validation sets, even though evolution is based on training sets. That is, somewhat contrarily to the prediction by Itzhaky introduced in Sect. 1, we found that there are strategies that tend to perform better for unforeseen problems, and we can find such strategies using evolutionary computation.

On the other hand, the order-only mutation and goal-specific rule-weight mutation resulted in less promising results. In particular, the goal-specific rule-weight mutation over-fitted to training data in Fig. 2 and Fig. 5, probably due to its capability to fine tune the strategy for our small dataset.

5   Discussion

The limited size of available dataset is the main challenge we faced in this project. This problem is partially unavoidable since program synthesis itself is still an emerging field in Computer Science. Other AI projects for interactive theorem provers take advantage of large existing proof corpora for training. For example, Nagashima built a tactic prediction tool, PaMpeR [16], for Isabelle/HOL by extracting 425,334 data points [13] from the Archive of Formal Proofs (AFP) [8]. Li *et al.* also mined the AFP and produced 820K training examples for conjecturing. For Coq, Yang *et al.* constructed a dataset containing 71K proofs from 123 projects [21], whereas Huang *et al.* [4] extracted a dataset consisting of 1,602 lemmas from the Feit-Thompson formalization. For HOL Light [3], The HOL-Step [6] used 1,013,046 training examples and 196,030 testing examples extracted from 11,400 proofs, while the HOList project presented a benchmark based on 2,199 definitions and 29,462 theorems and lemmas. These projects managed to gather large data sets since their underlying theorem provers, Isabelle/HOL, Coq, and HOL Light, have a larger user base than SuSLik [19] does.

For the moment, our framework improves *static* parameters for SuSLik. That is, the resulting weights and rule orders are fixed for all intermediate synthesis problems. Our evaluation has shown that our static parameter optimisation (general rule-weight mutation) using evolutionary computation generalises well: a SuSLik instance that performs well for a training dataset tends to perform well for an evaluation dataset. We expected that we could achieve even better performance by producing *dynamic* parameters (goal-specific rule-weight) for SuSLik: functions that inspect a node at hand and decide on a promising rule order and weights for that node. Our efforts in this direction are, unfortunately, unsuccessful so far. We hope that a larger training dataset would allow for such optimisation in the future.

6   Related Work

Even though there was an attempt to use reinforcement learning [20] for a connection-style proof search [7]; we mindfully chose evolutionary computation over reinforcement learning: since we do not have a changing environment in our setting, it is unclear if we gain any benefits from having two metrics, reward function for the long term goal and value function for the short term benefit. Instead, we improved SuSLik's default search strategy for randomly chosen fixed training problem sets and measured how the improvement generalizes to validation sets.

When implementing our framework for evolutionary computation, we took the advantage of a Python framework for evolutionary computation called DEAP [2], even though SuSLik itself is implemented in Scala.

Previously, we attempted to improve proof strategies [17] for Isabelle/HOL using evolutionary computing [11]. However, the focus of that project shifted to the prediction of induction arguments [14,15] using meta-languages [10,12].

Nawaz *et al.* used a genetic algorithm to evolve random proof sequences to target proofs. The drawback of their approach is that the fitness function used in the genetic algorithm relies on the existence of a proof for a given problem. Therefore, this framework is not applicable to open conjectures without existing proofs [18].

References

1. Fogel, L., Owens, A.J., Walsh, M.J.: Artificial intelligence through simulated evolution (1966)
2. Fortin, F.A., De Rainville, F.M., Gardner, M.A., Parizeau, M., Gagné, C.: DEAP: evolutionary algorithms made easy. J. Mach. Learn. Res. **13**, 2171–2175 (2012)
3. Harrison, J.: HOL light: a tutorial introduction. In: Srivas, M., Camilleri, A. (eds.) FMCAD 1996. LNCS, vol. 1166, pp. 265–269. Springer, Heidelberg (1996). https://doi.org/10.1007/BFb0031814
4. Huang, D., Dhariwal, P., Song, D., Sutskever, I.: GamePad: a learning environment for theorem proving. In: 7th International Conference on Learning Representations, ICLR 2019, New Orleans, LA, USA, 6–9 May 2019. OpenReview.net (2019). https://openreview.net/forum?id=r1xwKoR9Y7
5. Itzhaky, S., Peleg, H., Polikarpova, N., Rowe, R.N.S., Sergey, I.: Deductive synthesis of programs with pointers: techniques, challenges, opportunities. In: Silva, A., Leino, K.R.M. (eds.) CAV 2021, Part I. LNCS, vol. 12759, pp. 110–134. Springer, Cham (2021). https://doi.org/10.1007/978-3-030-81685-8_5
6. Kaliszyk, C., Chollet, F., Szegedy, C.: HolStep: a machine learning dataset for higher-order logic theorem proving. In: 5th International Conference on Learning Representations, ICLR 2017, Toulon, France, 24–26 April 2017, Conference Track Proceedings. OpenReview.net (2017). https://openreview.net/forum?id=ryuxYmvel
7. Kaliszyk, C., Urban, J., Michalewski, H., Olšák, M.: Reinforcement learning of theorem proving. In: Bengio, S., Wallach, H.M., Larochelle, H., Grauman, K., Cesa-Bianchi, N., Garnett, R. (eds.) Advances in Neural Information Processing Systems 31: Annual Conference on Neural Information Processing Systems 2018, NeurIPS 2018, Montréal, Canada, 3–8 December 2018, pp. 8836–8847 (2018). https://proceedings.neurips.cc/paper/2018/hash/55acf8539596d25624059980986aaa78-Abstract.html
8. Klein, G., Nipkow, T., Paulson, L., Thiemann, R.: The Archive of Formal Proofs (2004). https://www.isa-afp.org/
9. Koza, J.R.: Genetic Programming - On the Programming of Computers by Means of Natural Selection. Complex Adaptive Systems. MIT Press, Cambridge (1993)
10. Nagashima, Y.: LiFtEr: language to encode induction heuristics for Isabelle/HOL. In: Lin, A.W. (ed.) APLAS 2019. LNCS, vol. 11893, pp. 266–287. Springer, Cham (2019). https://doi.org/10.1007/978-3-030-34175-6_14
11. Nagashima, Y.: Towards evolutionary theorem proving for Isabelle/HOL. In: López-Ibáñez, M., Auger, A., Stützle, T. (eds.) Proceedings of the Genetic and Evolutionary Computation Conference Companion, GECCO 2019, Prague, Czech Republic, 13–17 July 2019, pp. 419–420. ACM (2019). https://doi.org/10.1145/3319619.3321921
12. Nagashima, Y.: Definitional quantifiers realise semantic reasoning for proof by induction. CoRR **abs/2010.10296** (2020). https://arxiv.org/abs/2010.10296
13. Nagashima, Y.: Simple dataset for proof method recommendation in Isabelle/HOL. In: Benzmüller, C., Miller, B. (eds.) CICM 2020. LNCS (LNAI), vol. 12236, pp. 297–302. Springer, Cham (2020). https://doi.org/10.1007/978-3-030-53518-6_21
14. Nagashima, Y.: Smart induction for Isabelle/HOL (tool paper). In: 2020 Formal Methods in Computer Aided Design, FMCAD 2020, Haifa, Israel, 21–24 September 2020, pp. 245–254. IEEE (2020). https://doi.org/10.34727/2020/isbn.978-3-85448-042-6_32

15. Nagashima, Y.: Faster smarter proof by induction in Isabelle/HOL. In: Zhou, Z. (ed.) Proceedings of the Thirtieth International Joint Conference on Artificial Intelligence, IJCAI 2021, Virtual Event / Montreal, Canada, 19-27 August 2021, pp. 1981–1988. ijcai.org (2021). https://doi.org/10.24963/ijcai.2021/273
16. Nagashima, Y., He, Y.: PaMpeR: proof method recommendation system for Isabelle/HOL. In: Huchard, M., Kästner, C., Fraser, G. (eds.) Proceedings of the 33rd ACM/IEEE International Conference on Automated Software Engineering, ASE 2018, Montpellier, France, 3–7 September 2018, pp. 362–372. ACM (2018). https://doi.org/10.1145/3238147.3238210
17. Nagashima, Y., Kumar, R.: A proof strategy language and proof script generation for Isabelle/HOL. In: de Moura, L. (ed.) CADE 2017. LNCS (LNAI), vol. 10395, pp. 528–545. Springer, Cham (2017). https://doi.org/10.1007/978-3-319-63046-5_32
18. Nawaz, M.Z., Hasan, O., Nawaz, M.S., Fournier-Viger, P., Sun, M.: Proof searching in HOL4 with genetic algorithm. In: Hung, C., Cerný, T., Shin, D., Bechini, A. (eds.) SAC 2020: The 35th ACM/SIGAPP Symposium on Applied Computing, online event, [Brno, Czech Republic], March 30–April 3 2020, pp. 513–520. ACM (2020). https://doi.org/10.1145/3341105.3373917
19. Polikarpova, N., Sergey, I.: Structuring the synthesis of heap-manipulating programs. Proc. ACM Program. Lang. 3(POPL), 72:1–72:30 (2019). https://doi.org/10.1145/3290385
20. Sutton, R.S., Barto, A.G.: Reinforcement learning: an introduction. IEEE Trans. Neural Netw. 9(5), 1054–1054 (1998). https://doi.org/10.1109/TNN.1998.712192
21. Yang, K., Deng, J.: Learning to prove theorems via interacting with proof assistants. In: Chaudhuri, K., Salakhutdinov, R. (eds.) Proceedings of the 36th International Conference on Machine Learning, ICML 2019, Long Beach, California, USA, 9–15 June 2019. Proceedings of Machine Learning Research, vol. 97, pp. 6984–6994. PMLR (2019). http://proceedings.mlr.press/v97/yang19a.html

Template-Based Conjecturing
for Automated Induction in Isabelle/HOL

Yutaka Nagashima[✉][iD], Zijin Xu[iD], Ningli Wang[iD], Daniel Sebastian Goc[iD],
and James Bang[iD]

Huawei Cambridge Research Centre, Cambridge, UK
yutaka.nagashima@huawei.com

Abstract. Proof by induction plays a central role in formal verification.
However, its automation remains as a formidable challenge in Computer
Science. To solve inductive problems, human engineers often have to
provide auxiliary lemmas manually. We automate this laborious process
with *template-based conjecturing*, a novel approach to generate auxiliary
lemmas and use them to prove final goals. Our evaluation shows that our
working prototype, TBC, achieved 50% point improvement of success
rates for problems at intermediate difficulty level.

1 Introduction

Consider the following definitions of add and even on natural numbers:

```
add        0  m = m
add (Suc n) m = Suc (add n m)


even               0  = True
even        (Suc 0)  = False
even (Suc (Suc n)) = even n
```

Intuitively, the following statement holds: even (add n n).

However, if we apply structural induction on n, the simplification based on
the definitions of add and even gets stuck at even (add n n) $\Rightarrow$ even (S (add
n (S n))) when attacking the induction step. This is due to the definition of
add, which does not allow us to operate on its second argument. Hence, if we
want to prove this statement, we need to introduce auxiliary lemmas.

What lemmas should we introduce? Empirically, we know various mathematical structures share well-known *algebraic properties* such as associativity and
commutativity. For example, our example problem uses add, which satisfies the
following properties:

```
add n (add m k) = add (add n m) k          (add is associative)
add n m = add m n                          (add is commutative)
```

© IFIP International Federation for Information Processing 2023
Published by Springer Nature Switzerland AG 2023
H. Hojjat and E. Ábrahám (Eds.): FSEN 2023, LNCS 14155, pp. 112–125, 2023.
https://doi.org/10.1007/978-3-031-42441-0_9

The commutative property of add allows us to operate on its second argument. Hence, if we prove this property, we can revert back to the original goal and finish its proof.

To automate this process, this paper introduces TBC, a tool that produces such template-based conjectures and attempts to prove them as well as the original proof goal in Isabelle/HOL [19]. For example, when applied to even (add n n), TBC first proves 10 conjectures then proves the original goal using two of them as shown in Program 4 in Appendix.

We chose Isabelle/HOL to exploit its powerful proof tactics and counter-example finders; however, the underlying idea of template-based conjecturing is not specific to Isabelle/HOL: we can build similar systems for other provers if they are equipped with equivalent tools. We developed TBC under the following research hypothesis:

> We can improve the proof automation of inductive problems by producing and proving conjectures based on fixed but general properties about relevant functions.

Our contributions are:

- the working prototype of a powerful inductive prover based on template-based conjecturing and newly developed default strategy (Sect. 2.1),
- the identification of useful properties (Sect. 2.2), and
- extensive evaluations of TBC to test our research hypothesis (Sect. 3).

2 System Description

2.1 Overview

Figure 1 shows how TBC attacks inductive problems using template-based conjecturing. Given an induction problem, the tool first attempts to prove the goal

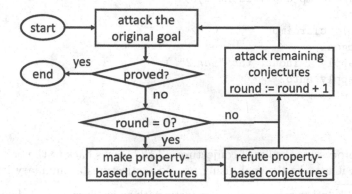

Fig. 1. Workflow of TBC

using a default strategy, TBC_Strategy, written in the proof strategy language, PSL [17]. As shown in Program 1, TBC_Strategy combines Isabelle's proof tactics, such as auto and clarsimp, and other sub-tools, such as smart induction [13–15] and Sledgehammer [21] to prove the goal completely. That is, PSL uses Sledgehammer as a sub-tool, even though Sledgehammer itself is a meta-tool that uses external provers and Isabelle's tactics to prove given problems.

As PSL is a new meta-tool, we first explain the language constructs in Program 1. Ors is a combinator for deterministic choice, whereas Thens and PThenOne combine sub-strategies sequentially. Subgoal lets PSL focus on the first sub-goal, temporarily hiding other sub-goals from the scope, while IsSolved checks if all proof obligations are solved within the current scope. Auto, Clarsimp, and Fastforce correspond to Isabelle's default tactics of the same name, while Hammer calls Sledgehammer [21] and Smart_Induct applies 5 promising candidates of proof by induction [14,15]. Essentially, this strategy applies increasingly expensive sub-strategies to solve proof goals using backtracking search.

If TBC_Strategy fails to prove the goal, it produces conjectures based on properties specified in advance, following the process explained in Sect. 2.2. Then, the tool attempts to refute the conjectures using Isabelle's counter-example generators: Quickcheck [2] and Nitpick [1]. After filtering out refuted conjectures, TBC attempts to prove the remaining conjectures using the default strategy. While doing so, TBC registers proved conjectures as auxiliary lemmas, so that it can use them to prove other conjectures.

For example, TBC_Strategy finds the following proof script for the commutativity of add. To demonstrate how TBC_Strategy finds proofs using backtracking search, we highlighted the parts of Program 1 that were *not* backtracked but resulted in this script. We invite readers to compare these highlighted parts in Program 1 against the resulting script and to find out which proof tactic Sledgehammer used to prove the corresponding sub-goal.[1]

```
lemma commutativity: "add var_1 var_2 = add var_2 var_1"
  apply ( induct_tac "var_1" )
    apply ( simp add : identity )
    subgoal
      apply clarsimp
      subgoal
        apply ( induct_tac "var_2" )
        apply auto
      done
    done
  done
```

After processing the list of conjectures, TBC comes back to the original goal. This time, it attacks the goal, using proved conjectures as auxiliary lemmas. If

---

[1] Answer: Sledgehammer used the simp tactic with an auxiliary lemma about identity. Furthermore, IsSolved resulted in the done command in the script.

Program 1 TBC_Strategy: TBC's default strategy.

```
Ors [
  Thens [Auto, IsSolved],
  PThenOne [Smart_Induct, Thens [Auto, IsSolved]],
  Thens [Hammer, IsSolved],
  PThenOne [
    Smart_Induct,
    Ors
      [Thens [
        Repeat (
          Ors [
            Fastforce,
            Hammer,
            Thens [ Clarsimp, IsSolved ],
            Thens [
              Subgoal,
              Clarsimp,
              Repeat (
                Thens [ Subgoal,
                        Ors [ Thens [Auto, IsSolved],
                              Thens [ Smart_Induct, Auto, IsSolved ] ] ]
              ),
              IsSolved
            ]
          ]
        ),
        IsSolved
      ]
    ]
  ]
]
```

TBC still fails to prove the original goal, it again attacks the remaining conjectures hoping that proved conjectures may help the strategy to prove remaining ones. By default, TBC gives up after the second round and shows proved conjectures and their proofs in Isabelle's standard editor's output pane, so that users can exploit them when attacking original goals manually.

The seamless integration of TBC into the Isabelle ecosystem lets users build TBC as an Isabelle theory using Isabelle's standard build command without installing additional software. Furthermore, when TBC finds a proof for the original goal, our tool shows the final proof as well as proved conjectures with their proofs in the output pane as shown in Fig. 2. Users can copy and paste them with a single click to the right location of their proof scripts. The produced scripts are human readable, and Isabelle can check them without TBC.

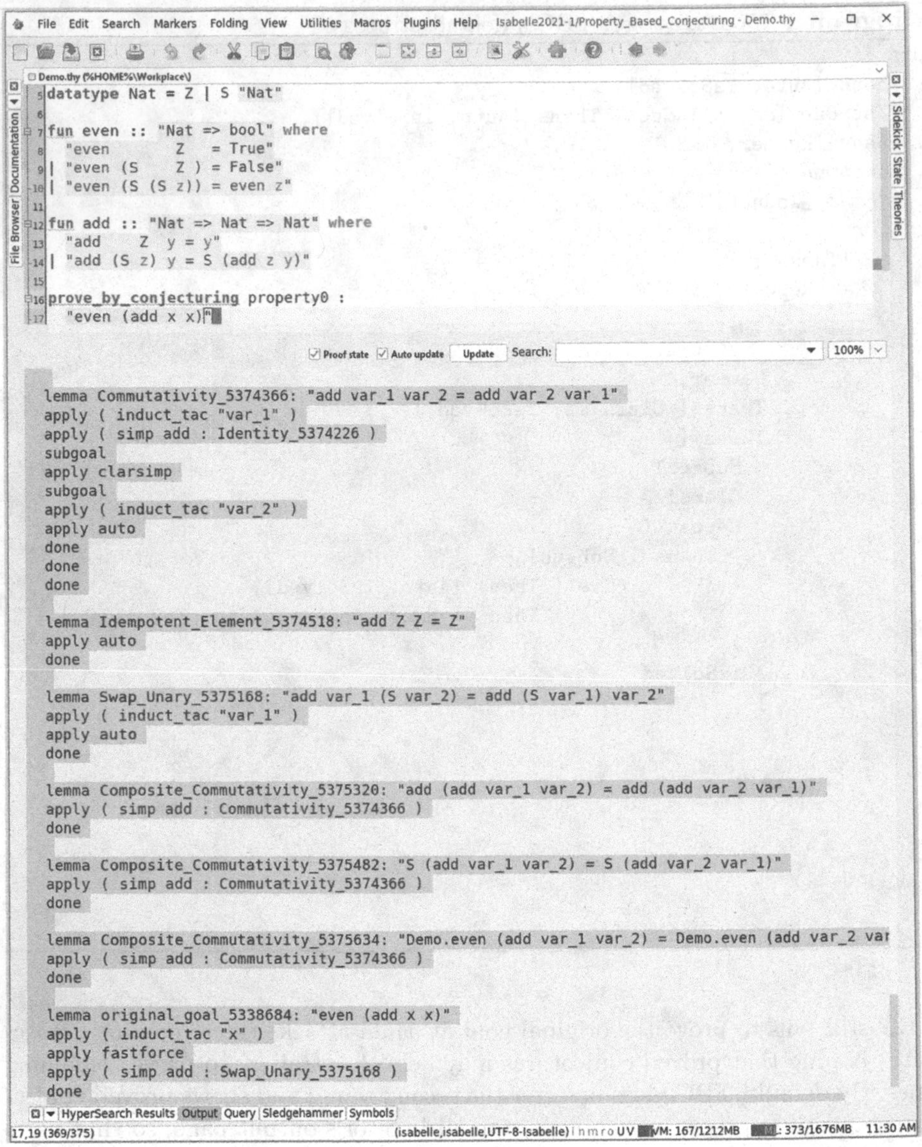

```
File  Edit  Search  Markers  Folding  View  Utilities  Macros  Plugins  Help    Isabelle2021-1/Property_Based_Conjecturing · Demo.thy    —   □   ×

  Demo.thy (%HOME%\Workplace\)
 5 datatype Nat = Z | S "Nat"
 6
 7 fun even :: "Nat => bool" where
 8   "even       Z    = True"
 9 | "even (S    Z ) = False"
10 | "even (S (S z)) = even z"
11
12 fun add :: "Nat => Nat => Nat" where
13   "add    Z  y = y"
14 | "add (S z) y = S (add z y)"
15
16 prove_by_conjecturing property0 :
17   "even (add x x)"

             ☑ Proof state  ☑ Auto update   Update    Search:                              ▼   100% ∨

  lemma Commutativity_5374366: "add var_1 var_2 = add var_2 var_1"
  apply ( induct_tac "var_1" )
  apply ( simp add : Identity_5374226 )
  subgoal
  apply clarsimp
  subgoal
  apply ( induct_tac "var_2" )
  apply auto
  done
  done
  done

  lemma Idempotent_Element_5374518: "add Z Z = Z"
  apply auto
  done

  lemma Swap_Unary_5375168: "add var_1 (S var_2) = add (S var_1) var_2"
  apply ( induct_tac "var_1" )
  apply auto
  done

  lemma Composite_Commutativity_5375320: "add (add var_1 var_2) = add (add var_2 var_1)"
  apply ( simp add : Commutativity_5374366 )
  done

  lemma Composite_Commutativity_5375482: "S (add var_1 var_2) = S (add var_2 var_1)"
  apply ( simp add : Commutativity_5374366 )
  done

  lemma Composite_Commutativity_5375634: "Demo.even (add var_1 var_2) = Demo.even (add var_2 var
  apply ( simp add : Commutativity_5374366 )
  done

  lemma original_goal_5338684: "even (add x x)"
  apply ( induct_tac "x" )
  apply fastforce
  apply ( simp add : Swap_Unary_5375168 )
  done

  □ ▼ HyperSearch Results  Output  Query  Sledgehammer  Symbols
17,19 (369/375)                       (isabelle,isabelle,UTF-8-Isabelle) i n m r o UV ■VM: 167/1212MB  ■■:373/1676MB  11:30 AM
```

Fig. 2. Screenshot of Isabelle/HOL with TBC. The upper pane shows the definition of a type and functions. The new command **prove_by_conjecturing** invokes TBC, which presents the proof script appearing in the lower pane.

Program 2 The Complete List of Template-Based Conjectures. We added the highlighted four conjectures after manually solving some benchmark problems. One can see that none of these conjectures are specific to particular problems.

`associativity`	$f (f (x, y), z) = f (x, f (y, z))$
`identity element`	$f (e, x) = x$ or $f (x, e) = x$ for some e
`commutativity`	$f (x, y) = f (y, x)$
`idempotent element`	$f (e, e) = e$ for some e
`idempotency`	$f (x, x) = x$
`distributivity`	$f (x, g (y, z)) = g (f (x, y), f (x, z))$
`anti-distributivity`	$f (g (x, y)) = g (f\ y, f\ x)$
`homomorphism`	$f (g (x, y)) = g (f\ x, f\ y)$
`transitivity`	$x\ R\ y \rightarrow y\ R\ z \rightarrow x\ R\ z$
`symmetry`	$x\ R\ y \rightarrow y\ R\ x$
`connexity`	$x\ R\ y \lor y\ R\ x \lor (x = y)$
`reflexivity`	$x\ R\ x$
`square`	$f (f\ x) = x$
`swap-unar`	$f (x, g\ y) = f (g\ x, y)$
`projection`	$f (f\ x) = f\ x$
`composite_commutativity`	$f (g (x, y)) = f (g (y, x))$

2.2 Template-Based Conjecturing

As mentioned in Sect. 2.1, our tool produces conjectures based on 16 templates specified in advance. 12 of them are either well-known algebraic properties, such as associative template, or relational properties, such as transitivity. Note that we added the 4 highlighted templates based on the feedback from students who manually solved several benchmark problems. None of these templates are specific to particular functions.

To produce conjectures for such templates, TBC first collects functions appearing in the original proof goal. Then, it looks for the definitions of these functions and adds functions in these definitions into the list of functions for conjecturing. Then, TBC filters out functions defined within the standard library since the standard library already contains useful auxiliary lemmas for them. Finally, TBC creates conjectures by filling templates with these functions.

3 Evaluation

3.1 Benchmark and Environment

We evaluated our tool using Tons of Inductive Problems (TIP) [6], which is a benchmark consisting of 462 inductive problems. TIP consists of three main problem sets: 85 problems in Isaplanner, 50 in Prod, and 327 in TIP15. Isaplanner is the easiest, whereas Prod contains problems at the intermediate difficulty level, and TIP15 has difficult problems, such as Fermat's Last Theorem.

The advantage of using TIP is that each problem is complete within a single file. That is, data types and functions are defined afresh within each problem file, instead of using the standard definition. For example, our running example problem from Sect. 1 is formalised as an independent Isabelle theory file in the Prod set in TIP. The functions, add and even, are defined afresh in this file, instead of using the default ones from the standard library. This allowed us to ignore manually developed lemmas for similar functions in the standard library. This way, by using TIP, we focused on TBC's conjecturing capability to prove the final goal.

In this experiment, we set the following timeouts for the counter-example generators: one second for Quickcheck, two seconds for Nitpick. The timeout for Sledgehammer is more flexible: 10 s when attacking conjectures in n-th round where n is an odd number, whereas 30 s when attacking conjectures in n-th round where n is an even number or attacking the original goals.

However, when measuring the performance of TBC against TIP15 problems, we set the following short timeouts to process 327 problems using computational resources available to us: 5 s for Sledgehammer to prove produced conjectures, 10 s for Sledgehammer to attack the original goal. Furthermore, We use 15 min as the overall timeout for each problem in TIP15.

We ran our evaluations on consumer-grade laptops. Specifically, we used a Lenovo Thinkpad T490s, with Intel Core i7-8665U CPU and 16GB of RAM. We used Windows 10 Pro as our evaluation operating system.

3.2   Results

Success Rates for Different Difficulty Levels. Fig. 3 shows the percentage of problems proved by each tool at each stage. We use an induction prover for Isabelle/HOL [16], TAP21, as our baseline prover. "Round0" represents the percentage of solved problems after the zeroth round of TBC, where TBC shows the percentage of solved problems after the second round for Isaplanner and Prod, but after the first round for TIP15 due to our limited computational resources.

The figure shows that TBC brought the largest improvement (50% points) to the Prod category. On the other hand, we can prove 60% of problems in Isaplanner without producing conjectures, while TBC struggles at harder problems in the TIP15 category.

Proof Completion Rates and Execution Time. Figures 4, 5, and 6 show the chances of solving a problem in each category relative to how long the program is run. For example, Fig. 5 illustrates that approximately 20% of the problems are solved within 5 min in the Prod category, and 60% of the problems are solved within 20 min of runtime. Beyond this time, the chances of producing a proof increase marginally, reaching 66% of problems after an hour.

Refuting and Proving. Figure 7 and Fig. 8 show how many conjectures TBC produced for each problem in Isaplanner and Prod and how it handled them, respectively. As shown in the figure, TBC did not produce any conjectures for some problems, since it proved these problems even before producing conjectures. Furthermore, the number of conjectures does not blow up in TBC, since TBC

Program 3 TAP_2021 is the strategy used in the baseline prover introduced by Nagashima [16]. Since we added minor improvements to Smart_Induct, we represent their version of Smart_Induct as Old_Smart_Induct in this paper.

```
Ors [
  Auto_Solve,
  PThenOne [Old_Smart_Induct, Auto_Solve],
  PThenOne [Old_Smart_Induct,
    Thens [ Auto, RepeatN (Hammer), IsSolved ]
  ]
]
```

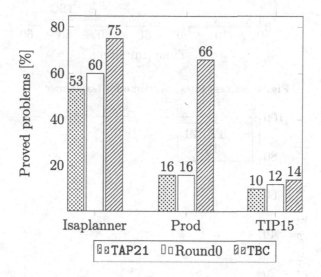

Fig. 3. Proof completion rates.

produces conjectures about commonly used properties only. Note that keeping the number of conjectures low is the main challenge in other conjecturing tools, as we discuss in Sect. 4. Moreover, these figures show that most conjectures are either proved or refuted for problems in Isaplanner and Prod, and only a few conjectures are left unsolved thanks to the strong default strategy and counter-example finders.

4   Related Work

Conjecturing. We have two schools of conjecturing to automate inductive theorem proving: top-down approaches and bottom-up approaches. Top-down approaches [3,4,18] create auxiliary lemmas from an ongoing proof attempt, whereas bottom-up approaches [5,10] produce lemmas from available functions and data types to enrich the background theory [11]. TBC falls into the latter

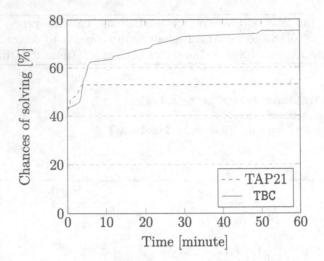

Fig. 4. Success rates over time for Isaplanner.

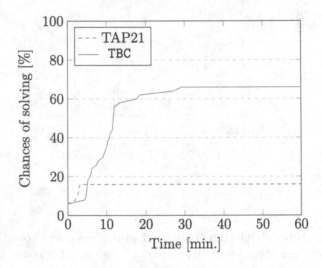

Fig. 5. Success rates over time for Prod.

category. While most bottom-up tools, such as HipSpec [5] and Hipster [10], produce conjectures randomly, TBC makes conjectures based on a fixed set of templates. Furthermore, Hipster aims to *discover* new lemmas, TBC checks for *known* properties to keep the number of conjectures low. In this respect, Rough-Spec [7] is similar to TBC: it produces conjectures based on templates, which describe important properties. Contrary to TBC, RoughSpec supports only equations as templates and is a tool for Haskell rather than a proof assistant.

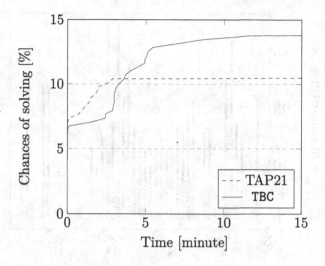

Fig. 6. Success rates over time for TIP15.

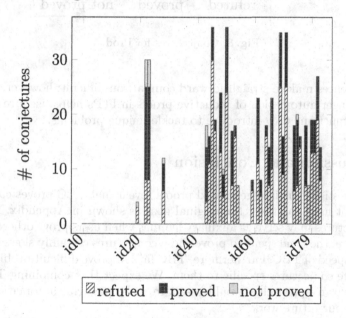

Fig. 7. Conjectures for Isaplanner.

Inductive Theorem Proving. TBC is an automatic tool developed for an interactive theorem prover (ITP) based on a higher-order logic. Others have introduced proof by induction for automatic theorem provers (ATPs) [9,12,20,22,23]. ATPs are typically based on less expressive logics and use different proof calculi compared to LCF-style provers. Moreover, ATPs are built for performance, whereas LCF-style provers are designed for high assurance and easy user-interaction.

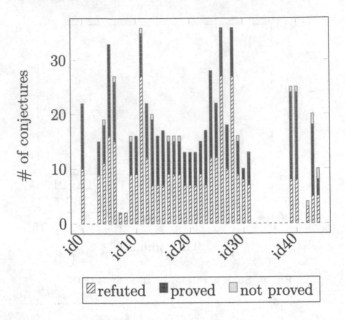

Fig. 8. Conjectures for Prod.

Such differences make a straightforward comparison difficult; however, we argue that a stronger automation of inductive proofs in ITPs helps users reason data types and functions they introduce to tackle unique problems.

5   Discussion and Conclusion

Careful investigations into generated proofs reveal that TBC proves conjectures that are not used to attack the original goal as shown in Appendix. Although such conjectures may serve as auxiliary lemmas when users prove other problems in the future, the time spent to prove these conjectures certainly slows down the execution speed of TBC. Furthermore, TBC fails to prove difficult problems since they require conjectures specific to them. We expect that combining TBC with other top-down approaches would result in more powerful automation, which remains as our future work.

This paper presented our template-based conjecturing tool, TBC. To the best of our knowledge, TBC is the only tool that achieved high proof completion rates for the TIP benchmarks while producing human readable proofs that are native to a widely used ITP.

In this work we used 12 commonly known algebraic properties and 4 manually identified useful conjectures as our templates. It remains our future work to incorporate templates that are found automatically by analysing large databases [8] into our framework.

Appendix

Program 4 Generated Proof Script for Our Running Example

```
lemma associativity_5382114:
  "add var_1 (add var_2 var_3) = add (add var_1 var_2) var_3"
  apply ( induct "var_1" arbitrary : var_2 ) apply auto done
lemma associativity_5382286:
  "add (add var_1 var_2) var_3 = add var_1 (add var_2 var_3)"
  apply ( induct "var_1" arbitrary : var_2 ) apply auto done
lemma identity_5382450: "add 0 var_1 = var_1" apply auto done
lemma identity_5382590: "add var_1 0 = var_1"
  apply ( induct_tac "var_1" ) apply auto done
lemma commutativity_5382730:
  "add var_1 var_2 = add var_2 var_1" apply ( induct_tac "var_1" )
  apply ( simp add : identity_5382590 )
  subgoal apply clarsimp subgoal apply ( induct_tac "var_2" )
  apply auto done done done
lemma idempotent_Element_5382882: "add 0 0 = 0" apply auto done
lemma swap_Unary_5383532: "add var_1 (S var_2) = add (S var_1) var_2"
  apply ( induct_tac "var_1" ) apply auto done
lemma composite_Commutativity_5383684:
  "add (add var_1 var_2) = add (add var_2 var_1)"
  apply ( simp add : commutativity_5382730 ) done
lemma composite_Commutativity_5383846:
  "S (add var_1 var_2) = S (add var_2 var_1)"
  apply ( simp add : commutativity_5382730 ) done
lemma composite_Commutativity_5383998:
  "even (add var_1 var_2) = even (add var_2 var_1)"
  apply ( simp add : commutativity_5382730 ) done
lemma original_goal_5347090: "even (add x x)" apply ( induct_tac "x" )
  apply fastforce apply ( metis Nat.distinct ( 1 ) Nat.inject
  even.simps(3) commutativity_5382730 add.elims ) done
```

Program 4 shows the output of TBC for our running example. The original goal is proved using `commutativity_5382730`, which is in turn proved using `identity_5382590`. 8 out of 10 proved conjectures are not used to prove the final goal; however, TBC outputs them, so that users may exploit them in future.

References

1. Blanchette, J.C., Nipkow, T.: Nitpick: a counterexample generator for higher-order logic based on a relational model finder. In: Kaufmann, M., Paulson, L.C. (eds.) ITP 2010. LNCS, vol. 6172, pp. 131–146. Springer, Heidelberg (2010). https://doi.org/10.1007/978-3-642-14052-5_11

2. Bulwahn, L.: The new quickcheck for isabelle. In: Hawblitzel, C., Miller, D. (eds.) CPP 2012. LNCS, vol. 7679, pp. 92–108. Springer, Heidelberg (2012). https://doi.org/10.1007/978-3-642-35308-6_10

3. Bundy, A., Basin, D.A., Hutter, D., Ireland, A.: Rippling - meta-level guidance for mathematical reasoning, Cambridge tracts in theoretical computer science, vol. 56. Cambridge University Press, Cambridge (2005)

4. Bundy, A., van Harmelen, F., Horn, C., Smaill, A.: The O^YS^TER-CL^AM system. In: Stickel, M.E. (ed.) CADE 1990. LNCS, vol. 449, pp. 647–648. Springer, Heidelberg (1990). https://doi.org/10.1007/3-540-52885-7_123

5. Claessen, K., Johansson, M., Rosén, D., Smallbone, N.: HipSpec: automating inductive proofs of program properties. In: Fleuriot, J.D., Höfner, P., McIver, A., Smaill, A. (eds.) ATx 2012/WInG'12: Joint Proceedings of the Workshops on Automated Theory eXploration and on Invariant Generation, Manchester, UK, June 2012. EPiC Series in Computing, vol. 17, pp. 16–25. EasyChair (2012). https://doi.org/10.29007/3qwr

6. Claessen, K., Johansson, M., Rosén, D., Smallbone, N.: TIP: tons of inductive problems. In: Kerber, M., Carette, J., Kaliszyk, C., Rabe, F., Sorge, V. (eds.) CICM 2015. LNCS (LNAI), vol. 9150, pp. 333–337. Springer, Cham (2015). https://doi.org/10.1007/978-3-319-20615-8_23

7. Einarsdóttir, S.H., Smallbone, N., Johansson, M.: Template-based theory exploration: discovering properties of functional programs by testing. In: Chitil, O. (ed.) IFL 2020: 32nd Symposium on Implementation and Application of Functional Languages, Virtual Event/Canterbury, UK, 2-4 September 2020, pp. 67–78. ACM (2020). https://doi.org/10.1145/3462172.3462192

8. Einarsdóttir, S.H., Johansson, M., Smallbone, N.: LOL: A library of lemma templates for data-driven conjecturing. In: Buzzard, K., Kutsia, T. (eds.) Work-in-progress papers presented at the 15th Conference on Intelligent Computer Mathematics (CICM 2022) Informal Proceedings (2022). http://www3.risc.jku.at/publications/download/risc_6584/proceedings-CICM2022-informal.pdf#page=28

9. Hajdú, M., Hozzová, P., Kovács, L., Voronkov, A.: Induction with recursive definitions in superposition. In: Formal Methods in Computer Aided Design, FMCAD 2021, New Haven, CT, USA, October 19-22, 2021, pp. 1–10. IEEE (2021). https://doi.org/10.34727/2021/isbn.978-3-85448-046-4_34

10. Johansson, M.: Automated theory exploration for interactive theorem proving. In: Ayala-Rincón, M., Muñoz, C.A. (eds.) ITP 2017. LNCS, vol. 10499, pp. 1–11. Springer, Cham (2017). https://doi.org/10.1007/978-3-319-66107-0_1

11. Johansson, M.: Lemma discovery for induction. In: Kaliszyk, C., Brady, E., Kohlhase, A., Sacerdoti Coen, C. (eds.) CICM 2019. LNCS (LNAI), vol. 11617, pp. 125–139. Springer, Cham (2019). https://doi.org/10.1007/978-3-030-23250-4_9

12. Kaufmann, M., Panagiotis Manolios, J.S.M. (ed.): Computer-Aided Reasoning ACL2 Case Studies. Advances in Formal Methods, Springer, New York, NY (2000). https://doi.org/10.1007/978-1-4757-3188-0

13. Nagashima, Y.: LiFtEr: language to encode induction heuristics for Isabelle/HOL. In: Lin, A.W. (ed.) APLAS 2019. LNCS, vol. 11893, pp. 266–287. Springer, Cham (2019). https://doi.org/10.1007/978-3-030-34175-6_14

14. Nagashima, Y.: Smart induction for Isabelle/HOL (tool paper). In: 2020 Formal Methods in Computer Aided Design, FMCAD 2020, Haifa, Israel, 21-24 September 2020, pp. 245–254. IEEE (2020). https://doi.org/10.34727/2020/isbn.978-3-85448-042-6_32

15. Nagashima, Y.: Faster smarter proof by induction in Isabelle/HOL. In: Zhou, Z. (ed.) Proceedings of the Thirtieth International Joint Conference on Artificial Intelligence, IJCAI 2021, Virtual Event / Montreal, Canada, 19-27 August 2021, pp. 1981–1988. ijcai.org (2021). https://doi.org/10.24963/ijcai.2021/273

16. Nagashima, Y.: Definitional quantifiers realise semantic reasoning for proof by induction. In: Kovács, L., Meinke, K. (eds.) Tests and Proofs - 16th International Conference, TAP 2022, Held as Part of STAF 2022, Nantes, France, July 5, 2022, Proceedings, LNCS, vol. 13361, pp. 48–66. Springer, Cham (2022). https://doi.org/10.1007/978-3-031-09827-7_4

17. Nagashima, Y., Kumar, R.: A proof strategy language and proof script generation for Isabelle/HOL. In: de Moura, L. (ed.) CADE 2017. LNCS (LNAI), vol. 10395, pp. 528–545. Springer, Cham (2017). https://doi.org/10.1007/978-3-319-63046-5_32

18. Nagashima, Y., Parsert, J.: Goal-oriented conjecturing for Isabelle/HOL. In: Rabe, F., Farmer, W.M., Passmore, G.O., Youssef, A. (eds.) CICM 2018. LNCS (LNAI), vol. 11006, pp. 225–231. Springer, Cham (2018). https://doi.org/10.1007/978-3-319-96812-4_19

19. Nipkow, T., Wenzel, M., Paulson, L.C. (eds.): Isabelle/HOL. LNCS, vol. 2283. Springer, Heidelberg (2002). https://doi.org/10.1007/3-540-45949-9

20. Passmore, G., et al.: The Imandra automated reasoning system (System description). In: Peltier, N., Sofronie-Stokkermans, V. (eds.) IJCAR 2020. LNCS (LNAI), vol. 12167, pp. 464–471. Springer, Cham (2020). https://doi.org/10.1007/978-3-030-51054-1_30

21. Paulson, L.C., Blanchette, J.C.: Three years of experience with sledgehammer, a practical link between automatic and interactive theorem provers. In: Sutcliffe, G., Schulz, S., Ternovska, E. (eds.) The 8th International Workshop on the Implementation of Logics, IWIL 2010, Yogyakarta, Indonesia, October 9, 2011. EPiC Series in Computing, vol. 2, pp. 1–11. EasyChair (2010). https://doi.org/10.29007/36dt

22. Reger, G., Voronkov, A.: Induction in saturation-based proof search. In: Fontaine, P. (ed.) CADE 2019. LNCS (LNAI), vol. 11716, pp. 477–494. Springer, Cham (2019). https://doi.org/10.1007/978-3-030-29436-6_28

23. Reynolds, A., Kuncak, V.: Induction for SMT solvers. In: D'Souza, D., Lal, A., Larsen, K.G. (eds.) VMCAI 2015. LNCS, vol. 8931, pp. 80–98. Springer, Heidelberg (2015). https://doi.org/10.1007/978-3-662-46081-8_5

Verification of the Busy-Forbidden Protocol
(using an Extension of the Cones and Foci Proof Framework)

P. H. M. van Spaendonck[✉][iD]

Department of Mathematics and Computer Science,
Eindhoven University of Technology, Eindhoven, Netherlands
P.H.M.v.Spaendonck@tue.nl

Abstract. The busy-forbidden protocol is a new readers-writer lock
with no resource contention between readers, which allows it to out-
perform other locks. For its verification, specifications of its implementation and its less complex external behavior are provided by the original
authors but are only proven equivalent for up to 7 threads.

We provide a general equivalence proof using the cones and foci proof
framework, which rephrases whether two specifications are branching
bisimilar as six properties on the data objects of the specifications. We
provide an extension of this framework consisting of four additional properties and prove that when the additional properties hold, the two systems are divergence-preserving branching bisimilar, a stronger version of
the aforementioned relation that also distinguishes livelocks.

Keywords: cones and foci proof framework · divergence-preserving
branching bisimulation · process algebra · protocol verification ·
readers-writer lock

1 Introduction

The readers-writer lock problem is a concurrency problem introduced and solved
by Courtois et al. [5]. The problem requires a synchronisation protocol that provides safe access to both a shared readers section, which can be used simultaneously by any number of threads, as well as an exclusive writer section, which
can not be used by more than one thread at any given time and only when the
readers section is not in use.

In [9], Groote et al. introduce a new readers-writer lock called the busy-
forbidden protocol. This locking protocol is of particular interest as it has no
resource contention between readers, and therefore provides a significant speedup
over other locks when having high readers section workloads.

To ensure the correctness of the protocol, the authors give process algebraic
specifications of both the implementation of the new algorithm as well as a

This publication is part of the PVSR project (with project number 17933) of the
MasCot research programme which is financed by the Dutch Research Council (NWO).

specification of its external behavior. The authors applied model checking and proved the implementation and external behavior equivalent for up to 7 threads using the mCRL2 toolset [4], but they were unable to do this for more concurrent threads due to the statespace of the implementation becoming too large.

But as readers-writer locks often use a large number of concurrent threads, a general correctness proof for the busy-forbidden protocol is desired. We opt to prove the process algebraic specifications of the implementation and external behavior to be equivalent. The advantage of this technique over contract-based approaches, such as Floyd-Hoare logic [12], and its extension for parallel composed systems by Owicki and Gries [15,16], is that the much smaller equivalent model can also be used for the modeling and verification of systems built on top of the busy-forbidden protocol. We consider this a significant advantage, as this is the typical use-case for readers-writer locks, e.g. the parallel term library which the protocol was originally designed for.

We prove the equivalence of the implementation and its external behavior by using the cones and foci proof framework, originally proposed in [11] by Groote and Springintveld and later generalized by Fokkink et al. in [6]. This framework simplifies the often complex and cumbersome branching bisimulation proof by reducing it to a small set of propositions on the data objects occurring in the implementation and specification. If these propositions are shown to hold, it follows that the two systems are equivalent modulo branching bisimulation.

The proof framework has already been used in several case studies to prove implementation and specification models equivalent, such as the verification of the 1-bit sliding window protocol in [2], a complex leader election protocol in [7], and a part of the IEEE P1394 high-speed bus protocol [1] in [17].

Since the equivalence relation proven by the cones and foci proof framework does not distinguish livelock, we first provide an extension to the framework such that it can also be used to prove equivalence modulo divergence-preserving branching bisimulation. This relation is a stronger version of branching bisimulation that does distinguish livelocks [8]. Our extension provides four additional propositions on the data objects in the implementation and specification models, that, when shown to also hold, imply the equivalence of the two processes modulo divergence-preserving branching bisimulation. We give a soundness proof of this extension and use it to prove the equivalence of implementation and specification of the busy-forbidden protocol.

2   The Busy-Forbidden Protocol

We first discuss the busy-forbidden protocol. An overview of its implementation using pseudocode is given in Table 1. The enter_- and leave_shared functions are used to have a thread p enter or leave the readers section. Similarly, enter_- and leave_exclusive provide functionality for safe access to the writer section.

The protocol uses two binary flags per thread and a single mutex. The first flag, the *busy* flag, indicates that a thread is either working or going to work inside of the readers section. The second flag, the *forbidden* flag, indicates that a thread is not allowed to enter the readers section. All flags are initially set to *false*. The mutex, called *mutex*, enforces exclusive access to the writer section.

Table 1. Pseudocode description of the busy-forbidden protocol

enter_shared(*thread p*) :	enter_exclusive(*thread p*) :
p.*busy* := *true*;	*mutex.lock*();
while p.*forbidden*	**while** exists *thread q* **with**
p.*busy* := *false*;	¬q.*forbidden*
if *mutex.timed_lock*()	**select** *thread r*
mutex.unlock();	r.*forbidden* := *true*;
p.*busy* := *true*;	**if** r.*busy* **or sometimes**
	r.*forbidden* := *false*;
leave_shared(*thread p*) :	leave_exclusive(*thread p*) :
p.*busy* := *false*;	**while** exists *thread q* **with**
	q.*forbidden*
	select *thread r*
	usually do
	r.*forbidden* := *false*;
	sometimes do
	r.*forbidden* := *true*
	mutex.unlock();

When entering the readers section, a thread sets its *busy* flag and enters iff its *forbidden* flag is *false*. If the *forbidden* flag is *true*, the *busy* flag is set back to *false* to avoid deadlock and the process is repeated again. To reduce resource contention on the flags, a *mutex.timed_lock*() can be used without altering the externally visible behavior of the protocol [9]. Upon leaving the readers section, the thread sets its *busy* flag back to false.

A thread that wants to enter the writer section must first acquire the mutex. This ensures that no other thread can be in the writer section simultaneously and that only the given thread is altering the *forbidden* flags. Once the mutex has been acquired, the thread sets the *forbidden* flag of each thread, but will immediately undo this if the *busy* flag of the same thread is *true*. To prevent a thread that is acquiring the writer section from locking out some reader threads while still waiting for others to leave the readers section, random *forbidden* flags can sometimes be set back to *false*. The writer section is entered once all *forbidden* flags are *true*. Upon leaving, all *forbidden* flags are set back to false and the mutex is released. During this, random *forbidden* flags can be set back to *true*. This prevents each iteration that occurs while leaving, from becoming externally visible and significantly reduces the number of states in the external specification.

The externally visible behavior of the protocol is given in Fig. 1 and, as we will prove later, provides an equivalent overview of how threads interact via the protocol. Individual threads move from node to node. Transition labels ending with `call` represent the identically named function being called by a thread moving across, and those ending with `return` represent those function calls terminating. All transitions not labeled as such represent some sequence of internal calculations that occurs during these function calls. Transitions labeled with a guard, i.e. starting with **if**, only allow a thread to progress if the given condition is met.

The *Free* node represents a thread not interacting with the protocol and being outside of any section. Each thread initially starts out in this node. The *Shared* and *Exclusive* nodes represent the readers and writer sections, respectively.

A thread starting to acquire the readers lock enters the *EnterShared (ES)* node. The thread stays in the *ES* node as long as its *forbidden* flag is *true*. As repeatedly checking the flag is discouraged through the *timed_lock* call, the internal loop is labeled as *improbable*. When the *forbidden* flag is evaluated to *false*, the thread moves to the *LockedOffExclusive (LOE)* node. After this, it is no longer possible for any other thread to enter the writer section until the readers section is completely freed. The *LeaveShared (LS)* node represents a thread leaving this section.

When a thread tries to acquire the writer lock, it enters the *EnterExclusive (EE)* node. Once the thread acquires the *mutex* variable, it will move to the *SetAllForbidden (SAF)* node and it will not be possible for any other thread to acquire the writer lock before it is released by this thread. The loop in the *SAF* node represents a *forbidden* flag being set back to *false*; this transition is labeled as *improbable* as this only rarely occurs. Once the last *busy* flag is evaluated to *false*, exclusive access is attained and the thread will move to the *LockedOutShared (LOS)* node before officially terminating the function call.

When the thread starts releasing the writer lock, it enters the *LeavingExclusive (LE)* node. Similar to the *SAF* node, a thread within the *LE* node can repeatedly turn the *forbid-*

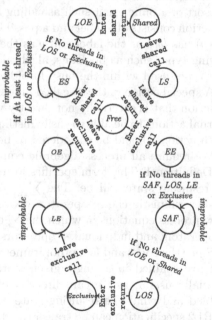

Fig. 1. The external behaviour

den flag off and on again, thus never fully opening up the readers section. Because a *forbidden* flag is only very rarely set back to *true* when releasing the lock, this transition is also labeled as *improbable*. Once the last *forbidden* flag is set to *false*, this is no longer possible and the thread moves to the *OpenedExclusive*

(*OE*) node, after which it will officially terminate the function call and move back to the *Free* node.

We can use the model of the external behavior to reason about certain safety properties. For example, from the guarded transitions from *ES* to *LOE* and from *SAF* to *LOS*, we can quickly see that the *Shared* and *Exclusive* sections can not be populated simultaneously, as they require the other respective section to be empty. The guarded transition from *EE* to *SAF* also assures that only a single thread can be present in the *Exclusive* section at any given time.

3 Linear Process Equations

Both the implementation of the pseudocode shown in Table 1 and the external behavior have been modeled in the mCRL2 language [10]. The mCRL2 language is based on the Algebra of Communicating Processes [3] and Calculus of Communicating Processes [14].

The mCRL2 language models processes using a combination of states and actions. States represent a collection of internal values that are used to calculate which actions can occur and what the resulting state will be. Actions represent any sort of atomic event such as calling a function, or setting or reading a flag. An action consists of a label and a possible set of data parameters, e.g. the action *lock*(*p*) has *lock* as the label and *p* as the data parameter. Parameters can be of varying types such as booleans, algebraic data types, and mappings. The exact data types used within the busy-forbidden models are given later.

A special action τ, the so-called hidden or internal action, is used to represent an action that is externally not directly visible. We use distinct action labels for internal actions to be able to easily distinguish between them. We explicitly state which actions should be considered to be τ actions.

We require all process algebraic equations to be in a clustered linear form, see Definition 1. This form specifies for each action when it can occur and what the resulting state will be. The $\sum_{e:S}$ operator models the application of the non-deterministic choice operator $+$ over all elements in some set S. We also allow process equations in which the $\sum$ operators are split into separate smaller $\sum$ operators and individual $+$ operators.

Since the cones and foci proof framework concerns itself only with the actions that are enabled in a single given state, the clustered normal form becomes especially useful, as we can directly infer for any given state if an action is enabled and what the resulting state will be. In [19], Usenko shows that any mCRL2 specification can be transformed into a clustered linear process equation.

Definition 1. A clustered linear process equation (LPE) is a process specification of the form:

$$X(d{:}D) = \sum_{a:Act} \sum_{e_a:E_a} c_a(d, e_a) \rightarrow a(f_a(d, e_a)) \cdot X(g_a(d, e_a)),$$

where D is the set of states, Act is the set of action labels including τ, E_a is an indexed set of all data types that need to be considered for label a, the boolean function $c_a(d, e_a)$ specifies when the action a with parameters resulting from the function $f_a(d, e_a)$ is enabled in state d, and $g_a(d, e_a)$ gives the resulting state from taking this action from state d.

Often we end up in a situation in which the set of states D also contains unreachable states. As we are only interested in the reachable states, we introduce the notion of an invariant in Definition 2. An invariant is a predicate on states in an LPE such that when it holds for a given state $d{:}D$, it also holds for all subsequent states.

Definition 2. Given a clustered *LPE* X as per Definition 1. A predicate $\mathcal{I}$ on the set of states D is called an invariant iff the following holds: for all $a{:}Act, d{:}D$ and $e_a{:}E_a$,

$$\mathcal{I}(d) \wedge c_a(d, e_a) \Rightarrow \mathcal{I}(g_a(d, e_a))$$

4   Equivalence and the Cones and Foci Proof Framework

As stated before, we prove the model of the implementation and the specification of the busy-forbidden protocol equivalent modulo divergence-preserving branching bisimulation. We define this equivalence relation in Definition 4, which is based on the definitions used in [13] and has been adapted to work with process equations instead of transition systems. In Definition 3, we provide some syntactic glue to make this shift between labeled transition systems and clustered LPEs more intuitive.

Definition 3. Given a clustered LPE as per Definition 1, states $d, d' \in D$, and action l, we define the following relations:

- $d \xrightarrow{l} d'$ iff there is an action a with an associated data type e_a such that $l = a(f_a(d, e_a))$, the condition $c_a(d, e_a)$ holds, and $g_a(d, e_a) = d'$.
- $d \xrightarrow{l}{}^* d'$ iff there is a finite sequence of states $d_0, \ldots, d_k$ such that $d_0 = d$, $d_k = d'$ and for all $0 \leq i < k$ we have $d_i \xrightarrow{l} d_{i+1}$.

Definition 4. Given two clustered LPEs as per Definition 1 with sets of states D and D'. A relation R on the states $D \times D'$ is a divergence-preserving branching bisimulation iff the following conditions for all states $s \in D$, $t \in D'$, and actions $l \in Act$ hold:

(B_1) If sRt and $s \xrightarrow{l} s'$ for some state $s' \in D$, then either $l = \tau$ and $s'Rt$, or there are states $t', t'' \in D'$ such that $t \xrightarrow{\tau}{}^* t' \xrightarrow{l} t''$, sRt', and $s'Rt''$.

(B_2) If sRt and $t \xrightarrow{l} t'$ for some state $t' \in D'$, then either $l = \tau$ and sRt', or there are states $s', s'' \in D$ such that $s \xrightarrow{\tau}{}^* s' \xrightarrow{l} s''$, $s'Rt$, and $s''Rt'$.

(D_1) If sRt and there is an infinite sequence of states $(s_n)_{n \in \mathbb{N}}$ such that $s = s_0$, and $s_k \xrightarrow{\tau} s_{k+1}$ and s_kRt for all $k \in \mathbb{N}$, then there is a state $t' \in D'$ such that $t \xrightarrow{\tau} t'$, and s_kRt' for some $k \in \mathbb{N}$.

(D_2) If sRt and there is an infinite sequence of states $(t_n)_{n\in\mathbb{N}}$ such that $t = t_0$, and $t_k \xrightarrow{\tau} t_{k+1}$ and sRt_k for all $k \in \mathbb{N}$, then there is a state $s' \in D$ such that $s \xrightarrow{\tau} s'$, and $s'Rt_k$ for some $k \in \mathbb{N}$.

Two clustered LPEs with respective initial states d_0 and d'_0 are *divergence-preserving branching bisimilar* iff there is a divergence-preserving branching bisimulation R such that $d_0 R d'_0$.

Note that in (divergence-preserving) branching bisimulation, τ-actions are said to be externally visible iff their begin- and endpoint are not equivalent.

In [11], it is noted that in communicating systems, equivalent states often have a "cone-like" structure as is shown in Fig. 2. In this figure, equivalent states are grouped together in the *cone C*. In the *focus point* state *fc*, all externally visible actions of said cone, i.e. a and b, are enabled. For all other states in which not all externally visible actions are simultaneously enabled, such as d or the states along the edges, there is always a path of *internal actions*, i.e. τ actions within the cone, that ends in the state *fc*. We show one such path for the state d, using the dashed arrows.

If a given system consists of such "cones", the cones and foci proof framework can be used to prove equivalence. To do so, we must provide a *state mapping* $h : D \to D'$ that maps states in the implementation to their equivalent state in the specification, a *focus condition* $FC : D \to \mathbb{B}$ that indicates if a state should be considered a focus point, i.e. all externally observable actions are enabled, and a

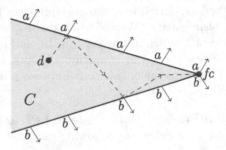

Fig. 2. A cone C with focus point fc

well-founded ordering $<_M$ on D that orders states by their distance to a focus point. We must then prove that a small set of requirements are met by the LPEs and the provided *state mapping, focus condition* and ordering.

Any τ action in the implementation that does not leave a cone, i.e. the state mapping h maps begin- and endpoint to the same state, is renamed to *int* (short for *internal* action). This allows us to easily distinguish between τ actions that are externally observable, i.e. that are preserved in our specification, and those that are not. While an *int* action is considered a τ action, we exclude them from the set of actions *Act*.

In Theorem 1, we extend the proof framework towards divergence-preserving branching bisimulation with a labeling p on cones that labels cones as either divergent (Δ) or non-divergent (∇), and four additional requirements on the LPEs. The divergent τ-loops in the specification, i.e. a τ transition with the same begin- and endpoint, are renamed to *int* to relate these to the divergent internal behavior in the implementation, i.e. repeatable paths of *int* actions.

Theorem 1. Consider a clustered linear process equation of an implementation with initial state d_0 and some invariant $\mathcal{I}$ that holds in d_0,

$$X(d{:}D) = \sum_{a:Act\cup\{int\}} \sum_{e_a:E_a} c_a(d, e_a) \rightarrow a(f_a(d, e_a)) \cdot X(g_a(d, e_a)),$$

and a clustered linear process equation of a specification with initial state d'_0,

$$Y(d'{:}D') = \sum_{a:Act\cup\{int\}} \sum_{e_a:E_a} c'_a(d', e_a) \rightarrow a(f'_a(d', e_a)) \cdot Y(g'_a(d', e_a)).$$

The LPEs X and Y are divergence-preserving branching bismilar if there is a *state mapping* $h : D \rightarrow D'$, a *focus condition* $FC : D \rightarrow \mathbb{B}$, a well founded ordering $<_M$ on D, and a cone labeling $p : D' \rightarrow \{\Delta, \nabla\}$ such that $h(d_0) = d'_0$ and the following requirements hold for all states $d{:}D$ in which invariant $\mathcal{I}$ holds:

I If not a focus point, there is at least one internal step such that the target state is closer to the focus point:

$$(\neg FC(d)) \Rightarrow (\exists e_{int}{:}E_{int}.\ c_{int}(d, e_{int}) \wedge g_{int}(d, e_{int}) <_M d)$$

II For every internal step, the mapping h maps source and target states to the same states in the specification:

$$\forall e_{int}{:}E_{int}.c_{int}(d, e_{int}) \Rightarrow h(d) = h(g_{int}(d, e_{int}))$$

III Every visible action in the specification must be enabled after a finite number of *int* actions for each corresponding focus point: For all $a{:}Act$

$$\forall e_a{:}E_a.(FC(d) \wedge c'_a(h(d), e_a)) \Rightarrow (\exists d_{int}{:}D.d \xrightarrow{int}{}^* d_{int} \wedge c_a(d_{int}, e_a))$$

IV Every visible action in the implementation must be mimicked in the corresponding state in the specification: For all $a{:}Act$

$$\forall e_a{:}E_a.c_a(d, e_a) \Rightarrow c'_a(h(d), e_a)$$

V Matching actions have matching parameters: For all $a{:}Act$

$$\forall e_a{:}E_a.c_a(d, e_a) \Rightarrow f_a(d, e_a) = f'_a(h(d), e_a)$$

VI For all matching actions in specification and implementation, their endpoints must be related: For all $a{:}Act$

$$\forall e_a{:}E_a.c_a(d, e_a) \Rightarrow h(g_a(d, e_a)) = g'_a(h(d), e_a)$$

I$_\Delta$ Any internal action in the specification is part of an *int*-loop:

$$\forall e_{int}{:}E_{int}.c'_{int}(h(d), e_{int}) \Rightarrow g'_{int}(h(d), e_{int}) = h(d)$$

II$_\Delta$ The cone labeling indicates whether or not a specification state allows an *int*-loop:

$$p(h(d)) = \Delta \Leftrightarrow (\exists e_{int}{:}E_{int}.\ c'_{int}(h(d), e_{int}))$$

III$_\Delta$ A cone is labelled as divergent if and only if it is possible to take an internal action in its focus points:

$$FC(d) \Rightarrow (p(h(d)) = \Delta \Leftrightarrow \exists e_{int}{:}E_{int}.c_{int}(d, e_{int}))$$

IV$_\Delta$ All internal transitions within a non-divergent cone must bring us closer to a focus point:

$$\forall e_{int}{:}E_{int}.((p(h(d)) = \nabla \wedge c_{int}(d, e_{int})) \Rightarrow g_{int}(d, e_{int}) <_M d)$$

Proof. We define $R \subseteq D \times D'$ as $\{\langle d, h(d)\rangle \mid d \in D \wedge \mathcal{I}(d)\}$.

Proving that R is a branching bisimulation, i.e. proving conditions B_1 and B_2 from Defininition 4, follows the same general proof structure as is used in both [6], and [11]. We give a concise proof sketch.

Condition B_1. Consider the states $d, d'{:}D$, and label $l{:}Act \cup \{int\}$ such that $d \xrightarrow{a} d'$. As per Requirement II , if $l = int$ then $h(d) = h(d')$. If $l \neq int$, then we have $h(d) \xrightarrow{l} h(d')$ as per Requirement IV , and VI.

Condition B_2. Consider the states $d{:}D, d'_2{:}D'$, and label $l{:}Act \cup \{int\}$ such that $h(d) \xrightarrow{l} d'_2$. If $l = int$, then $h(d'_2) = h(d)$, as per Requirement I$_\Delta$. If $l \neq int$, then there is a state $d_2{:}D$ such that $d \xrightarrow{int}{}^* d_2$ and $FC(d_2)$ as per Requirement I and $<_M$ being well founded. As per Requirements III and VI, there are states $d_3, d_4{:}D$ such that $d \xrightarrow{int}{}^* d_2 \xrightarrow{int}{}^* d_3 \xrightarrow{l} d_4$ and $h(d_4) = d'_2$. From Requirement II follows that all states along the *int* path are related to $h(d)$.

We show that the branching bisimulation R is also divergence-preserving by proving the two remaining conditions.

Condition D_1. Consider the pair $\langle d, h(d)\rangle \in R$ and an infinite sequence $(d_n)_{n\in\mathbb{N}}$ over states in D such that $d_0 = d$ and for any $n \in \mathbb{N}$ we have $h(d_n) = h(d)$ and $d_n \xrightarrow{int} d_{n+1}$. We show that there is some $e_{int}{:}E_{int}$ such that $c'_{int}(h(d), e_{int})$ and $g'_{int}(h(d), e_{int}) = h(d)$. If $h(d)$ is labeled Δ then this directly follows from Requirements I$_\Delta$, and II$_\Delta$.

Assume, for sake of contradiction, that $h(d)$ is labeled as ∇ instead. Since $<_M$ is a well-founded ordering on D, the sequence $(d_n)_{n\in\mathbb{N}}$ contains some minimal element $d_\perp$ such that no other element in the sequence is smaller than $d_\perp$. However, as per Requirement IV$_\Delta$, any outgoing *int* action from $d_\perp$ must have an endpoint that is smaller than $d_\perp$, and thus the state that comes directly after $d_\perp$ in the sequence would have to be smaller, contradicting that $d_\perp$ is the minimal element.

Condition D_2. Consider the pair $\langle d, h(d)\rangle \in R$ and an infinite sequence $(d'_n)_{n\in\mathbb{N}}$ over states in D' such that $d'_0 = h(d)$ and for any $n \in \mathbb{N}$ we have $d\ R\ d'_n$, i.e. $d'_n = h(d)$, and $d'_n \xrightarrow{int} d'_{n+1}$.

Since $h(d)$ allows an int-loop, we have $p(h(d)) = \Delta$ as per Requirement II$_\Delta$. If d is not a focus point then this action is enabled as per Requirement I. If d is a focus point then this action is enabled as per Requirement III$_\Delta$, since its corresponding cone is labeled as Δ. Requirement II gives us that the endpoint of this internal action is related to $h(d)$. Thus, if a state in the specification diverges then so do the related states in the implementation.

We thus conclude that the relation R is a divergence-preserving branching bisimulation.   □

5 Models of the Specification and the Implementation

We now discuss the models of the specification and implementation of the busy-forbidden protocol, such that we can use the extended proof framework to prove them equivalent in Sect. 6. From here on, we use N to denote the number of concurrent threads and we define $P = \{p_1, \ldots, p_N\}$ to be the set containing all N threads.

The linear process equation of the external behavior of the busy-forbidden protocol is given in Table 9 in the appendix [18]. The set S contains the nodes shown in Fig. 1. Each state in the specification is represented using a mapping s that maps each thread to its current node, with each thread starting in the *Free* node. The set of specification states for N threads is denoted by D'_N. Note that each condition in the specification is the same as the conditions shown in Fig. 1. The *improbable* actions are considered to be *int* actions.

The linear process equation of the implementation is given in Table 10 in the appendix [18]. All non-typewriter font actions are considered to be τ actions and *italicized* actions are specifically considered to be *int* actions. The set of implementation states D_N is given in Definition 5. A part of each state consists of N substates, with each substate giving the state of that specific thread. The set of substates is given in Definition 6, in which substates corresponding to the same node are grouped together.

Definition 5. Each state in the linearized process of the busy-forbidden implementation for N threads is defined as the tuple

$$d = \langle d_{p_1}, d_{p_2}, \ldots, d_{p_N}, busy, forbidden, mtx \rangle : D_N, \text{ in which:}$$

- $d_{p_1}, d_{p_2}, \ldots, d_{p_N}$ are the substates of threads 1 through N.
- $busy : P \to \mathbb{B}$ is the mapping that keeps track of all the busy flags, in which $busy(p)$ is the current value of the busy flag of thread p.
- $forbidden : P \to \mathbb{B}$ is the mapping that keeps track of all the forbidden flags in the same way as the $busy$ mapping.
- mtx is a boolean that indicates whether the mutual exclusion variable mtx is locked or unlocked.

Definition 6. The set of substates for each individual process is defined as the union of the following sets:

- $Free = \{Free\}$, $ES = \{ES_1, ES_2, ES_3, ES_4\}$, $LOE = \{LOE\}$,
  $Shared = \{Shared\}$, $LS = \{LS_1, LS_2\}$, $EE = \{EE\}$, $LOS = \{LOS_1, LOS_2\}$,
  $Exclusive = \{Exclusive\}$, and $OE = \{OE_1, OE_2\}$,
- $SAF = \{SAF_U | U \subset P\} \cup \{SAF_{p_x,U} | p_x{:}P, U \subset P\} \cup \{SAF_{p_x,U}^{undo} | p_x{:}P, U \subset P\}$,
- and $LE = \{LE_U | U \subseteq P \wedge U \neq \emptyset\}$.

Note that the singleton sets, such as *Free*, contain a single state with the same name as the set and do not contain themselves.

In the initial state of the implementation for N threads, all substates are set to *Free*, *busy* and *forbidden* map each thread p to *false* and *mtx* is set to *false*.

Since the state tuple contains a large number of elements, we use a shorthand notation for writing down the resulting state. All elements which remain the same are not listed and are abbreviated with "*etc.*". A substate or the *mtx* variable being changed in the resulting state is denoted with the "=" operator, where the lefthand side is assigned the value on the righthand side, e.g. $d_p = ES_2$ indicates that the substate of thread p becomes ES_2 in the next state. The function update $f[e \mapsto n]$ specifies that in the next state $f(x)$ equals the new value n if $x \approx e$ and otherwise equals its original value.

We introduce the Invariants 1, 2, and 3. These exclude some unreachable states and show that for any given state, the exact values of *busy*, *forbidden*, and *mtx* can be inferred from just the set of substates, i.e. $d_{p_1}, d_{p_2}, \ldots, d_{p_N}$. In the proof of Invariant 1, we show that the value of *mtx* can be inferred from just the set of substates and that it is not possible to have multiple threads simultaneously present in the set of states fenced off by the mutex operations. We show that the values of the *busy* and *forbidden* flags can also be inferred from just the set of substates in the proofs of Invariants 2 and 3.

The exact proofs for these invariants can be found in the appendix [18]. All of them follow the same general structure. Namely, the actions that result in a thread entering or leaving the given set of states, e.g. B, are the exact same actions that result in the value, e.g. *busy(p)*, being altered. And thus the exact values can be inferred from just the set of substates.

Invariant 1. The following invariant holds in the initial state and all subsequent states of the implementation: Given any state $d{:}D$ as per Definition 5,

$$\exists p{:}P.\ d_p \in M \Leftrightarrow mtx, \text{ and } \forall p_x, p_y{:}P.\ d_{p_x}, d_{p_y} \in M \Rightarrow p_x = p_y,$$

where $M = SAF \cup LOS \cup Exclusive \cup LE \cup \{OE_2\}$.

Invariant 2. The following invariant holds in the initial state and all subsequent states of the implementation: Given any state $d{:}D$ as per Definition 5,

$$\forall p{:}P.d_p \in B \Leftrightarrow busy(p), \text{ where } B = LOE \cup Shared \cup \{ES_1, ES_4, LS_2\}.$$

Invariant 3. The following invariant holds in the initial state and all subsequent states of the implementation: Given any state $d{:}D$ as per Definition 5,

$$\forall p{:}P.forbidden(p) \Longleftrightarrow \exists q{:}P.d_q \in F,$$

where $F = LOS \cup Exclusive \cup \{LE_U | U \subsetneq P \wedge p \in U\} \cup \{SAF_U | U \subset P \wedge p \in U\} \cup \{SAF_{p,U} | U \subset P\} \cup \{SAF_{p,U}^{undo} | U \subset P\}$.

6 Correctness of the Busy-Forbidden Protocol

The state mapping, focus condition, state ordering and cone labeling used during the equivalence proof are given in Definitions 7, 8, 9, and 10, respectively. These data objects only need to use substates since the values of the *busy, forbidden,* and *mtx* data objects can be directly inferred from the substates in any given state.

Definition 7. We define our state-mapping $h : D_N \to D'_N$ as follows:

$$h(\langle d_1, d_2, \ldots, d_N, busy, forbidden, mtx \rangle) = s \text{ where } s(p) = h_P(d_p) \text{ for any } p{:}P.$$

The mapping h_P, referred to as the substate-mapping, maps each substate to the specification state with the same name as the set, shown in Definition 6, that it belongs to, e.g. $h_P(ES_3) = ES$ and $h_P(SAF_{\{p_1,p_3,p_4\}}) = SAF$.

Definition 8. We define our focus condition $FC : D_N \to \mathbb{B}$ as follows:

$$FC(\langle d_{p_1}, d_{p_2}, \ldots, d_{p_N}, busy, \text{ } forbidden, \text{ } mtx \rangle) = \bigwedge_{p_x:P} FC_{p_x}(d_{p_x}),$$

where $FC_{p_x}(d_{p_x}) \overset{def}{=} p_x \in \{Free, ES_1, LOE, Shared, LS_1, EE, SAF_\emptyset, LOS_1, Exclusive, LE_{\{p_x\}}, OE_1\}$. We refer to the predicate FC_{p_x}, for any given $p_x{:}P$, as the sub-focus condition.

Definition 9. Given two states $d = \langle d_{p_1}, d_{p_2}, \ldots, d_{p_N}, busy, forbidden, mtx \rangle$ and $d' = \langle d'_{p1}, d'_{p2}, \ldots, d'_{pN}, busy', forbidden', mtx' \rangle$, we define the ordering on these states as follows:

$$d <_M d' \overset{def}{=} \bigwedge_{p:P} d_p <_p d'_p,$$

where, given some thread $p{:}P$, the ordering $<_p$ on its substates is defined such that only the following holds:

- $ES_1 <_p ES_2 <_p ES_3 <_p ES_4$, $LS_1 <_p LS_2$, $LOS_1 <_p LOS_2$, and $OE_1 <_p OE_2$,
- $SAF_{p_x,U} <_p SAF_U$ iff $p_x \in U$ for any given $U{:}\mathcal{P}(P)$ and $p_x{:}P$, $SAF_{U \setminus \{p_x\}} <_p SAF_{p_x,U}$ for any given $U{:}\mathcal{P}(P)$ and $p_x{:}P$, $SAF_U < SAF_{p_x,U'}^{undo}$ for any given given $U, U'{:}\mathcal{P}(P)$ and $p_x{:}P$,
- $LE_U <_p LE_{U'}$ iff $U \subset U' \wedge p \in U$ or $p \in U \wedge p \notin U'$ for any given $U, U'{:}\mathcal{P}(P)$

Definition 10. We define the cone labeling $p : D'_N \to \{\triangle, \nabla\}$ as follows: Given any state $s{:}D'_N$, $p(s) = \triangle$ iff $\exists q{:}P.s(q) \in \{SAF, LE\} \vee (\exists q : P.s(q) = ES \wedge \exists q'{:}P.q' \in \{LOS, Exclusive\})$ otherwise $p(s) = \nabla$.

The specification indicates that if there is one thread in the ES node and one thread in the SAF node, either one of them should be able to progress to the next node. This is not simultaneously possible in the implementation, as progressing to the LOE node requires the $busy$ flag to be $true$ and the $forbidden$ flag to be $false$, while progressing to the LOS node requires all $busy$ flags to be $false$ and all $forbidden$ flags to be $true$. Thus, the subfocus point of each node is chosen such that the external actions are enabled directly given that they would also be enabled in the specification, with the exception of $SAF_\emptyset$ which is used as the focus point of the SAF node.

We show that there is a path of int actions from this to some state d_{int} in which the transition to LOE is enabled. This is outlined in Theorem 2 for which the proof is given in the appendix [18]. The general idea behind the proof is that if the $forbidden$ flag is set before it is read by the thread in the ES node, the $busy$ flag will be set back to false. Repeating this, leads to all $busy$ flags being $false$ and all $forbidden$ flags being $true$, thus enabling the transition to LOE.

We now conclude by proving the implementation and specification of the busy-forbidden protocol equivalent in Theorem 3.

Theorem 2. Given some state $d{:}D$, some thread $p_{SAF}{:}P$, and some data configuration $e_\tau{:}E_\tau$ such that $FC(d)$ and $c'_\tau(h(d), e_\tau)$ hold, $h(d)(p_{SAF}) = SAF$ and $g'_\tau(h(d), e_\tau) = LOE$. There must be some state $d_{int}{:}D$ such that $d \xrightarrow{int}{}^* d_{int}$ and $c_\tau(d_{int}, e_\tau)$ hold and $h(g_\tau(d_{int}, e_\tau))(p_{SAF}) = LOE$.

Theorem 3. The LPE of the implementation given in Table 10 and the LPE of the specification given in Table 9 are divergence-preserving branching bisimilar.

Proof. To prove the aforementioned equivalence, we show that all ten requirements given in Theorem 1 hold using Invariants 1, 2, and 3, and the state mapping, focus condition, ordering and cone labeling, given in Definitions 7, 8, 9, and 10, respectively. From the linear process equation, it is relatively easy to see that Requirements I, II, V, VI, I_Δ, and II_Δ are not invalidated. As such, we refer the reader to their extended proofs, found in the appendix [18].

Both the implementation and specification contain exactly three externally observable actions that are not always enabled. For these actions, we show that if the action in the specification is enabled, the same action is also enabled in the corresponding focus point in the implementation, and if the action in the implementation is enabled, the corresponding specification action is also enabled, thus showing that Requirements III, and IV hold.

The first action is the $load(Forbidden(p), false, p)$ action in ES_2 and the τ transition from the ES to the LOE node in the specification. The $load$ action is only enabled when $forbidden(p)$ is $false$, and the τ transition in the specification is only enabled if there are no threads in LOS or $Exclusive$ node. As per Invariant 3, these conditions hold exactly when they hold in the corresponding focus points.

The second action is the $lock(p)$ action in EE and the τ transition in the EE node in the specification. The $lock$ action is only enabled when mtx is $false$, and the τ transition in the specification is only enabled if there is no thread in the *SAF*, *LOS*, *Exclusive*, and *LE* node. As per Invariant 1, these conditions, again, hold exactly when they would hold in the corresponding focus points of the implementation.

The third action is the load($Busy(p_x), false, p$) action in $SAF_{p_x,U}$ and the τ transition from the *SAF* to the *LOS* node in the specification. The *load* action is only enabled when $Busy(p)$ is *false* and the τ transition is only enabled if there is no thread in the *LOE* and *Shared* nodes. As per Invariant 2, if $busy(p)$ is *false* then the *LOE* and *Shared* node are empty and thus, if the action is enabled in the implementation, it is also enabled in the specification. As per the same invariant, the only focus points in which the action would not be enabled while it would be in the corresponding specifications state, are the ones in which a thread is in the *SAF* node, i.e. some thread $p{:}P$ has the substate $SAF_\emptyset$. In these cases, as per Theorem 2, there must be some finite path of *int* actions to some state d_{int} in which this action is enabled.

In the corresponding focus points for the *SAF* and *LE* cone, there is always at least one internal action enabled. In the focus point for the *ES* cone, the load($Forbidden(p), true, p$) action is enabled iff $forbidden(p)$ is *true*. As per Invariant 3, the only focus points in which $Forbidden(p)$ is *true* are the ones in which the *LOS* or *Exclusive* node are occupied. In all other focus points, there are no further internal actions enabled. Thus Requirement III$_\Delta$ holds.

If a cone is labelled as non-diverging (∇), then each thread should be in one of the following nodes: *Free*, *LOE*, *Shared*, *LS*, *EE*, *LOS*, *Exclusive*, or *OE*, or *ES*, given that there are no threads present in either *LOS* or *Exclusive*. With the exception of the load($Forbidden(p), true, p$) action in the *ES* node, all the internal actions within these nodes take us closer to a focus point. As per Invariant 3, *forbidden* is *true* only if there is a thread present in either the *LOS* or *Exclusive*, *LE*, or *SAF* node, which are known to be empty. Thus Requirement IV$_\Delta$ also holds and the implementation and specification are divergence-preserving branching bisimilar as per Theorem 1.   □

7   Conclusion and Future Work

We have extended the cones and foci proof framework [6,11] with four additional requirements, i.e. Requirements I$_\Delta$, II$_\Delta$, III$_\Delta$, and IV$_\Delta$, such that it can be used to prove divergence-preserving branching bisimulation. We have proven this extension to be sound and have used it to prove the implementation and specification of the novel busy-forbidden protocol [9] to be equivalent.

We note some opportunities to extend upon the work in this paper:

- The completeness of the extended cones and foci proof framework has not been formally proven. We assume its completeness due to the weakening of Requirement III, and it is of similar interest as to whether this Requirement can be made stronger without loss of our assumed completeness.
- As mentioned before, the original cones and foci proof framework has been used for the verification of the sliding window protocol [2]. The communication channels used by this protocol are unreliable and thus allow divergence.

As such, the sliding window protocol could provide an interesting case study for our extension of the cones and foci proof framework.

– The diverging loops in the external behavior are considered to be *improbable*, as such, we abstract away any actual, but potentially informative, probabilistic analysis of the protocol.

References

1. IEEE standard for a high performance serial bus. IEEE Std 1394–1995, pp. 1–384 (1996). https://doi.org/10.1109/IEEESTD.1996.81049
2. Badban, B., Fokkink, W., Groote, J.F., Pang, J., Pol, J.V.d.: Verification of a sliding window protocol in μcrl and pvs. FAC **17**(3), 342–388 (2005). https://doi.org/10.1007/s00165-005-0070-0
3. Baeten, J., Weijland, W.: Process algebra, Cambridge tracts in theoretical computer science, vol. 18. Cambridge University Press (1990). https://doi.org/10.1017/CBO9780511624193
4. Bunte, O., et al.: The mCRL2 toolset for analysing concurrent systems. In: Vojnar, T., Zhang, L. (eds.) TACAS 2019. LNCS, vol. 11428, pp. 21–39. Springer, Cham (2019). https://doi.org/10.1007/978-3-030-17465-1_2
5. Courtois, P.J., Heymans, F., Parnas, D.L.: Concurrent control with "readers" and "writers". Commun. ACM **14**(10), 667–668 (1971). https://doi.org/10.1145/362759.362813
6. Fokkink, W., Pang, J., van de Pol, J.: Cones and foci: a mechanical framework for protocol verification. Formal Methods Syst. Des. **29**(1), 1–31 (2006). https://doi.org/10.1007/s10703-006-0004-3dBLP:journals/fmsd/FokkinkPP06
7. åke Fredlund, L., Groote, J.F., Korver, H.: Formal verification of a leader election protocol in process algebra. Theor. Comput. Sci. **177**(2), 459–486 (1997). https://doi.org/10.1016/S0304-3975(96)00256-3
8. van Glabbeek, R., Luttik, B., Trcka, N.: Computation tree logic with deadlock detection. Logical Methods Comput. Sci. **5**(4) (2009). https://doi.org/10.2168/LMCS-5(4:5)2009
9. Groote, J.F., Laveaux, M., van Spaendonck, P.H.M.: A thread-safe term library, pp. 422–459 (2022). https://doi.org/10.1007/978-3-031-19849-6_25
10. Groote, J.F., Mousavi, M.R.: Modeling and Analysis of Communicating Systems. The MIT Press, Cambridge (2014)
11. Groote, J., Springintveld, J.: Focus points and convergent process operators?: a proof strategy for protocol verification. J. Logic Algebraic Program. **49**, 31–60 (2001). https://doi.org/10.1016/S1567-8326(01)00010-8
12. Hoare, C.A.R.: An axiomatic basis for computer programming. Commun. ACM **12**(10), 576–580 (1969). https://doi.org/10.1145/363235.363259
13. Luttik, B.: Divergence-preserving branching bisimilarity. EPTCS **322**, 3–11 (2020). https://doi.org/10.4204/EPTCS.322.2
14. Milner, R. (ed.): A Calculus of Communicating Systems. LNCS, vol. 92. Springer, Heidelberg (1980). https://doi.org/10.1007/3-540-10235-3
15. Owicki, S., Gries, D.: An axiomatic proof technique for parallel programs i. Acta informatica **6**(4), 319–340 (1976). https://doi.org/10.1007/BF00268134
16. Owicki, S., Gries, D.: Verifying properties of parallel programs: An axiomatic approach. Commun. ACM **19**(5), 279–285 (1976)

17. Shankland, C., Van Der Zwaag, M.: The tree identify protocol of IEEE 1394 in μcrl. Formal Aspects Comput. **10**(5), 509–531 (1998)
18. van Spaendonck, P.H.M.: Verification of the busy-forbidden protocol, August 2022. https://doi.org/10.48550/arxiv.2208.05334
19. Usenko, Y.S.: Linearization of μcrl specifications. In: Proceedings of 3rd Workshop on Verification and Computational Logic, Technical Report DSSE-TR-2002-5. Department of Electronics and Computer Science, University of Southampton. Citeseer (2002)

kProp: Multi-neuron Relaxation Method for Neural Network Robustness Verification

Xiaoyong Xue, Xiyue Zhang, and Meng Sun[✉]

School of Mathematical Sciences, Peking University, Beijing 100871, China
{xuexy,zhangxiyue,sunm}@pku.edu.cn

Abstract. With the increasing application of neural networks in safety-critical domains, their robustness becomes a crucial concern. In this paper, we present a multi-neuron relaxation-based verification framework *kProp* for ReLU neural networks with adversarial distortions in general norms. In contrast with existing verification methods tackling general distortion norms, the proposed multi-neuron relaxation method is able to capture the relations among a group of neurons, thus providing tighter convex relaxations and improving verification precision. In addition, existing methods based on linear relaxation may include infeasible inputs to the neural network for robustness verification, which further leads to verification precision loss. To address this problem, we propose a region clipping method to exclude infeasible inputs to further improve the verification precision. We implement our verification framework and evaluate its performance on open-source benchmarks. The experiments show that *kProp* can produce precise verification results where existing verification methods fail to produce conclusive results, and can be applied to neural networks with more than 4k neurons in general distortion norms.

Keywords: Robustness · Verification · Neural network

1 Introduction

Neural networks (NNs) have been increasingly used in a broad range of applications and made inspiring breakthroughs in many safety-critical domains, such as autonomous driving, drone control, and medical diagnosis [1,3,10]. Meanwhile, a lot of studies have highlighted the vulnerability of neural networks against adversarial attacks. Adversarial attacks can be performed by applying small imperceptible perturbations to alter the NN's prediction result on the original image [9]. In addition, more practical attacks can be achieved by adding real-world physical perturbations [5]. With the increasing deployment of neural networks into safety-critical tasks, rigorous verification of NN's robustness against adversarial perturbations has gained substantial momentum in recent years.

Verification methods for neural networks mainly fall into two categories – complete and incomplete. Complete verification methods based on satisfiability

Current Address: Department of Computer Science, University of Oxford, Oxford, UK.

H. Hojjat and E. Ábrahám (Eds.): FSEN 2023, LNCS 14155, pp. 142–156, 2023.
https://doi.org/10.1007/978-3-031-42441-0_11

modulo theories (SMT) [4,11] or mixed integer linear programming (MILP) [13] can provide an exact answer of whether a neural network is robust. However, robustness verification of neural networks even with the piece-wise linear function ReLU (Rectified Linear Unit) is an NP-hard problem [11]. The worst-case exponential complexity severely restricts the application of such complete verifiers. In contrast, incomplete methods leverage various approximation techniques to attain better scalability. Approximation techniques include abstract interpretation [8,14–16] which captures the propagation from inputs to outputs in symbolic shapes, and linear relaxation [18–20] which computes linear upper and lower bounds for non-linear activation functions.

Given a neural network, the (local) robustness verification problem is to ensure that the neural network has the same prediction (such as predicted labels) on the neighborhood of an arbitrary input. Generally, the neighborhood of an input is characterized by an ℓ_p ball for a given radius $\epsilon \in \mathbb{R}^+$ with the input as the center. The aforementioned verification methods based on abstract interpretation, e.g. kPoly [15] and PRIMA [14], only consider ℓ_∞ perturbation neighborhood. However, some real-life perturbations such as adding black and white stickers [5] cannot be characterized by this formalization. It is more appropriate to capture such distortion in the form of ℓ_1 or ℓ_2 ball. Verification methods based on linear relaxation are able to verify robustness for general ℓ_p norms. The commonly-used Δ-relaxation [4] in these methods offers the tightest possible relaxation for one single neuron. However, due to the ignorance of the constraints between multiple neurons, methods based on Δ-relaxation still suffer from precision loss. In addition, verification methods based on linear relaxation make use of *Hölder Inequality* to calculate the global bounds. In this computation process, infeasible input regions are considered to derive the global bounds, which leads to more approximation loss.

In this work, we propose a propagation algorithm based on multi-neuron relaxation method to produce tighter relaxations for ReLU neural networks in Sect. 3. The overall framework of this algorithm is to propagate the verification objective from the output layer to the input layer, which yields a linear over-approximation of the original neural network and thus is able to apply to general ℓ_p distortions. The key insight of this algorithm is multi-neuron relaxation, shown in Sect. 4, to capture the relations among a group of neurons (in the same layer), which naturally leads to tighter approximation and increased verification precision. Moreover, we propose a region clipping method for infeasible input removal in Sect. 5 to further improve the verification precision.

2   Preliminary

In this section, we provide the preliminaries about neural networks, the local robustness property, and two kinds of polyhedron representation.

2.1   Neural Network

Neural networks are sequential programs that consist of an input layer, several hidden layers, and an output layer. The adjacent layers are connected with weighted edges. A neural network N with n-dimensional input and m-dimensional output can be regarded as a function $f : \mathbb{R}^n \rightarrow \mathbb{R}^m$. For every neuron in hidden layers, we split it into the pre-activation neuron and the post-activation neuron. The neural network $y = f(x)$ can be formulated as follows:

$$z_{0,i} = x_i \qquad \forall i = 1 \ldots n \qquad (1)$$

$$\hat{z}_{l,i} = \sum_{j=1}^{n_{l-1}} w_{i,j}^l z_{l-1,j} + b_i^l \qquad \forall l = 1 \ldots L, i = 1 \ldots n_l \qquad (2)$$

$$z_{l,i} = \sigma(\hat{z}_{l,i}) \qquad \forall l = 1 \ldots L, i = 1 \ldots n_l \qquad (3)$$

$$y_i = z_{L,i} \qquad \forall i = 1 \ldots m \qquad (4)$$

The input layer is represented in Eq. (1), where each neuron takes one-dimensional value of the input data. This network has $L - 1$ hidden layers and n_l neurons for layer l. Equations (2) and (3) describe the behavior of affine transformations and non-linear transformations in terms of activation functions. Here $z_{l,i}$ is the output of the i-th neuron in layer l and $\hat{z}_{l,i}$ is the corresponding pre-activation output value. $w_{i,j}^l$ and b_i^l denote the connection weights and biases between neurons of adjacent layers. The activation function that we consider in this paper is ReLU, that is $\sigma(x) = max\{0, x\}$. Equation (4) represents the output layer where the i-th dimension of the output is y_i, also denoted as $f_i(x)$. In classification tasks, for a given input x, the neural network determines that x belongs to class t if $f_t(x) > f_k(x), \forall k \neq t, 1 \leq k \leq m$.

2.2 Robustness Property

In real-world deployment, neural networks are expected to stay stable when small perturbations occur to the input data. This safety property is referred to as local robustness [20], which states that all data that is close to the original input x_0 has the same prediction label as x_0.

Specifically, local robustness can be formalized as follows. Given a neural network f, its input domain D_f, an input data x_0 with ground-truth label l, and the distortion radius ϵ, we say the neural network satisfies local robustness in the neighborhood $\mathbb{B}_p(x_0, \epsilon)$ if

$$\forall x' \in D_f, ||x' - x_0||_p \leq \epsilon, \forall j \neq l : f_l(x') > f_j(x'). \qquad (5)$$

The local robustness is represented by the conjunction of a set of inequalities, which can be verified by checking the satisfiability of each constraint.

2.3 Polyhedron Representation

The abstract domain of polyhedron is generally used in abstract interpretation for neural network verification. A bounded polyhedron can be represented as the intersection of a set of half-spaces, or the convex hull of a set of points. The former representation is called the H-representation, and the latter one is called the V-representation. Here are the formal definitions of these two representations.

Definition 1 (H-representation). *A is an $m \times n$-matrix, and b is a column vector in $\mathbb{R}^m$. A polyhedron in H-representation is a region $P \subseteq \mathbb{R}^n$ that satisfies a set of linear constraints.*

$$P = \{x \in \mathbb{R}^n \mid Ax \le b\}$$

Definition 2 (V-representation). *Let $R = \{r_1, r_2, \ldots, r_m\}$ be a set of points in $\mathbb{R}^n$. A bounded polyhedron in V-representation is the convex hull of R.*

$$P = \{x \in \mathbb{R}^n \mid x = \sum_{i=1}^{m} \lambda_i r_i, \ \sum_{i=1}^{m} \lambda_i = 1, \lambda_i \ge 0, i = 1 \ldots m\}$$

Both representations can describe a polyhedron, but each has its advantages and disadvantages. Computing intersection of polyhedra is simpler in H-representation. And the V-representation makes it easier to compute the convex hull. We can use the Double Description Method [6] to transform one to another.

3 Propagation Framework

In this section, we present the general propagation framework with multi-neuron relaxation and region clipping to compute tighter convex relaxation of neural networks and more precise verification results against adversarial distortions in general ℓ_p norms, which is shown in Fig. 1.

The idea of layer-by-layer propagation from output to the input has been widely used in many neural network verification methods [16,17,19,20]. As shown in Fig. 1, the propagation procedure begins from the output layer. Specifically, the verification objective $t = y_o - y_l$ is characterized by the linear inequalities in Eq. (5), where l is the prediction label of the given input and $o \ne l$. If $t < 0$, then the local robustness of the neural network on the given input data within the adversarial distortions is guaranteed.

The verification objective t is then propagated from the output to the input layer by layer. However, the non-convexity of activation functions is the obstacle in the backward propagation of the linear objective. Therefore, in this process,

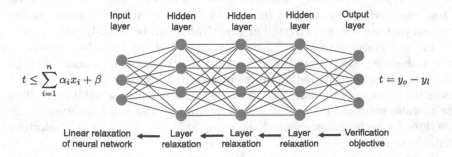

Fig. 1. Backward propagation framework

we maintain an over-approximation of t by performing linear relaxations for the activation functions in each hidden layer. In this way, we can transform the linear inequalities to the input layer and obtain a linear relaxation of the neural network. When the verification objective is propagated to the input layer, the over-approximation of t is a linear combination of input variables. We then calculate the upper bound of t restricted by the input constraints.

The most crucial part in the propagation framework is the linear relaxation. For neuron $\hat{z}_{k,i}$, we compute its two scalar bounds $ub_{k,i}$ and $lb_{k,i}$ that satisfy $lb_{k,i} \leq \hat{z}_{k,i} \leq ub_{k,i}$ for any $x' \in \mathbb{B}_p(x, \epsilon)$. The neurons of hidden layers can be categorized into three types according to the scalar bounds.

- If the neuron is always activated ($lb_{k,i} \geq 0$), we have $z_{k,i} = \hat{z}_{k,i}$.
- If the neuron is always deactivated ($ub_{k,i} \leq 0$), we have $z_{k,i} = 0$.
- If the neuron is unstable ($lb_{k,i} < 0 < ub_{k,i}$), we perform linear relaxation.

Existing verification methods use an upper bounding function $\mathcal{U}_{k,i}$ and a lower bounding function $\mathcal{L}_{k,i}$ for each unstable neuron $z_{k,i}$. These two functions are subject to the following inequality: $\mathcal{L}_{k,i}(\hat{z}_{k,i}) \leq \sigma(\hat{z}_{k,i}) \leq \mathcal{U}_{k,i}(\hat{z}_{k,i})$. The most frequently used bounding functions are linear functions, which can be calculated based on the scalar bounds of the pre-activation neurons as follows:

$$\mathcal{U}_{k,i}(\hat{z}_{k,i}) = \frac{ub_{k,i}}{ub_{k,i} - lb_{k,i}}(\hat{z}_{k,i} - lb_{k,i}) \quad \mathcal{L}_{k,i}^1(\hat{z}_{k,i}) = \hat{z}_{k,i} \quad \mathcal{L}_{k,i}^2(\hat{z}_{k,i}) = 0$$

The above bounding functions are used in many verification methods [16,20]. Generally, the upper bounding function has only one candidate. But the lower bounding functions are adaptively selected from $\mathcal{L}_{k,i}^1$ and $\mathcal{L}_{k,i}^2$. The bounding function that minimizes the area between the activation function and lower bound is chosen, which means $\mathcal{L}_{k,i}(\hat{z}_{k,i}) = \hat{z}_{k,i}$ is selected if $ub_{k,i} + lb_{k,i} \geq 0$, and $\mathcal{L}_{k,i}(\hat{z}_{k,i}) = 0$ is selected if $ub_{k,i} + lb_{k,i} < 0$.

Existing works mentioned above only consider the relaxation on one single neuron, losing sight of relations among neurons in the same hidden layer. We aim to capture the relations between multiple neurons and obtain tighter convex relaxation by calculating the joint bounding function for a group of neurons.

We propose a multi-neuron relaxation based verification framework as shown in Algorithm 1. To calculate joint bounding functions for a group of neurons, the first step is to compute bounding functions for each single neuron through a fast linear relaxation method (line 1). In the backward propagation process, neurons that are always activated or deactivated can be directly propagated to the pre-activation layer (line 5 - 8). For the remaining unstable neurons, we gather them together (line 9) and perform multi-neuron relaxation (line 10 - 15). Computing joint bounding functions for all unstable neurons is practically infeasible for large-scale neuron networks. To achieve better scalability, we divide the unstable neurons into several non-overlapping groups and calculate bounding functions for each neuron group. Each group is formed by randomly selecting k unstable neurons.

Based on the multi-neuron relaxation method, we can propagate the verification objective to the preceding layer according to Eq. (2) (line 17). Through

---

Algorithm 1: Propagation Framework

Input: Verification objective $t = \sum_{i=1}^{n_{L-1}} c_{L-1,i} z_{L-1,i} + \beta_{L-1}$,
    the given input x_0, radius ϵ, norm p, weights $w_{i,j}^l$, biases b_i^l,
    number of neurons in a group k

Output: An upper bound of t

  1   $ub, lb, \mathcal{U}, \mathcal{L} \leftarrow$ InitalBounding(x_0, ϵ, p)
  2   **for** $l \leftarrow L\text{-}1, \ldots, 1$ **do**
  3   unstable_neurons $\leftarrow \{\}$
  4   **for** $i \leftarrow 1$ **to** n_l **do**
  5   **if** $lb_{l,i} \geq 0$ **then**
  6              $t \leftarrow t - c_{l,i} z_{l,i} + c_{l,i} \hat{z}_{l,i}$
  7   **else if** $ub_{l,i} \leq 0$ **then**
  8              $t \leftarrow t - c_{l,i} z_{l,i} + 0 \cdot \hat{z}_{l,i}$
  9   **else** add $z_{l,i}$ to unstable_neurons
10   **while** unstable_neurons *is not empty* **do**
11   Pop k neurons $z_{l,u_1}, z_{l,u_2}, \ldots, z_{l,u_k}$ from unstable_neurons
12   U_group $\leftarrow [\, \mathcal{U}_{l,u_1}, \mathcal{U}_{l,u_2}, \ldots, \mathcal{U}_{l,u_k} \,]$
13   L_group $\leftarrow [\, \mathcal{L}_{l,u_1}, \mathcal{L}_{l,u_2}, \ldots, \mathcal{L}_{l,u_k} \,]$
14   upper_bound $\leftarrow$ JointBound$(\sum_{i=1}^{k} c_{l,ui} z_{l,ui}$, U_group, L_group, $x_0, \epsilon, p)$
15          $t \leftarrow t - \sum_{i=1}^{k} c_{l,ui} z_{l,ui} +$ upper_bound
16   **for** $i \leftarrow 1$ **to** n_l **do**
17          $t \leftarrow t - \hat{c}_{l,i} \hat{z}_{l,i} + \sum_{j=1}^{n_{l-1}} \hat{c}_{l,i} w_{i,j}^l z_{l-1,j} + \hat{c}_{l,i} * b_i^l$
18 res $\leftarrow$ GlobalBound(t, x_0, ϵ, p)
19 **return res**

---

repeating the above procedure for every hidden layer in a backward manner, we can obtain a linear relaxation of the verification objective, which is in the form of $t \leq \alpha_1 x_1 + \alpha_2 x_2 + \cdots + \alpha_n x_n + \beta$.

The last step of this algorithm is to find a global upper bound, the maximum value of t, with regard to the input perturbations. For any input x_0, we can use *Hölder Inequality* to find the solution in $\mathbb{B}_p(x_0, \epsilon)$ [20]. However, some regions of this ball are not included in the input domain of the neural network. To address this problem, we propose the region clipping method in Sect. 5.

4   Multi-neuron Relaxation

In this section, we introduce the insight of multi-neuron relaxation over single neuron relaxation and how to calculate the multi-neuron relaxation for a group of unstable neurons.

4.1 Motivation Example

We first show the superiority of multi-neuron relaxation with a simple example.

Example 1. Consider a neural network with one hidden layer. It has three neurons in the input layer, two neurons in the hidden layer, and two neurons in the output layer. The structure of this neural network is illustrated with the following equations and figure.

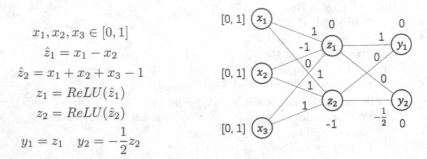

$$x_1, x_2, x_3 \in [0, 1]$$
$$\hat{z}_1 = x_1 - x_2$$
$$\hat{z}_2 = x_1 + x_2 + x_3 - 1$$
$$z_1 = ReLU(\hat{z}_1)$$
$$z_2 = ReLU(\hat{z}_2)$$
$$y_1 = z_1 \quad y_2 = -\frac{1}{2}z_2$$

The range of each input neuron is $[0, 1]$. In this example, we attempt to find the upper bound of $t = y_1 - y_2 = z_1 + \frac{1}{2}z_2$.

We first perform single neuron relaxation using the bounding functions shown in Sect. 3. According to the value range of x_1, x_2, x_3, we can calculate that the lower scalar bound and upper scalar bound of $\hat{z}_1$ are $-1, 1$, and those of $\hat{z}_2$ are $-1, 2$. The single-neuron upper bounding function for z_1 and z_2 are $\mathcal{U}_1 = \frac{1}{2}\hat{z}_1 + \frac{1}{2}$ and $\mathcal{U}_2 = \frac{2}{3}\hat{z}_2 + \frac{2}{3}$.

With the above bounding function we have $t \leq \frac{1}{2}\hat{z}_1 + \frac{1}{3}\hat{z}_2 + \frac{5}{6}$. By substituting $\hat{z}_1, \hat{z}_2$ with x_1, x_2, x_3, we have $t \leq \frac{5}{6}x_1 - \frac{1}{6}x_2 + \frac{1}{3}x_3 + \frac{1}{2}$. Considering the input range, the upper bound of t with single neuron relaxation is $\frac{5}{3}$.

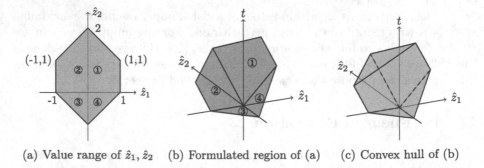

(a) Value range of $\hat{z}_1, \hat{z}_2$ (b) Formulated region of (a)   (c) Convex hull of (b)

Fig. 2. Relations of hidden neurons in Example 1

In single neuron relaxation, we only make use of the scalar upper and lower bounds. The pre-activation neurons $\hat{z}_1$ and $\hat{z}_2$ are treated to be independent of each other. However, they are not independent. In this example, the values

---

Algorithm 2: Computing Joint Bound

Input: Function $t = \sum_{i=1}^{k} c_i z_i$, upper bounding functions U_group, lower
      bounding functions L_group, the given input x_0, radius ϵ, norm p
Output: An upper bounding function of t

1   octahedron ← OCTAHERALABSTRACTION(U_group, L_group, x_0, ϵ, p)
2   segments ← SPLIT(octahedron, k)
3   generators ← {}
4   for each segment in segments do
5   vertices ← GETVERTICES(segment)
6   for each $(v_1, \ldots, v_k)$ in vertices do
7   lifted_v ← $(v_1, \ldots, v_k, \sum_{i=1}^{k} \text{ReLU}(v_i))$
8   add lifted_v to generators

9   bounds ← GETFACETS(generators)
10 upper_bound ← BOUNDSELECTION(bounds, generators)
11 return upper_bound

---

of $\hat{z}_1$ and $\hat{z}_2$ are taken from blue region as shown in Fig. 2(a). Then the image
of function $t = ReLU(\hat{z}_1) + \frac{1}{2}ReLU(\hat{z}_2)$ over the blue region is illustrated in
Fig. 2(b). This image is composed by four planes as the function is linear in each
quadrant. As this function is piece-wise linear, the formulated region in $(\hat{z}_1, \hat{z}_2, t)$-
space is non-convex. To calculate the joint bounding functions, we calculate the
convex hull of this region as shown in Fig. 2(c) where each facet of the convex
hull can be transformed into a bounding function.

Considering the orientations of facets in Fig. 2(c), we can obtain two upper
bounding functions. Using the bound selection algorithm (Sect. 4.3), $t \leq \frac{1}{2}\hat{z}_1 +$
$\hat{z}_2 + \frac{1}{2}$ is selected to be the upper bounding function. After propagating this
joint bound to the input layer, we have $t \leq x_1 + \frac{1}{2}x_3$. The upper bound of t is
then calculated to be $\frac{3}{2}$ with multi-neuron relaxation, which is tighter than the
obtained upper bound with single neuron relaxation.

4.2 Joint Bounding Function

In this subsection we present how to compute the joint bounding functions for
multi-neuron relaxation.

The multi-neuron relaxation algorithm is shown in Algorithm 2. It can
be divided into three steps: determining the value range of the pre-activation
neurons, constructing the corresponding region in the $(\hat{\mathbf{z}}, t)$-space where $\hat{\mathbf{z}} =$
$(\hat{z}_1, \ldots, \hat{z}_k)$, and computing the convex hull of this region.

We use octahedral abstraction [14,15] to determine the value range of the
pre-activation neurons (line 1). Specifically, the octahedral abstraction is represented by a series of linear inequalities that over-approximate the values of
a group of neurons, i.e., $\{\sum_{i=1}^{k} d_i \hat{z}_i \leq e_i \mid d_i \in \{-1, 0, 1\}, d_i$ are not all zero.$\}$.
The constant term e_i is generated by computing the upper bound of $\sum_{i=1}^{k} d_i \hat{z}_i$,
which utilizes the single neuron bounding functions.

Next we construct the region in the $(\hat{z}, t)$-space, which corresponds to the value range of pre-activation neurons (line 2 - 7). As ReLU is linear in each orthant, the input domain is split into a list of subregions by adding constraints $\hat{z}_i \geq 0$ or $\hat{z}_i \leq 0$ (line 2). If there are k neurons in a group, the number of produced subregions is at most 2^k.

Example 2. The value range of $\hat{z}_1, \hat{z}_2$ in Example 1 can be described with the following linear inequalities.

$$\hat{z}_1 \leq 1, -\hat{z}_1 \leq 1, \hat{z}_1 \leq 2, -\hat{z}_1 \leq 1, \hat{z}_1 + \hat{z}_2 \leq 2, -\hat{z}_1 + \hat{z}_2 \leq 2, \hat{z}_1 - \hat{z}_2 \leq 1, -\hat{z}_1 - \hat{z}_2 \leq 1$$

This can be split into 4 subregions by adding inequalities like $\hat{z}_1 \sim 0$, $\hat{z}_2 \sim 0$ ($\sim$ is $\leq$ or $\geq$). For example, by adding $\hat{z}_1 \geq 0$, $\hat{z}_2 \geq 0$ the upper right quadrant (after simplification) is $\hat{z}_1 \leq 1$, $-\hat{z}_1 \leq 0$, $-\hat{z}_2 \leq 0$, $\hat{z}_1 + \hat{z}_2 \leq 2$.

In each subregion, as the activation function is linear, the constituted region in $(\hat{z}, t)$-space is a plane, which can be represented with linear inequalities, i.e., H-representation. For the convenience of computing the convex hull of the constituted region in $(\hat{z}, t)$-space, we transform this into the V-representation. We firstly use the Double Description Method to transform the subregion into the V-presentation and get its vertices (line 5). Then for each vertex v, we compute its corresponding t value and concatenate it with v (line 7). In this way, we lift this vertex to the $(\hat{z}, t)$-space, and we get the V-representation of the formulated region in the $(\hat{z}, t)$-space.

Example 3. The vertices of the quadrant in Example 2 are $(0, 2)$, $(0, 0)$, $(1, 0)$, $(1, 1)$. The output function is $t = ReLU(\hat{z}_1) + \frac{1}{2}ReLU(\hat{z}_2)$. For vertex $(0, 2)$, we have $t = ReLU(0) + \frac{1}{2}ReLU(2) = 1$. Concatenate this with $(0, 2)$, and we can get the lifted vertex $(0, 2, 1)$. In the same way, the other three lifted vertices are $(0, 0, 0)$, $(1, 0, 1)$, $(1, 1, \frac{3}{2})$. The corresponding region of the upper right quadrant in $(\hat{z}_1, \hat{z}_2, t)$-space is represented as the convex hull of these 4 lifted points, i.e., V-representation.

The last step is to compute the convex hull of all subregions in $(\hat{z}_1, \ldots, \hat{z}, t)$-space. Since all formulated subregions are in V-representation, we just need to gather all the vertices (line 8) to get the V-representation of the convex hull. Then we can use Double Description Method again to transform the convex hull into H-representation (line 9). Each inequality of the H-representation is a facet of the convex hull, and thus a bounding function in multi-neuron relaxation. We can determine the orientation of a facet with the coefficient of the output variable.

Example 4. By gathering all the vertices, we can get the V-representation of the convex hull in Fig. 2(c). And with Double Description Method, we can get the facets of this convex hull.

$$-\hat{z}_1 + 2t \leq 2, \quad -\hat{z}_1 - \hat{z}_2 + 2t \leq 1$$
$$-t \leq 0, \quad \hat{z}_1 - t \leq 0, \quad \hat{z}_2 - t \leq 0, \quad 2\hat{z}_1 + \hat{z}_2 - 2t \leq 0$$

The coefficients of t in the first two inequalities are positive, thus they are the upper bounding functions.

4.3 Bounding Function Selection

We have introduced how to compute the bounding functions in the previous subsection. Note that the convex hull of the constructed region may have more than one facet, and thus the bounding functions may not be unique. For example, there are two upper bounding functions in Example 4. However, only one bounding function can be adopted in the propagation framework for computational efficiency. To address this problem, we propose an approach to select the bounding functions (line 10).

Similar to the adaptive selection in single neuron relaxation, we choose the bounding function that minimizes the difference between the bounding function and the original activation function. Specifically, we measure the difference between the bounding function and activation function on the region vertices. After splitting the value range of the pre-activation neurons, we can gather the vertices of all subregions together. We then calculate the sum of the differences between the bounding function and activation function on these vertices.

$$\text{difference} = \sum_{p \in \text{generators}} |bounding(p) - activation(p)|$$

The bounding function with the minimum difference is chosen to be the best and applied in the propagation framework.

Example 5. There are two upper bounding functions in Example 4: $f_1 = \frac{1}{2}\hat{z}_1 + \frac{1}{2}\hat{z}_2 + \frac{1}{2}$, and $f_2 = \frac{1}{2}\hat{z}_1 + 1$ The vertices are $(0,2)$, $(1,1)$, $(1,0)$, $(0,0)$, $(0,-1)$, $(-1,0)$, $(-1,1)$. For bounding function $f_1 = \frac{1}{2}\hat{z}_1 + \frac{1}{2}\hat{z}_2 + \frac{1}{2}$,

$$diff_1 = |\frac{3}{2} - 1| + |\frac{3}{2} - \frac{3}{2}| + |1 - 1| + |\frac{1}{2} - 0| + |0 - 0| + |0 - 0| + |\frac{1}{2} - \frac{1}{2}| = 1$$

For bounding function f_2, we have $diff_2 = 3$ in the same way. The first bounding function is closer to the activation function than the second one. Therefore, we choose f_1 as the upper bounding function in Example 1.

5 Region Clipping

As introduced in Sect. 3, simply using *Hölder Inequality* may lead to verification precision loss because the derived global upper bound of the neural network may take infeasible inputs into consideration. For example, as shown in Fig. 3, when the given data point (black dot) lies on the boundary of the input region, some portion of the ℓ_p ball (red part) is not included in the neural network's input domain.

For robustness verification, we only need to consider the intersection of the neural network's input domain and the distortion neighborhood, which is represented by the blue region in Fig. 3. Clipping out infeasible inputs to the neural network can assist in computing a tighter global upper bound, thus increasing the verification precision.

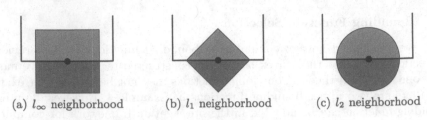

(a) l_∞ neighborhood   (b) l_1 neighborhood   (c) l_2 neighborhood

Fig. 3. The neighborhood of a borderline input.

Without loss of generality, we assume the value range of each input neuron is $[0,1]$. Considering robustness verification with respect to $\mathbb{B}_p(x_0, \epsilon)$, computing the global bound of the neural network in the clipped input region can be formulated as the following constrained optimization problem

$$\gamma = \max_{x'} \sum_{i=1}^{n} \alpha_i x_i' + \beta \quad s.t. \; x_i' \in [0,1], \; ||x' - x_0||_p \leq \epsilon$$

We can reformulate the above problem by setting $v_i = x_i' - x_{0,i}$.

$$\gamma = \max_{v} \sum_{i=1}^{n} \alpha_i v_i + \sum_{i=1}^{n} \alpha_i x_{0,i} + \beta \quad s.t. -x_{0,i} \leq v_i \leq 1 - x_{0,i}, \; \sum_{i=1}^{n} |v_i|^p \leq \epsilon^p$$

The last two terms of γ are constants. So we just need to find the maximum value of the first term. Solving this optimization problem with respect to l_∞ neighborhood is trivial. We just need to clip the illegal value range of each input variable and the resulted feasible region is still a box. However, for the other cases, the feasible region is irregular. Next we propose the region clipping methods for ℓ_1 neighborhood and ℓ_p ($p \geq 2$) neighborhood separately.

For ℓ_1 neighborhood, we sort the perturbation variables in non-increasing order according to the absolute values of their coefficients. This is because variable with larger absolute value of coefficient has more influence on the optimization objective. Therefore, we maximize the perturbation variables one by one in this order until either reaching the boundary of the feasible region or exhausting the allowed distortions.

Region clipping for ℓ_p ($p \geq 2$) neighborhood is presented in Algorithm 3. As with region clipping for ℓ_1 neighborhood, we only maximize the first term of γ. This optimization problem can be solved by Lagrange multiplier method. We can construct the Lagrangian function and obtain the Karush-Kuhn-Tucker (KKT) conditions. As the objective function is linear and the inequality constraints are continuously differentiable convex functions, the satisfaction of KKT conditions are sufficient and necessary conditions for the optimal solution. We can find the optimal solution along with the direction of the gradient. If the boundary of a linear constraint is encountered, we fix the corresponding distortion v_i and optimize the remaining variables. The solution found by Algorithm 3 satisfies the KKT conditions, thus is the optimal solution.

Algorithm 3: Region clipping for l_p neighborhood

Input: The objective function $\sum_{i=1}^{n} \alpha_i v_i$, the given data point x_0, neighborhood radius ϵ, norm p

Output: the maximum value of $\sum_{i=1}^{n} \alpha_i v_i$

1 $r_i \leftarrow 0$ for all $i = 1, \ldots, n$
2 **for** $i \leftarrow 1 \ldots n$ **do**
3   **if** $\alpha_{k_i} > 0$ **then**
4           $r_i \leftarrow 1 - x_{0,i}$
5   **else**
6           $r_i \leftarrow -x_{0,i}$

7 $q \leftarrow \frac{1}{p-1}$
8 $\{\alpha_{k_1}, \ldots, \alpha_{k_n}\} \leftarrow$ sort $\{\alpha_1, \ldots, \alpha_n\}$ in non-decreasing order according to $\frac{r_i}{\alpha_i^q}$
9 remain, $\gamma \leftarrow \epsilon^p, 0$
10 **for** $i = 1$ **to** n **do**
11   **if** $\frac{r_{k_i}^p}{\alpha_{k_i}^{pq}} \sum_{j=i}^{n} \alpha_{k_j}^{pq} \geq$ remain **then**
12           $\gamma \leftarrow \gamma + (\sum_{j=i}^{n} \alpha_{k_j}^{pq})^{\frac{1}{pq}} \cdot$ remain$^{\frac{1}{p}}$
13   break
14   **else**
15           $\gamma \leftarrow \gamma + \alpha_{k_i} \cdot r_{k_i}$
16   remain $\leftarrow$ remain $- r_{k_i}^p$

17 **return** γ

---

6 Experiments

We implement the propagation framework with multi-neuron relaxation and region clipping as *kProp*. To show the effectiveness of our algorithm, we compare *kProp* with two widely-used robustness verifiers, DeepPoly [16] and CROWN [20]. DeepPoly is an efficient verifier with high precision, but it can only be used for distortions of l_∞ norm. CROWN can verify the robustness of neural networks with regard to general l_p norms. But CROWN simply uses *Hölder Inequality* to calculate the global bound of the final optimization problem. Both of them adopt the single neuron relaxation.

Neural Networks and Datasets. The neural networks used in our experiments are well-trained models from the publicly available ERAN dataset [7]. We conduct experiments on both feed-forward neural networks (FNNs) and convolutional neural networks (CNNs) trained on MNIST [12] and CIFAR-10 [2] datasets. The feed-forward neural network with a hidden layers and b neurons per hidden layer is denoted as $a \times b$. The convolutional neural network denoted as Conv has two convolutional layers and two fully-connected layers. For each neural network, we use the first 1000 images from the corresponding test data as the test images and filter out the misclassified images.

Problem Settings. The properties considered in the experiments are local robustness with respect to distortions in ℓ_∞, ℓ_1 and ℓ_2 norms. The radius of ℓ_p ball ϵ is set to different values in different settings to avoid meaningless results. Experiments conducted on neural networks with respect to l_∞ norm are set to smaller radius than those with respect to l_1 norm. The detailed radius settings ϵ are shown in Table 1. For all neural networks and norms, we use $k = 3$ in $kProp$ to balance precision and time cost. This is shown in Table 2.

Table 1. Number of verified local robustness properties.

Dataset	Model	ℓ_∞ norm			ℓ_1 norm			ℓ_2 norm		
		ϵ	$kProp$	DeepPoly	ϵ	$kProp$	CROWN	ϵ	$kProp$	CROWN
MNIST	6×100	0.026	174	160	2.5	350	223	0.3	546	287
	9 × 100	0.026	186	182	2.5	309	219	0.3	456	272
	6 × 200	0.015	303	292	2	303	144	0.25	342	116
	9 × 200	0.015	262	259	2	188	132	0.25	276	112
	Conv	0.12	158	158	1.5	766	367	0.6	486	137
CIFAR-10	6 × 100	0.002	55	54	1	112	97	0.07	106	99
	9 × 200	0.002	63	63	1	136	112	0.07	127	123
	Conv	0.01	274	256	0.5	303	268	0.12	307	280

Experiment Results. Table 1 shows the number of verified local robustness properties for common distortions in terms of ℓ_∞, ℓ_1, and ℓ_2 norms based on different verification algorithms. In general, our method demonstrates better verification precision and outperforms DeepPoly and CROWN or achieves comparable performance for all verification problems.

For ℓ_1 and ℓ_2 norms, $kProp$ shows great superiority over CROWN with tighter convex relaxation through the multi-neuron relaxation method and tighter global bounds through region clipping. For MNIST dataset, the number of verified properties by $kProp$ is at least 40% more than those of CROWN. The precision gain is especially noticeable on convolution neural networks. $kProp$ successfully verifies 766 problems for ℓ_1 norm and 486 problems for ℓ_2 norm, whereas CROWN verifies 367 and 486 problems respectively. For the CIFAR-10 dataset, the improvements on convolutional neural networks are also more significant compared with FNNs. For ℓ_∞ norm, we only perform comparison experiments with DeepPoly as it demonstrates better verification performance than CROWN in this case. DeepPoly also performs region clipping for distortions of ℓ_∞ norm. Therefore, the results mainly demonstrate the effect of multi-neuron relaxation. We can see that $kProp$ is able to verify more robustness problems than DeepPoly which indicates that multi-neuron relaxation can provider tighter bounds than single neuron relaxation. The computational cost of $kProp$ is acceptable. For the most complicated verification task, robustness of CNN trained on CIFAR-10 with respect to ℓ_2 norm, the average runtime cost of each problem is less than 12 min. For verification tasks on FNNs with respect to ℓ_1 or ℓ_∞ norms, $kProp$ is able to finish in a few seconds.

The Choice of k. To explore the influence of parameter k in *kProp*, we perform experiments on the 6×100 FNN and MNIST dataset for different k. The number of verified properties and corresponding runtime are shown in Table 2. With a larger k, we can capture more complicated relations among neurons, and thus generate tighter bounding functions. However, this can take plenty of time. On the contrary, smaller k costs less time but provides looser bounding functions. To balance precision and efficiency, we chose $k = 3$ in the previous experiment.

Table 2. Number of verified properties of 6×100 FNN and runtime for $k = 2, 3, 4$.

Norm	ϵ	$k{=}2$		$k{=}3$		$k{=}4$	
		verified(#)	time(s)	verified(#)	time(s)	verified(#)	time(s)
ℓ_∞	0.026	166	1.99	174	4.61	174	187.71
ℓ_1	2.5	344	5.90	350	9.83	351	131.92
ℓ_2	0.3	546	35.33	550	56.87	550	180.06

7 Conclusion

We presented a multi-neuron based robustness verification framework *kProp* to verify the local robustness of neural networks for general ℓ_p norms. *kProp* is featured with constraint propagation, multi-neuron relaxation, and region clipping. The propagation framework enables *kProp* to verify robustness properties for general ℓ_p norms. The multi-neuron relaxation and region clipping together improve the verification precision. We implement our algorithm and evaluate it on a set of neural networks with different sizes, which demonstrates the effectiveness of our method. In the future, we would like to extend the application range of our method to more activation functions and network architectures.

Acknowledgements. This research was sponsored by the National Natural Science Foundation of China under Grant No. 62172019, 61772038, and CCF-Huawei Formal Verification Innovation Research Plan.

References

1. Amato, F., López, A., Peña-Méndez, E.M., Vaňhara, P., Hampl, A., Havel, J.: Artificial neural networks in medical diagnosis. J. Appl. Biomed. **11**(2), 47–58 (2013)
2. Carlini, N., Wagner, D.: Towards evaluating the robustness of neural networks. In: 2017 IEEE Symposium on Security and Privacy (SP), pp. 39–57. IEEE (2017)
3. Chen, Z., Huang, X.: End-to-end learning for lane keeping of self-driving cars. In: 2017 IEEE Intelligent Vehicles Symposium (IV), pp. 1856–1860. IEEE (2017)

4. Ehlers, R.: Formal verification of piece-wise linear feed-forward neural networks. In: D'Souza, D., Narayan Kumar, K. (eds.) ATVA 2017. LNCS, vol. 10482, pp. 269–286. Springer, Cham (2017). https://doi.org/10.1007/978-3-319-68167-2_19

5. Eykholt, K., et al.: Robust physical-world attacks on deep learning visual classification. In: Proceedings of the IEEE Conference on Computer Vision and Pattern Recognition (CVPR), pp. 1625–1634 (2018)

6. Fukuda, K., Prodon, A.: Double description method revisited. In: Deza, M., Euler, R., Manoussakis, I. (eds.) CCS 1995. LNCS, vol. 1120, pp. 91–111. Springer, Heidelberg (1996). https://doi.org/10.1007/3-540-61576-8_77

7. Gagandeep, S., et al.: Eran verification dataset. https://github.com/eth-sri/eran

8. Gehr, T., Mirman, M., Drachsler-Cohen, D., Tsankov, P., Chaudhuri, S., Vechev, M.: AI2: safety and robustness certification of neural networks with abstract interpretation. In: 2018 IEEE Symposium on Security and Privacy (SP), pp. 3–18. IEEE (2018)

9. Goodfellow, I.J., Shlens, J., Szegedy, C.: Explaining and harnessing adversarial examples. In: 3rd International Conference on Learning Representations (ICLR), Conference Track Proceedings (2015)

10. Julian, K.D., Lopez, J., Brush, J.S., Owen, M.P., Kochenderfer, M.J.: Policy compression for aircraft collision avoidance systems. In: 2016 IEEE/AIAA 35th Digital Avionics Systems Conference (DASC), pp. 1–10. IEEE (2016)

11. Katz, G., Barrett, C., Dill, D.L., Julian, K., Kochenderfer, M.J.: Reluplex: an efficient SMT solver for verifying deep neural networks. In: Majumdar, R., Kunčak, V. (eds.) CAV 2017. LNCS, vol. 10426, pp. 97–117. Springer, Cham (2017). https://doi.org/10.1007/978-3-319-63387-9_5

12. LeCun, Y., Bottou, L., Bengio, Y., Haffner, P.: Gradient-based learning applied to document recognition. Proc. IEEE 86(11), 2278–2324 (1998)

13. Lomuscio, A., Maganti, L.: An approach to reachability analysis for feed-forward ReLU neural networks (2017). https://arxiv.org/abs/1706.07351

14. Müller, M.N., Makarchuk, G., Singh, G., Püschel, M., Vechev, M.: PRIMA: general and precise neural network certification via scalable convex hull approximations. Proc. ACM Program. Lang. 6(POPL), 1–33 (2022)

15. Singh, G., Ganvir, R., Püschel, M., Vechev, M.: Beyond the single neuron convex barrier for neural network certification. In: Advances in Neural Information Processing Systems (NeurIPS), vol. 32, pp. 15072–15083 (2019)

16. Singh, G., Gehr, T., Püschel, M., Vechev, M.: An abstract domain for certifying neural networks. Proc. ACM Program. Lang. 3(POPL), 1–30 (2019)

17. Wang, S., Pei, K., Whitehouse, J., Yang, J., Jana, S.: Efficient formal safety analysis of neural networks. In: Advances in Neural Information Processing Systems (NeurIPS), vol. 31, pp. 6369–6379 (2018)

18. Wang, S., et al.: Beta-CROWN: efficient bound propagation with per-neuron split constraints for neural network robustness verification. In: Advances in Neural Information Processing Systems (NeurIPS), vol. 34, pp. 29909–29921 (2021)

19. Weng, L., et al.: Towards fast computation of certified robustness for ReLU networks. In: Proceedings of the 35th International Conference on Machine Learning (ICML), vol. 80, pp. 5276–5285. PMLR (2018)

20. Zhang, H., Weng, T.W., Chen, P.Y., Hsieh, C.J., Daniel, L.: Efficient neural network robustness certification with general activation functions. In: Advances in Neural Information Processing Systems (NeurIPS), vol. 31, pp. 4944–4953 (2018)

Author Index

© IFIP International Federation for Information Processing 2023
Published by Springer Nature Switzerland AG 2023
H. Hojjat and E. Ábrahám (Eds.): FSEN 2023, LNCS 14155, p. 157, 2023.
https://doi.org/10.1007/978-3-031-42441-0

Printed in the United States
by Baker & Taylor Publisher Services